THE PHONOLOGY OF THE WORLD'S LANGUAGES

Series Editor: Jacques Durand, Université de Toulouse-le-Mirail

━━━━━━━

The Phonology of Portuguese

THE PHONOLOGY OF THE WORLD'S LANGUAGES

The phonology of most languages was once and to a large extent still is available only in a fragmented way, through unpublished theses, or articles scattered in more or less accessible journals. Each volume in this series offers an extensive treatment of the phonology of one language within a modern theoretical perspective, and provides comprehensive references to recent and more classical studies of the language. The following are normally included: an introduction situating the language geographically and typologically, an overview of the theoretical assumptions made by the author, a description of the segmental system and of the rules or constraints characterizing the language, an outline of syllable structure and domains above the syllable, a discussion of lexical and postlexical phonology, an account of stress and prominence, and, if space allows, some overview of the intonational structure of the language.

Each volume is cast in a modern theoretical framework, but there has been and will always be scope for a diversity of approach which reflects variations between languages and in the methodologies and theoretical preoccupations of the authors.

Published in the series:

The Phonology of Norwegian
Gjert Kristoffersen

The Phonology of Hungarian
Péter Siptár and Miklós Törkenczy

The Phonology of Portuguese
Maria Helena Mateus and Ernesto d'Andrade

The Phonology of English
Michael Hammond

The Phonology of Dutch
Geert Booij

The Phonology of Armenian
Bert Vaux

The Phonology of German
Richard Wiese

The Phonology and Morphology of Kimatuumbi
David Odden

The Lexical Phonology of Slovak
Jerzy Rubach

THE
PHONOLOGY
OF
PORTUGUESE

——

Maria Helena Mateus
and
Ernesto d'Andrade

UNIVERSITY PRESS

OXFORD
UNIVERSITY PRESS

Great Clarendon Street, Oxford OX2 6DP

Oxford University Press is a department of the University of Oxford.
It furthers the University's objective of excellence in research, scholarship,
and education by publishing worldwide in

Oxford New York

Athens Auckland Bangkok Bogotá Buenos Aires Calcutta
Cape Town Chennai Dar es Salaam Delhi Florence Hong Kong Istanbul
Karachi Kuala Lumpur Madrid Melbourne Mexico City Mumbai
Nairobi Paris São Paulo Singapore Taipei Tokyo Toronto Warsaw

with associated companies in Berlin Ibadan

Published in the United States
by Oxford University Press Inc., New York

British Library Cataloguing in Publication Data

Data available

Library of Congress Cataloging in Publication Data

Data applied for

ISBN 0-19-823581-X

1 3 5 7 9 10 8 6 4 2

Typeset in Times
by Regent Typesetting
Printed in Great Britain
on acid-free paper by
Biddles Ltd., Guildford and King's Lynn

PREFACE

In this book the reader will find a broad concept of phonology: syllable, stress and segments, as well as morphological aspects implying phonological processes. The work presents an overview of the field, putting together and enlarging partial analyses, our own and those of colleagues, most of which have so far been presented in Portuguese only. To make available to students of phonology and to linguists a substantial body of relevant data and analyses, and to raise crucial questions and suggest directions for alternative interpretations of this data, has presented us with a pleasurable challenge. To support our analyses we have relied on those theories which in our view best explain language design and structure in relation to the facts of phonology.

European and Brazilian Portuguese are somewhat different at the phonetic level. Thus we have tried to present a comparative account of both varieties, to allow readers to appreciate their common underlying system.

We hope that the book will provide relevant information, new insights, and suggestive ideas for those who wish to deepen their knowledge of the phonology of Portuguese.

ACKNOWLEDGEMENTS

We owe a debt of gratitude to all those colleagues, students, and audiences who discussed many parts of the book with us while it was in preparation and whose remarks led us to improve upon earlier versions of the text.

We would especially like to thank Amália Andrade for her contribution in refining the style and the analyses proposed in Chapter 2. We are also indebted to Alan Kihm, Alina Villalva, Bernard Laks, Maria do Céu Viana, Maria João Freitas, and Marina Vigário.

We sincerely thank Jacques Durand, the series editor, for his constant support and his readiness to discuss various aspects of the work. Finally, we appreciate the assistance that was provided in the final stages of preparing the typescript by the editorial team of OUP.

CONTENTS

1

INTRODUCTION

1.1. AIM AND THEORETICAL FRAMEWORK

The aim of this book is to describe the phonological system of Portuguese and to discuss its functioning in the light of recent phonological theories. Chapters 1 and 2 are introductory: they describe some of the phonetic, phonological and morphological characteristics of European Portuguese (henceforth EP), where relevant including data from Brazilian Portuguese (henceforth BP). Chapter 2 also deals with theoretical aspects such as feature geometry and underspecification. Some of this material will be further discussed in later chapters. From Chapter 3 onwards, the analyses are based on autosegmental theory, and Portuguese phonological processes, both segmental and prosodic, are set out in terms of a multilinear structural organization. The discussion of nasalization, phonological and morphological processes, syllable and stress presupposes such a theoretical framework. All the models we use are from the same theoretical background and have been chosen for their explanatory power.

1.2. RELEVANT HISTORICAL MILESTONES AND SYNCHRONIC VARIATION

Portuguese is a Romance language closely linked to Castilian and Catalan. In Europe, Portuguese is spoken in Portugal. In traditional studies on dialectology, and for historical reasons, the dialects spoken in Galicia (Spain) have been grouped with the Galician-Portuguese dialects (see Cintra, 1971a). We shall not consider them here. It was in Galicia, which was founded in the third century and was a part of the Roman-occupied lands of Gallaecia and Asturica, that the Portuguese language emerged from Vulgar Latin. The inhabitants of this peripheral and inaccessible area retained in their language the typical characteristics of the archaic Low Latin spoken by their colonizers.

The languages spoken on the Iberian Peninsula during the Roman occupation influenced the phonological differentiation between the Hispanic languages and dialects. According to authors such as Baldinger (1958), this influence, for example, suppressed the initial etymological [f] in Castilian and the fricative pronunciation of the Latin plosive [b], which was common to both the northern

Portuguese and the Castilian dialects. Between the fifth and the seventh centuries, the Peninsula was invaded by Germanic peoples, and a Suebic kingdom was established in the northwest of the Peninsula. The region became increasingly isolated so that the type of Latin spoken there grew to be unique. When the Visigoths overthrew the Suebic rulers in the seventh century, some of the phonological characteristics that set Galician-Portuguese apart from Castilian had already formed. The intervocalic pronunciation of Latin [n] and [l] had disappeared and the Latin clusters [pl], [kl] and [fl] had become palatalized. At the same time, the classical Latin vowel system had reached the end of its progression with the loss of quantity opposition and, in Portuguese, there was a replacement of the short [e] and [o] vowels by the corresponding open vowels [ɛ] and [ɔ], although no diphthongization occurred, as happened in Castilian.

Earlier texts written in Portuguese date back to 1175—*Notícia de Fiadores*—and 1214–16—*Notícia do Torto* and the *Testamento de D. Afonso II*.[1]

The spread of the Portuguese language kept pace with the conquest of Portugal from the Moors during the thirteenth century, extending right down to the province of Algarve in the extreme south of the country. Later, Portuguese spread to every continent in the world and at the end of the sixteenth century and during the seventeenth, apart from being spoken in Brazil, it served as a *lingua franca* along the West-African coast and in the ports of India (Indo-Portuguese) and South-East Asia (Malay-Portuguese).

Today, Portuguese is the national language of Portugal and Brazil. It has been made the official language of Angola, Mozambique, the Cape Verde islands, Guinea-Bissau, and the São Tomé and Príncipe Islands. In Asia, only Macao has officially kept Portuguese, which is also spoken in the eastern part of the island of Timor. Large communities of emigrants keep Portuguese alive in North America and in various countries in Europe.

The two most important varieties of Portuguese, which define so-called educated standards of the language, are European Portuguese and Brazilian Portuguese. The most obvious differences between these two varieties are located in the unstressed vowel system—the vowels are more audible in BP than in EP.

With regard to dialects, there are no striking differences between the dialects in either Portugal or Brazil. In European Portuguese there are two main groups of dialects: northern Portuguese and central-southern Portuguese. The distinction between these groups lies mainly in the fricative consonant system, traditionally called 'sibilants': the northern dialects have kept their Latin apico-alveolar fricatives, as is also the case in northern Castilian, and in some areas, these consonants coexist with the dental ones, so reflecting the distinction shown in the written form (*passo* 'step', an apico-alveolar, and *paço* 'palace or court', a dental); in the central-southern dialects these fricatives have been replaced by the dental ones although the different forms of spelling have been kept. The dialects on the archipelagos of Madeira and the Azores, while they have their own peculiarities, share the general characteristics of the central-southern dialects.

[1] See Cintra (1971b), Costa (1977), and Martins (1999).

According to Nascentes (1953), there are two groups of dialects in Brazilian Portuguese: the ones from the north (the Amazon, the north and the north-east) and those from the south (the central and southern regions). The Northern dialects tend to have more open prestressed vowels. There are several linguistic atlases, many monographs and quite a number of general articles available on the Portuguese Brazilian dialects. However, Cunha and Cintra (1984) believe that the sheer vastness of Brazil has made the job of presenting an organized, detailed study of all the existent dialect variations extremely difficult. Even if the variation in dialects is not very great, the enormous variation in sociolects presents the Brazilian school with a formidable challenge.

In the Portuguese-speaking African countries, the number of Portuguese speakers is still fairly low, although it is increasing slowly as more children attend school. The lack of systematic, exhaustive research into the type of Portuguese spoken in these countries has made it impossible to draw up a profile. Nevertheless, in very general terms, it can be said, that the unstressed vowels are more audible in Africa than in European Portuguese.

In Angola and Mozambique, Portuguese coexists with other national languages, mainly belonging to the Bantu group. In Guinea-Bissau, the São Tomé and Príncipe islands and the Cape Verde islands different Creoles have grown from Portuguese. The Creoles spoken in São Tomé and in Cape Verde are national languages and are the only ones standing on an equal footing with Portuguese in these two countries.

1.3. STUDIES ON PORTUGUESE

The first Portuguese grammars date from the sixteenth century: Fernão de Oliveira (1536) and João de Barros (1540). These compilations naturally provide one of the most valuable sources of knowledge about the history of the Portuguese phonology. Barbosa's grammar (1822), written in emulation of Arnauld and Lancelot's *Grammaire Générale et Raisonnée* (1660), is the most important philosophical grammar of Portuguese. Philosophical orientation notwithstanding, it provides insights on the Portuguese prosody.

At the beginning of the twentieth century, several historical grammars were published. They are vital for understanding the development of the phonology of Portuguese both in Portugal and in Brazil. It is worth singling out from among them Said Ali (1921–3), Nunes (1919) and Williams (1938). Pre-theoretical studies on Portuguese phonology are those of Viana (1883), who shows remarkable phonological intuition, and, among others, Vasconcellos (1901), who throws much light on Portuguese dialects.

Extremely full structural descriptions of the phonology of present-day Portuguese are to be found in Barbosa (1965) for European and Câmara (1953 and 1970) for Brazilian Portuguese. Cunha and Cintra's work (1984) looks at both varieties from a traditional stance.

In the last twenty years, work published on the Portuguese language has taken into account standard generative grammar and related theories. In Portugal, phonological studies have been appearing since the mid-1970s, for example, Mateus (1975) and Andrade (1977), who write on the phonology of European Portuguese in the *Sound Pattern of English* model (henceforth SPE), and Callou and Leite (1990), who study the phonology of Brazilian Portuguese.

The Proceedings of the Portuguese and Brazilian Linguistic Associations (APL and ABRALIN) contain some enlightening articles on the current state of research. Many studies in Portuguese phonetics have been published since 1980, e.g. Delgado-Martins on the phonetic study of prosodic facts (1982 and 1983), Viana (1987) and A. Andrade (1987). A few articles are dedicated to applying metrical and autosegmental theories to Portuguese phonology: Andrade (1983), Andrade and Viana (1988a, b), Andrade and Laks (1987, 1991, 1996), Abaurre (1991), Bisol (1989) and Wetzels (1991).

The present study of the Portuguese phonological system is based on European Portuguese and presents data from Brazilian Portuguese either to argue in favour of certain proposals or to explain different phonological processes. European Portuguese data will be taken from the standard dialects spoken in Lisbon and Coimbra, which are accepted in Portugal as a reference for teaching Portuguese as a second language and are the most commonly heard on radio and television. Some remarks about other dialects will be made on appropriate occasions. For Brazilian Portuguese, in which there is more than one standard, the widely diffused dialect spoken in Rio de Janeiro ('carioca') will be referred to.

The most complete monolingual dictionaries of Portuguese (Figueiredo, 1899; Silva, 1948–59; Aurélio, 1986) do not include phonetic transcriptions. Only Vilela (1990), a small dictionary compiled for pedagogical purposes, gives instruction on pronouncing words. Viana (1883) contains some interesting remarks about the pronunciation of vowels and sequences of vowels.

1.4. OVERVIEW OF THE BOOK

The present chapter briefly surveys the historical aspects and synchronic variations of the language which are relevant to an understanding of the contemporary Portuguese. The description of the phonological system included in Chapter 2 illustrates the distribution and the phonetic characteristics of consonants, vowels and glides in Portuguese, employing a wide range of data. We take an autosegmental perspective in the analysis of the segments and propose an organization of the features which accords with the feature geometry model. We also adopt the underspecification view, and we state the underspecification of Portuguese consonants and vowels.

Chapter 3 looks at prosodic structure. After a phonotactic description, the non-linear theoretical model is introduced to account for the behaviour of the segments with respect to the internal structure of the syllable and the phonological word.

In Chapters 4 and 5 we present the general characteristics of Portuguese morphology—nominal and verbal systems—in the framework of lexical phonology. Chapter 4 concerns inflectional processes in which morphology interacts with phonology to affect the application of several phonological rules. Chapter 5 analyses derivational processes and discusses morphophonological phenomena occurring in derivational processes. Chapter 6 deals with word stress—main, secondary and echo—using the 'grid only' model as our analytical tool. The focus of Chapter 7 is on phonological processes that are not related to the morphological structure of the word. Here the rules applied on final syllable consonants and the very peculiar process of nasalization are analysed. We also deal with the reduction of unstressed vowels which occurs in European Portuguese. The last part of the chapter reviews the consequences of applying external sandhi rules.

1.5. PHONETIC TRANSCRIPTION AND CONVENTIONS

The phonetic transcriptions included throughout this work are broad and, up to a point, abstract transcriptions representing a class of individual realizations. Although they vary in phonetic details, these differences are not deemed linguistically relevant. The notation used is that of the most recent version (1993) promulgated by the International Phonetic Association (IPA). Following usual conventions, the phonetic transcriptions are written in square brackets and the underlying representations are enclosed in slashes. Sigma (σ) is the symbol for syllables. Whenever necessary, morpheme boundaries (+) word boundaries (#) and syllable boundaries (– or $) will be used. Primary stress is indicated by the diacritic (´) usually placed over the stressed vowel.

Italics represent a sound that may be interpreted as being etymological. Orthographic transcriptions are enclosed in angles. Examples that occur in running text are given in italic and referred to in their orthographic form. Sometimes a word in its orthographic form will contain one or more sounds represented in phonetic transcription (e.g. am[ó]r).

The lateral [ł] used in the EP dialects is a velarized consonant. It is pronounced by raising of the tongue body towards the velum (as in pronouncing the English 'dark l').

In the standard varieties of EP and BP described here we seldom find, in word-initial position or between vowels, the typical alveolar trill that implies 'usually three vibrating movements' (Ladefoged, 1975). It can be found in some dialects of Portugal and in the south of Brazil. Fairly often, an uvular fricative occurs instead, being represented by the symbol [ʁ]. The alveolar trill, a very short one where there is only a single vibrating movement (almost an alveolar tap), is denoted here by [ɾ]. In some Brazilian dialects it can occur as a retroflex sound. The symbol [χ] represents a voiceless uvular fricative which is usually pronounced in syllable-final position in BP.

1.6. A WORD ON ORTHOGRAPHY

Portuguese spelling is phonological; it is also fairly conservative. The spelling system of the vowels has single symbols. The five letters, ⟨a, e, i, o, u⟩ represent in fact nine vowels: [a], [ɐ], [ɛ], [e], [i], [ɔ], [o], [u] (and [ɨ] in European Portuguese). The glides [j] and [w] are usually represented by ⟨i⟩ and ⟨u⟩ (but they may also be denoted by ⟨e⟩ and ⟨o⟩). The correspondence between letters and vowels and glides, and the different pronunciation in the two varieties, is given in (1) below:

(1) ⟨a⟩ → [a] *caso* [kázu] 'case'
     ⟨a⟩ → [ɐ] *café* [kɐfé] (EP) 'coffee'
     ⟨a⟩ → [ɐ] *sopa* [sópɐ] 'soup'

     ⟨e⟩ → [ɛ] *belo* [bɛ́lu] 'beautiful'
     ⟨e⟩ → [e] *seco* [séku] 'dry'
     ⟨e⟩ → [i] *ermida* [iɾmídɐ] 'small church'
     ⟨e⟩ → [i] *estar* [iʃtáɾ] (BP) 'to be'
     ⟨e⟩ → [i] *nove* [nɔ́vi] (BP) 'nine'
     ⟨e⟩ → [ɨ] *dever* [dɨvéɾ] (EP) 'duty'
     ⟨e⟩ → [ɨ] *nove* [nɔ́vɨ] (EP) 'nine'
     ⟨e⟩ → [i]/[j] *cear* [siáɾ]/[sjáɾ] 'to have supper'

     ⟨i⟩ → [i] *vi* [ví] 'I saw'
     ⟨i⟩ → [i] *tirar* [tiɾáɾ] 'to take'
     ⟨i⟩ → [j] *pai* [páj] 'father'
     ⟨i⟩ → [i]/[j] *pior* [piɔ́ɾ]/[pjɔ́ɾ] 'worst'

     ⟨o⟩ → [ɔ] *bola* [bɔ́lɐ] 'ball'
     ⟨o⟩ → [o] *força* [fóɾsɐ] 'strength'
     ⟨o⟩ → [u] *poder* [pudéɾ] (EP) 'power'
     ⟨o⟩ → [u] *pato* [pátu] 'duck'
     ⟨o⟩ → [u]/[w] *voar* [vuáɾ]/[vwáɾ] 'to fly'

     ⟨u⟩ → [u] *tudo* [túdu] 'everything'
     ⟨u⟩ → [u] *murar* [muɾáɾ] 'to enclose'
     ⟨u⟩ → [w] *pau* [páw] 'stick'
     ⟨u⟩ → [u]/[w] *suor* [suɔ́ɾ]/[swɔ́ɾ] 'sweat'

The plosive consonants generally do not have different pronunciations in the two varieties. They are represented by the following letters:

(2) ⟨p⟩ → [p] *pá* [pá] 'spade'
     ⟨b⟩ → [b] *boa* [bóɐ] 'good' (fem.)

⟨t⟩ → [t] *u* [tú] 'you'
⟨d⟩ → [d] *dar* [dáɾ] 'to give'
⟨c^{a,o,u}⟩ → [k] *casa* [kázɐ] 'house'
⟨g^{a,o,u}⟩ → [g] *gato* [gátu] 'cat'

(i) The letter ⟨q⟩ can be used to represent the sound [k] but it is always followed by ⟨u⟩ which is normally not pronounced (*quero* [kéɾu] 'I want'). The letter ⟨g⟩ placed before ⟨e⟩ and ⟨i⟩ represents a plosive only if it makes a string with ⟨u⟩ which does not need to be pronounced either (*guita* [gítɐ] 'string'). However, in these two cases the ⟨u⟩ represents a glide in some words, as in *quarto* [kwáɾtu] 'room' and in *linguística* [lĩgwíʃtikɐ] 'linguistics', or in BP *questão* [kweʃtɐ̃w̃] 'question'.

(ii) In some Brazilian dialects, ⟨t⟩ and ⟨d⟩ placed before ⟨i⟩ represent the affricates [t͡ʃ] and [d͡ʒ] as in *tia* [t͡ʃíɐ] 'aunt', *dia* [d͡ʒíɐ] 'day' (see 2.1.2. below). The fricative dental and palatal consonants maintain a difference in orthography due to a different pronunciation that has disappeared from most dialects (see 2.1.1 (iv) concerning the different pronunciation of these fricatives, except for voiced palatals, in some dialects).

(3) ⟨ss⟩ → [s]   *passo* [pásu] 'step'
   ⟨ç⟩ → [s]   *paço* [pásu] 'palace'
   ⟨c^{e,i}⟩ → [s]   *cego* [ségu] 'blind'
   ⟨s⟩ → [s]   *saber* [sɐbéɾ] 'knowledge'
   ⟨s⟩ → [z]   *casa* [kázɐ] 'house'
   ⟨s⟩ → [ʃ]   *pás* [páʃ] 'spades'
   ⟨z⟩ → [z]   *gozo* [gózu] 'joy'
   ⟨z⟩ → [ʃ]   *paz* [páʃ] 'peace'
   ⟨ch⟩ → [ʃ]   *chá* [ʃá] 'tea'
   ⟨x⟩ → [ʃ]   *xá* [ʃá] 'Shah'
   ⟨x⟩ → [s]   *sintaxe* [sĩtásɨ]/[sĩtási] 'syntax'
   ⟨x⟩ → [z]   *êxodo* [ézudu] 'exodus'
   ⟨x⟩ → [ks]   *táxi* [táksi] 'taxi'
   ⟨g^{e,i}⟩ → [ʒ]   *gingar* [ʒĩgáɾ] 'to roll'
   ⟨j⟩ → [ʒ]   *jacto* [ʒátu] 'jet'

⟨l⟩ and ⟨lh⟩ represent lateral consonants in syllable-initial position. At the end of the syllable only ⟨l⟩ occurs and it represents the velarized lateral [ɫ] (EP) or the glide [w] (BP) (for more on the distribution of the laterals see 2.2.2(ii)).

(4) ⟨l⟩ → [l]   *mala* [málɐ] 'bag'
   ⟨l⟩ → [ɫ]   *mal* [máɫ] (EP) 'evil'
   ⟨l⟩ → [w]   *mal* [máw] (BP) 'evil'
   ⟨lh⟩ → [ʎ]   *alho* [áʎu] 'garlic'

The liquids [ɾ] and [ʀ] are represented respectively by ⟨r⟩ and ⟨rr⟩ except word-initially, where the uvular trill is denoted by one single ⟨r⟩. See (5).

(5) ⟨r⟩ → [ɾ]   *caro* [káɾu] 'expensive'
     ⟨r⟩ → [ʀ]   *rato* [ʀátu] 'mouse'
     ⟨rr⟩ → [ʀ]   *carro* [káʀu] 'car'

⟨m⟩, ⟨n⟩, ⟨nh⟩ represent nasal consonants in syllable-initial position. In syllable-final position (before a consonant or word-finally), ⟨m⟩ and ⟨n⟩ represent the vowel nasalization: ⟨m⟩ before ⟨p⟩, ⟨b⟩ and word-finally, ⟨n⟩ before the other consonants; ⟨nh⟩ does not occur in this position.[2]

(6) a.   ⟨m⟩   →   [m]   *mama* [mɐ́mɐ] 'mamma'
           ⟨n⟩   →   [n]   *mana* [mɐ́nɐ] 'sister'
           ⟨nh⟩   →   [ɲ]   *manha* [mɐ́ɲɐ] 'slyness'

    b.   ⟨am⟩   →   [ɐ̃]   *campina* [kɐ̃pínɐ] 'level land'
           ⟨am⟩   →   [ɐ̃w̃]   *falam* [fálɐ̃w̃] 'they speak'
           ⟨em⟩   →   [ẽ]   *embora* [ẽbɔ́ɾɐ] 'even so'
           ⟨em⟩   →   [ẽj]   *viagem* [viáʒẽj] (EP) 'trip'
           ⟨em⟩   →   [ẽj̃]   *viagem* [viáʒẽj̃] (BP) 'trip'
           ⟨im⟩   →   [ĩ]   *assim* [ɐsĩ́] 'so'
           ⟨en⟩   →   [ẽ]   *pensar* [pẽsáɾ] 'to think'
           ⟨on⟩   →   [õ]   *contar* [kõtáɾ] 'to count'

The practice of writing the nasal consonants which merely indicate that the vowel is nasal although they are not pronounced as such is another example of the phonological nature of written Portuguese.

    The letter ⟨h⟩ never represents an aspiration: either it represents nothing (*humano* [umɐ́nu] 'human'), or it is the second item in a sequence ⟨ch⟩, ⟨nh⟩, ⟨lh⟩ which indicates palatalization.

    The diacritics have three aims: the tilde (˜) indicates the nasal sound of [ɐ] and [o] vowels in the absence of a nasal consonant (*limão* [limɐ́w̃], *limões* [limṍjʃ] 'lemon(s)'); the diacritic (ˆ) indicates closed [ɐ], [e] and [o] vowels in words where the stress is either on the last or on the antepenultimate syllable (*pânico* [pɐ́niku] 'panic', *mês* [méʃ] 'month', *avô* [ɐvó] 'grandfather', *estômago* [ʃtómɐgu] (EP) / [iʃtómagu] (BP) 'stomach'); the diacritic (´) denotes the stressed vowel in words that have traditionally failed to comply with the language's general rules (words with an antepenultimate stress such as *fábrica* [fábɾikɐ] 'factory', *cómico* [kɔ́miku] 'comic', *ética* [étikɐ] 'ethics', *dúvida* [dúvidɐ] 'doubt'; words with the stress on the penultimate syllable such as *nível* [nívɛɫ] 'level', *órfão* [ɔ́ɾfɐ̃w̃] 'orphan'; words with a last stressed syllable such as *café* [kɐfé] 'coffee', *avó* [ɐvɔ́] 'grandmother'). The diacritic (`) is only used in words resulting from the contraction of the preposition *a* with the definite article and pronouns beginning with *a* (*à* [a] 'to', *àquele* [akélɨ] (EP) / [akéli] (BP) 'to that', etc.). In Brazil, the 'trema' or 'umlaut' is also used to indicate the pronunciation of the glide [w] following a ⟨q⟩ or a ⟨g⟩ (*lingüística* [lĩgwíʃtikɐ] 'linguistics').

───────────

[2] In a very few cultivated words ending in ⟨en⟩, the consonant is pronounced (e.g. *abdómen* [ɐbdɔ́men] 'abdomen').

European Portuguese and Brazilian Portuguese have two notable differences in orthography: (a) consonants that are not pronounced are still written in Portugal but have been suppressed in Brazil (e.g. *direcção* (EP) / *direção* (BP) [dirɛsẽ̃w] 'direction', *óptico* (EP) / *ótico* (BP) [ɔtiku] 'opticist'); (b) words stressed on the antepenultimate syllable whenever the penultimate begins with a nasal consonant have the diacritic (´) in EP and (^) in BP, corresponding to two different pronunciations of the vowel (e.g. *cómodo* [kɔmudu] / *cômodo* [kómudu] 'comfortable').

THE PHONOLOGICAL SYSTEM OF PORTUGUESE

2.1. INTRODUCTION

This chapter is divided into three sections. After presenting the phonetic data including salient differences betweeen EP, BP and other dialects of the language (2.2), we describe, in 2.3, the EP sound system within the framework of feature geometry (see Clements and Hume, 1995) going on to consider segmental representation in the light of radical underspecification theory (2.4).

2.2. PORTUGUESE CONSONANTS, VOWELS AND GLIDES: A TRADITIONAL APPROACH

The main purpose of this chapter is to describe the sound system of standard European Portuguese (Lisbon region). To begin with, we identify the consonants (C), vowels (V) and glides (G) that occur in this variety of the language at the phonetic level, and point out their distributional characteristics.

Along with the segmental description, we briefly point out some questions of phonological interest. Most of these have already been the object of discussion in previous analyses of Portuguese phonology (e.g. Morais Barbosa, 1965; Mateus, 1975; Andrade, 1977).

2.2.1. Consonants

2.2.1.1. Inventory

Examples in (1a, b and c) provide the inventory of EP consonants which contrast word-initially (# – V), word-medially (V – V) and word-finally (V – #).

(1) a. Word-initial consonants (# – V)
        [p] *pala* [pálɐ] 'visor; peak'   [b] *bala* [bálɐ] 'bullet'
        [t] *tom* [tõ] 'tone'   [d] *dom* [dõ] 'gift'
        [k] *calo* [kálu] 'corn'   [g] *galo* [gálu] 'cock'
        [f] *fala* [fálɐ] 'speech'   [v] *vala* [válɐ] 'trench'
        [s] *selo* [sélu] 'seal'   [z] *zelo* [zélu] 'care'
        [ʃ] *chá* [ʃá] 'tea'   [ʒ] *já* [ʒá] 'already'

[m] *mata* [mátɐ] 'wood'   [n] *nata* [nátɐ] 'cream'
[l] *lato* [látu] 'large'   [ʀ] *rato* [ʀátu] 'mouse'

The uvular trill [ʀ] co-occurs with other back variants in modern EP, namely the voiced uvular fricative [ʁ] or the voiceless one, [χ]; the alveolar trill [r] is common in dialects other than the one under consideration. There is some reason to believe that the voiced uvular fricative [ʁ] is in the process of becoming dominant, today, in the Lisbon region; however, we will use the representation of the uvular trill, rather than the uvular fricative in this book. The reason for this choice lies in our conviction that place, but not stridency[1] plays a pertinent role in the distinction between the two rhotics. In fact, the consonant behaves like a sonorant in the phonological processes.

b. Word-medial consonants, between vowels (V – V)
  [p] *ripa* [ʀípɐ] 'chip'   [b] *riba* [ʀíbɐ] 'cliff'[2]
  [t] *lato* [látu] 'wide'   [d] *lado* [ládu] 'side'
  [k] *vaca* [vákɐ] 'cow'   [g] *vaga* [vágɐ] 'wave'
  [f] *estafa* [ʃtáfɐ] 'fatigue'   [v] *estava* [ʃtávɐ] 's/he was'
  [s] *caça* [kásɐ] 'hunt'   [z] *casa* [kázɐ] 'house'
  [ʃ] *acha* [áʃɐ] 's/he finds'   [ʒ] *haja* [áʒɐ] 'there may be'(subj.)
  [l] *mala* [málɐ] 'bag'   [ʎ] *malha* [máʎɐ] 'mesh'
  [m] *gama* [gémɐ] 'range'   [n] *gana* [génɐ] 'will, energy'
  [ɲ] *sanha* [séɲɐ] 'fury'   [n] *sana* [sénɐ] 's/he heals'
  [ɾ] *caro* [káɾu] 'expensive'   [ʀ] *carro* [káʀu] 'car'

c. Word-final consonants (V – #)
  [ɫ] *mal* [máɫ] 'evil'
  [ɾ] *mar* [máɾ] 'sea'   [ʃ] *más* [máʃ] 'bad'(fem.pl.)

It may be inferred from the examples listed above that EP possesses 19 distinct consonants. All of them occur word-medially and most of them also contrast word-initially. The absolute final subset of consonants is significantly restricted to a fricative and two liquids.

Word-initially, the palatal [ʎ] is limited to a very small number of lexical morphemes, of which all but the pronoun 'lhe' are rarely used loan-words. The nasal palatal [ɲ] may also fill word initial position, but again, it is confined to a few loan-words.[3] As for the alveolar flap ([ɾ]), it is simply not allowed word-initially, in any dialect.

Portuguese only allows three consonants in word-final position, namely the flap, the non-palatal lateral, and the voiceless alveolo-palatal fricative.[4] We should

---

[1] Stridency is associated with the occurrence of noise characterized by a relatively high amplitude.
[2] As a matter of fact, in northern and central EP dialects, voiced stops may be realized as the correspondent non-strident fricatives, [β], [δ], [γ], except in phrase-initial position and after an homorganic non-continuant.   [3] These are more common in BP than in EP.
[4] Actually, the alveolo-palatals [ʃ] and [ʒ] can be classified as palatals, together with [ɲ] and [ʎ], in Portuguese. We therefore label them as 'palatal' henceforth. Similarly we will not distinguish between dental and alveolar articulations.

specify here, in parenthesis, that phonetically any consonant may be found in word final position, in EP (not in BP). As will become clearer in 2.3.2, this fact, however, is a consequence of phenomena associated with deletion of unstressed vowels. Now, going back to the three word-final consonants in question, the final lateral is systematically velarized ([ɫ]) in EP. In BP the positional modification has gone a step further: with the loss of its consonantal character, the lateral liquid has given way to the velar glide [w].[5] Thus, for instance, *mal* 'evil, badly' is realized as [máɫ] in EP and as [máw] in BP.[6] The EP final flap corresponds, in BP, to [R], [x] or [h], or it is simply deleted as in *amar*, 'to love' [ɐmáɾ] in EP as compared with [amáR]/[amáx]/[amáh]/[amá] in BP (Callou and Leite, 1990, 72–6).

The phenomena just observed in association with word final position are also found in syllable final position (coda), in both dialects. The items in (1d) support our assertion with respect to EP. The ones in (1e) indicate further that the coda sibilant agrees in voicing with the following context.

d. Segments in coda and in word-final positions

EP	BP
[ʃ] *pasto* [páʃtu]	[ʃ] *pasto* [páʃtu] 'pasture'
[ʃ] *paz* [páʃ]	[ʃ] *paz* [páʃ] 'peace'
[ʒ] *Lisboa* [liʒbóɐ]	[ʒ] *Lisboa* [liʒbóɐ] 'Lisbon'
[ɫ] *caldo* [káɫdu]	[w] *caldo* [káwdu] 'broth'
[ɫ] *sal* [sáɫ]	[w] *sal* [sáw] 'salt'
[ɾ] *porto* [póɾtu]	[R]/[x] *porto* [póRtu]/[póxtu] 'harbour'
[ɾ] *ter* [téɾ]	[R]/[x] *ter* [téR]/[téx] 'to have'

e. Voicing agreement in syllable coda

[ʃ] *rasca* [Ráʃkɐ] '(of) bad quality'	[ʒ] *rasga* [Ráʒgɐ] 's/he tears'
[ʃ] *suspiro* [suʃpíɾu] 'sigh'	[ʒ] *Lisboa* [liʒbóɐ] 'Lisbon'
[ʃ] *pasta* [páʃtɐ] 'paste, suitcase'	[ʒ] *desdém* [dɨʒdéj̃] 'disdain'
[ʃ] *asfalto* [ɐʃfáɫtu] 'asphalt'	[ʒ] *mesma* [méʒmɐ] 'the same'
[ʃ] *ascético* [ɐʃsétiku] 'ascetic'	[ʒ] *desviar* [dɨʒvjáɾ] 'to remove'
	[ʒ] *Israel* [iʒRɐéɫ] 'Israel'
	[ʒ] *Islão* [iʒléw̃] 'Islam'

It is worth pointing out, at this point, that the voicing assimilation effect undergone by the fricative also takes place at word boundaries, that is, when the word is followed by another word, in an utterance (e.g. *maus dias* [máwʒdíɐʃ] 'bad days'; *maus tempos* [máwʃtẽpuʃ] 'bad times'; see Chapter 7). The fricative followed by a word-initial vowel is realized as a [z] (e.g. *maus amigos* [máwzɐmíguʃ] 'bad friends'; see more about this in Chapter 7).

---

[5] This phenomenon is also found in some regions of northern Continental Portugal.
[6] Final [ɫ], rather than [w], occurs in some southern Brazil dialects.

2.2.1.2. *Further comments*

• *Context-dependent variation common to EP and BP*

Let us summarize what has been said so far about non-labial fricatives. EP distinguishes two sibilants produced in the dento-alveolar region ([s], [z]), and two others in the post-alveolar region ([ʃ], [ʒ]), word-initially (# −) and intervocalically (V − V). BP converges with EP in this respect. In coda position, both word-medially and word-finally, we find sibilant neutralization with respect to place and voicing. With respect to place, this fact was commonly viewed in previous generative studies as a process of palatalization of an underlying /s/. Examples are given in (2).

(2) Sibilant distribution in EP and BP

[s]	*selo*	[sélu] 'seal'		[z]	*zelo*	[zélu] 'care'	
[ʃ]	*chá*	[ʃá] 'tea'		[ʒ]	*já*	[ʒá] 'already'	

[s] *selo* [sélu] 'seal'　　　　　　[z] *zelo* [zélu] 'care'
[ʃ] *chá* [ʃá] 'tea'　　　　　　　[ʒ] *já* [ʒá] 'already'

[s] *assa* [ásɐ] 's/he roasts'　　[z] *asa* [ázɐ] 'wing'
[ʃ] *acha* [áʃɐ] 's/he finds'　　[ʒ] *haja* [áʒɐ] 'there may be' (subj.)

[ʃ] *rasca* [ʀáʃkɐ] '(of) bad quality'　[ʒ] *rasga* [ʀázgɐ] 's/he tears'
[ʃ] *artista* [ɐɾtíʃtɐ] 'artist'　　[ʒ] *carisma* [kɐɾíʒmɐ] 'carisma'
[ʃ] *lápis* [lápiʃ] 'pencil'

As we saw in (1e), syllable final fricatives agree in voicing with the following context: they are voiceless when followed by a voiceless consonant or by silence, in absolute final position. With respect to this, EP and BP converge.[7]

• *Sibilants: regional sub-systems*

In some regions of (northern) Portugal, the sibilant system is more complex than that just described for EP and BP. In fact, there are dialects that distinguish two pairs of sibilants in the dento-alveolar region, rather than one: a laminal pair and an apical pair, which we symbolize as [s], [z] and [ʂ], [ʐ], respectively. In terms of the passive articulators, it is said that the former are dental ([s̪], [z̪]) and that the latter are alveolar, but may involve varying degrees of palatalization (e.g. Cintra, 1971a). Unlike EP and BP, such dialects contrast, for instance, *paço* [pásu] 'palace' with *passo* [páʂu] 'step', and *cozer* [kuzéɾ] 'to boil' with *coser* [kuʐéɾ] 'to sew' ([pásu] and [kuzéɾ] in EP); they also distinguish two sibilants in a word like *social* [ʂusjáɫ] 'social' ([susjáɫ] in EP).

Moreover, some of these dialects also possess the affricate [t͡ʃ]; its alternation with [ʃ] secures contrasts like that between *buxo* [búʃu] 'box tree' and *bucho* [bút͡ʃu] 'stomach' (both [búʃu] in EP).

The dialects in question can be labelled as more conservative than EP, for they are closer to the following consonants of early Portuguese: [ʂ], [ʐ], [s], [z], [ʃ], [ʒ], [t͡ʃ]. As the reader may observe in the examples above, the distinctions are recoverable from the orthography, which preserves their etymological origin. Table 2.1 summarizes the correspondence between the early Portuguese system and its source—mainly Latin.

---

[7] In certain BP dialects, including the São Paulo dialect, this palatalization does not exist.

TABLE 2.1

Early Portuguese	Source
1. [ş]	< Lat. [ş] (or retroflex [ṣ]?), word initially, or inter-vocalically before any vowel but [i], when the fricative was tense(?)
saber [sabéɾ] 'knowledge'	< *sapere*
fosse [fósi] 'it were' (subj.)	< *fuisset*
2. [ẕ]	< Lat. [ş] (or retroflex [ṣ]?), word initially, or inter-vocalically before any vowel but [i] (?), when the fricative was lax
causa [káwẕɐ] 'cause'	< *causa* (Lat.)
3. [s]	< Lat. [k] (orth. ⟨c⟩) initial?, before ⟨i, e, æ⟩, < Lat. [t] before [i],
cego [ségu] 'blind'	< *caecus*
cerca [sérkɐ] 'about'	< *circa*
palácio [pɐlásju] 'palace'	< *palatium*
4. [z]	< Lat. [k] (orth. ⟨c⟩) before a front vowel (⟨i, e, æ⟩), in intervocalic position
azedo [ɐzédu] 'acidic'	< *acidu*
5. [ʒ]	< Lat. [g] before [i, e], or < Lat. [j] which strengthened into a consonant
gelar [ʒeláɾ] 'to freeze'	< *gelare*
janeiro [ʒɐnéjɾu] 'january'	< *januariu*
6. [t͡ʃ]	< Lat. [pl], [kl], [fl] (the processes involved in this change are not yet well understood)
chuva [t͡ʃúvɐ] 'rain'	< *pluvia*
chamar [t͡ʃamár] 'call'	< *clamare*
chama [t͡ʃámɐ] 'flame'	< *flamma*
7. [ʃ][8]	< Lat. [ş] before [i] or before [k]
paixão [pajʃɛ̃́] 'passion'	< *passione*
mexer [mɨʃéɾ] 'to mix'	< *miscere*
	< Arab [ʃ]
xarope [ʃɐɾɔ́pɨ] 'syrup'	<*šarab*

This seven consonant sub-system dominated Portuguese everywhere with a significant degree of stability until the sixteenth century. Nowadays, the complete primitive system is only preserved in small regions of northern Portugal. Variants of it exist in several regions. The affricate appears to be the most unstable element of all, as it is a socially stigmatized mark, associated with members of the older generation.

[8] It should be noted that this fricative has two sources: a Latin one and an Arabic one.

• *Further comments on the rhotics*

We observed previously that the two liquids [R] and [ɾ] contrast intervocalically (e.g. *carro* [káRu] 'car' versus *caro* [káɾu] 'dear, expensive'), but that their distinction is neutralized at word boundaries: [ɾ] does not occur word-initially and [R] does not occur word-finally (e.g. *calor* [kɐlóɾ] 'heat' vs. *Roma* [Rómɐ] 'Rome').

However, at the phonetic level there are other contexts for the occurrence of rhotics. See the items in (3a and b) for the contexts where rhotics appear.

(3) a. Distribution of [R]
   [R] *honrar* [õRáɾ] 'to honour'
   [R] *enredo* [ẽRédu] 'plot (of a story)'
   [R] *palra* [páɫRɐ] 's/he chatters'
   [R] *Israel* [iʒRɐéɫ] 'Israel'
   [R] *desregrado* [dɨʒRɨgɾádu] 'unruly'
   [R] *roda* [Rɔdɐ] 'wheel'
   [R] *carro* [káRu] 'car'

   b. Distribution of [ɾ]
   [ɾ] *parar* [pɐɾáɾ] 'to stop'
   [ɾ] *sardinha* [sɐɾdíɲɐ] 'sardine'
   [ɾ] *arco* [áɾku] 'arch, arc'
   [ɾ] *atributo* [ɐtɾibútu] 'attribute'
   [ɾ] *praça* [pɾásɐ] 'square'
   [ɾ] *caro* [káɾu] 'dear, expensive'
   [ɾ] *mar* [máɾ] 'sea'

These data lead us to think that rhotic occurrence is predictable in certain contexts. In fact, the examples show that whenever the rhotic is word-initial (*roda* [Rɔdɐ]) or syllable-initial preceded by a syllable-final consonant (*palra* [páɫRɐ], *desregrado* [dɨʒRɨgɾádu]), it is realized as [R].The rhotic is a simple alveolar flap when it is word-final (*mar* [máɾ]) or syllable-final (*sardinha* [sɐɾdíɲɐ], *arco* [áɾku]), or when it belongs to the same syllable as the precedent consonant (branching onset) (*atributo* [ɐtɾibútu]).

When the rhotic follows a nasal vowel, [ɾ] is not licensed and only [R] occurs (*honrar* [õRáɾ]). This fact is justified by some proposals about the lexical representation of nasality. In previous generative studies (e.g. Mateus, 1975; Andrade, 1977), it has been argued that phonetically nasalized vowels in Portuguese are actually derived from an underlying non-nasal vowel followed by a nasal segment (see 2.2.2.1 and 2.2.2.4 on nasal vowels; see also Barbosa (1965:187–208) and Câmara (1953) for the structural view of the liquids). As a first approach, we take the view that cases like *honrar* [õRáɾ] are not exceptional, since underlyingly the rhotic is not preceded by a vocalic segment.

• *Occurrence of both rhotics between vowels* (e.g. *carro* [káRu] vs. *caro* [káɾu]). We propose that the first syllable of *carro* [káRu] and similar words has a flap in the coda at the underlying level, and the second syllable has a flap in the onset which entails the realization of the latter as a [R]. The syllable coda flap is then erased. The occurrence of this underlying coda is supported by the fact that words having intervocalic trill never can be stressed on the antepenultimate syllable because the penultimate has a final consonant and is thus heavy. The same happens with words having diphthongs or another consonant in coda in the penultimate syllable (see 2.2.2.4).

Thus, we propose a single underlying rhotic, which is the flap. This consonant triggers specific rules in the following contexts: (a) word-initially (*rodar* [Rudáɾ]), (b) when preceded by a nasal autosegment (*enredo* [ẽRédu]); (c) when preceded by a consonant in coda (*palra* [páɬRɐ], Israel [iʃRɐéɬ], *carro*, [káRu]). In other words, the flap is the unmarked rhotic, the trill is the exceptional one, and its phonetic realization depends on the application of specific rules.

Bonet and Mascaró (1997) argue in favour of the opposite position, basing their proposal on the sonority principle and the dispersion principle (dissimilarity condition). They show that the contrast (or distance) between the trill as an onset and the vocalic nucleus is preferred to the contrast between the flap and the vowel, from a syllabic point of view. We agree with this preference, but we think that the arguments supporting our proposal are stronger, even from a syllabic point of view. It is generally accepted that codas may not have C-place (see 2.4 and Chapter 3). If this is true, and given that that flap is an unmarked consonant (see again 2.4), it is preferable to have an underspecified flap in coda and fill it with default rules than to specify it with a new feature, [+f] (as Bonet and Mascaró propose), even if this specification is restricted to the contrasting contexts.

Furthermore, in connected speech the flap is maintained when it is both word-final and followed by a word beginning with a vowel (e.g. *mar azul* [máɾɐzúɬ], *[máRɐzúɬ] 'blue sea'). We assume that in case of sandhi it is the underlying flap that is realized, and the same happens with the other liquid, the lateral /l/ (e.g. *mal amado* [málɐmádu] vs. * [maɬɐmádu] 'badly loved'). In any case, in the languages having contrasting rhotics, there are so many different realizations for the flap and the trill that the question of the underlying representation is much harder to solve.

• *Stop affrication in Brazilian dialects*[9]

One of the phonetic characteristics of the BP (Rio de Janeiro) dialect and several other Brazilian dialects is the alternation of the dento-alveolar plosives, [t] and [d], with the affricates [t͡ʃ] and [d͡ʒ].[10] As may be observed in the examples of (4a and b), the occurrence of the affricates is context dependent: in fact they are determined by the presence of a following [i]. This fact is generally described as a palatalization phenomenon undergone by the plosives. (4a) compares EP and BP realizations.

---

[9] See also Mateus (1975) and Andrade (1977) on the questions concerning all these subsystems of consonants within the SPE model and the formulation of rules.

[10] They do not occur, for instance, in São Paulo.

(4) a. Differences between EP and BP

EP	BP
tia [tíɐ]	[t͡ʃíɐ] 'aunt'
dia [díɐ]	[d͡ʒíɐ] 'day'
pote [pɔ́tɨ]	[pɔ́t͡ʃi] 'pot'
pode [pɔ́dɨ]	[pɔ́d͡ʒi] 's/he can'

  b. Palatalization of BP dental stops

tia [t͡ʃíɐ] 'aunt'	*tom* [tṍ] 'tone'
dia [d͡ʒíɐ] 'day'	*dom* [dṍ] 'gift'
bate [bát͡ʃi] 's/he beats'	*bato* [bátu] 'I beat'
arde [áɾd͡ʒi] 's/he burns'	*ardo* [áɾdu] 'I burn'

2.2.2. Vowels and glides

2.2.2.1. Inventory

In order to describe the EP vowel system, a distinction between stressed and unstressed vowels must be made, given the close relation existing between vowel quality and word-stress in this variety of the language. Vowel quality is significantly more independent from word-stress in BP than in EP. This fact entails considerable difference between the two varieties at the phonetic level when it comes to the atonic sub-system.

Stressed vowels (see (5)) and unstressed vowels (see (6) and (7)), as well as nasal vowels (see (8)) are considered separately. In Portuguese, word-final position only allows a limited set of unstressed vowels (see (7)). The difference between EP and BP is specially striking with respect to the non-final unstressed positions (see (6)). Nasal vowels are the same in both varieties.

(5) Stressed vowels

  a. Similarities between EP and BP
   [í] *silo* [sílu] 'silo'
   [é] *selo* [sélu] 'seal'
   [ɛ́] *selo* [sɛ́lu] 'I stamp'
   [á] *bala* [bálɐ] 'bullet'
   [ɔ́] *bola* [bɔ́lɐ] 'ball'
   [ó] *bola* [bólɐ] 'a kind of cake'
   [ú] *bula* [búlɐ] 'bull'

  b. Differences between EP and BP

EP	BP
[é] *telha* [téʎɐ][11]	[é] *telha* [téʎɐ] 'roof-tile'
[é] *lei* [léj]	[é] *lei* [léj] 'law'

---

[11] Unlike the standard variety of Lisbon, on which we base this book, that of Coimbra maintains stressed [e] in the context of a non-nasal palatal (*telha* t[é]lha).

(6)   Unstressed non-final vowels

    a.   Prestressed position

EP	BP
[i] *mirar* [miɾáɾ]	[i] [miɾáɾ] 'to look at'
[u] *morar* [muɾáɾ]	[o] [moɾáɾ] 'to live'
[u] *murar* [muɾáɾ]	[u] [muɾáɾ] 'to enclose'
[ɐ] *pagar* [pɐgáɾ]	[a] [pagáɾ] 'to pay'
[ɨ] *pegar* [pɨgáɾ]	[e] [pegáɾ] 'to take'

    b.   Post-stressed position

EP	BP
[i] *dúvida* [dúvidɐ]	[i] *dúvida* [dúvidɐ] 'doubt'
[u] *pérola* [péɾulɐ]	[u] *pérola* [péɾulɐ] 'pearl'
[u] *báculo* [bákulu]	[u] *báculo* [bákulu] 'stick'
[ɐ] *ágape* [ágɐpɨ]	[a] *ágape* [ágapi] 'agape'
[ɨ] *cérebro* [séɾɨbɾu]	[e] *cérebro* [séɾebɾu] 'brain'

(7)   Unstressed vowels in final position

EP	BP
[i] *júri* [ʒúɾi]	[i] *júri* [ʒúɾi] 'jury'
[ɨ] *jure* [ʒúɾɨ]	[i] *jure* [ʒúɾi] 's/he swears' (subj.)
[u] *juro* [ʒúɾu]	[u] *juro* [ʒúɾu] 'I swear'
[ɐ] *jura* [ʒúɾɐ]	[ɐ] *jura* [ʒúɾɐ] 's/he swears'

In EP the unstressed vowel [ɨ] is usually deleted in colloquial speech (*dever* [dɨvéɾ] / [dvéɾ] 'duty'; *bate* [bátɨ] / [bát] 's/he beats').[12] Word-final unstressed [u] can also be deleted (*bato* [bátu] / [bát] 'I beat'), but this is not such a frequent phenomenon as [ɨ] deletion.

It is worth noting that, in BP, the unstressed vowel [ɐ] only occurs in word-final position.

(8)   Nasal vowels

[ĩ] *cinto* [sĩtu] 'belt'	[ẽ] *sento* [sẽtu] 'I seat'
[ẽ] *canto* [kẽtu] 'corner'	[õ] *conto* [kõtu] 'story'
[ẽ] *mando* [mẽdu] 'I order'	[ũ] *mundo* [mũdu] 'world'

(9) Glides

[j] *pai* [páj] 'father'	[w] *pau* [páw] 'stick'

Glides are also nasalized in nasal diphthongs, as in *mão* [mẽw̃] 'hand' or *viagem* [viáʒẽj̃] 'trip'.[13]

---

[12] See Miguel (1993) and A. Andrade (1994) on this.

[13] In EP northern dialects we find low nasal vowels as [ã], [ɛ̃] and [ɔ̃] namely in verb forms when the vowel is stressed (e.g. *canto* [kãtu] 'I sing', *sento* [ɛ̃] 'seat', *conto* [kɔ̃tu] 'I count').

2.2.2.2. *Vowel alternations and variation in stressed position*

As we saw in (5a), EP and BP have the same set of stressed vowels at the phonetic level: [i, e, ɛ, a, ɔ, o, u]. (5b) contains examples of a contrast occurring in EP but not in BP, namely that between [á] and [ɐ́] However, this contrast is only apparent, for stressed [ɐ] is an alternative realization of other stressed vowels in certain contexts. In fact, this vowel occurs in three types of contexts in EP:

- before a palatal consonant (*telha* [tɐ́ʎɐ] 'tile', *fecho* [fɐ́ʃu] 'bolt', *cereja* [sɨɾɐ́ʒɐ] 'cherry', *senha* [sɐ́ɲɐ] 'signal');
- before the palatal (front) glide (*lei* [lɐ́j] 'law');
- before a nasal consonant (*cama* [kɐ́mɐ] 'bed', *cana* [kɐ́nɐ] 'reed', *manha* [mɐ́ɲɐ] 'astuteness').

In each of these contexts it can be shown to alternate with either [a] or [e]. Let us look at the two first cases.

As has already been pointed out, before palatals there is no [e] in EP (see note 11). On the other hand, words derived from base words possessing a stressed [ɐ́] have an [ɨ] in the corresponding unstressed position (e.g. *telhado* [tɨʎádu] 'roof', derived from *telha* [tɐ́ʎɐ] 'tile'; *fechado* [fɨʃádu] 'closed', derived from *fecho* [fɐ́ʃu] 'bolt'). Usually, [ɨ] alternates in unstressed position with stressed [é] and [ɛ́] (for instance, *selo* [sélu] 'seal' and *selo* [sɛ́lu] 'I stamp' vs. *selar* [sɨláɾ] 'to stamp'). This fact shows that stressed [ɐ́] alternates with stressed [é] and [ɛ́] when these vowels occur before palatal consonants and the front glide. However, stressed [ɛ́] occurs in the same context (*velha* [vɛ́ʎɐ] 'old woman', *mecha* [mɛ́ʃɐ] 'wick'),[14] which means that stressed [ɐ́] can only alternate with [é], in this context. Some examples are given in (10).

(10)   Alternation between [ɐ́] and [ɨ]

telha [tɐ́ʎɐ] 'tile'	*telhado* [tɨʎádu] 'roof'
abelha [ɐbɐ́ʎɐ] 'bee'	*abelhinha* [ɐbɨʎíɲɐ] 'little bee'
fecho [fɐ́ʃu] 'bolt'	*fechado* [fɨʃádu] 'closed'
venho [vɐ́ɲu] 'I come in'	*venhamos* [vɨɲémuʃ] 'we come in'
lei [lɐ́j] 'law'	*legal* [lɨgáɫ] 'legal'

The case of [ɐ́] followed by a nasal is somewhat different. In EP, words derived from base-words as *cama* [kɐ́mɐ] 'bed' (e.g. *caminha* [kɐmíɲɐ] 'little bed') or *cana* [kɐ́nɐ] 'reed' (e.g. *canavial* [kɐnɐviáɫ] 'reed patch'), which have [ɐ] in stressed and unstressed syllables, allow us to infer that [ɐ] alternates with [a] because it is followed by a nasal consonant. This is confirmed by the fact that in Portuguese, all nasal vowels, either stressed or unstressed, are [–low].[15]

---

[14] Probably for socio-cultural reasons, there seems to be an ongoing change in the sense that, under the same circumstances, /ɛ/ may be realized as [ɐ́] (e.g. *velha* v[ɐ́]lha).

[15] In BP, at least stressed vowels followed by a nasal consonant may be nasalized (*cama* [kɐ̃mɐ], *cana* [kɐ̃nɐ]).

2.2.2.3. *Unstressed vowels*

The EP and BP systems of unstressed vowels are very different from each other. Examples of unstressed vowels occurring in different positions can be observed above, in (6) and (7).

In non-final positions, the EP vowel system has just two degrees of openness, rather than the three degrees found in stressed position: three high vowels ([i], [ɨ], [u]) and one mid vowel ([ɐ]). In BP the three degrees of height are maintained: two high vowels ([i], [u]), two mid vowels ([e], [o]), and one low one ([a]). In word-final position, the two varieties have fewer distinctions than in other unstressed positions: two high vowels ([ɨ] EP or [i] BP and [u]) and one mid vowel ([ɐ]).

Unstressed [ɐ] always alternates with stressed [a] (see, for example, the alternation in the words *pagar* [pɐgáɾ] 'to pay' vs. *paga* [págɐ] 's/he pays'; *parar* [pɐɾáɾ] 'to stop' vs. *paro* [páɾu] 'I stop'). Stressed [i] and [u] do not alternate with other vowels when unstressed (for example *viver* [vivéɾ] 'to live' vs. *vivo* [vívu] 'I live; *subir* [subíɾ] 'to go up' vs. *subo* [súbu] 'I go up'). As far as the remaining vowels are concerned, European and Brazilian Portuguese have different realizations:

- In EP stressed [ɛ] and [e] correspond to a high and central vowel [ɨ] (either in pre or post-stressed position) which, in most cases, is deleted in colloquial speech (e.g. *selo* [sélu] 'seal' and *selo* [sɨ́lu] 'I stamp' vs. *selar* [sɨláɾ], [sláɾ] 'to stamp'; *devo* [dévu] 'I owe' vs. *dever* [dɨvéɾ], [dvéɾ] 'to owe'); stressed [ɔ] and [ó] correspond to [u] (e.g. *forço* [fɔ́ɾsu] 'I oblige' and *força* [fóɾsɐ] 'strength' vs. *forçar* [fuɾsáɾ] 'to oblige');
- In BP stressed [ɛ] and [e] correspond to [e] in pre-stressed position, and to [i] in post-stressed position (e.g. *selar* [seláɾ] 'to stamp'/ *sele* [séli] 'you stamp');[16] stressed [ɔ] and [o] correspond to [o] in pre-stressed position, and to [u] in post-stressed position (e.g. *forçar* [foɾsáɾ] 'to oblige' and *forço* [fɔ́ɾsu] 'I oblige').

So, keeping [a] apart, it may be said that the distinction between low and mid vowels is neutralized in unstressed position in both varieties: they are realized as mid in BP, and as high in EP;[17] only [i] and [u] are found in word-final position in BP.

2.2.2.4. *Nasal vowels*

Portuguese nasal vowels raise difficult questions. As we can see in the data presented below (11), at the phonetic level the two varieties have the same nasal vowels. These are always [–low]. Nasal vowels in non-final stressed and prestressed syllables are exemplified in (11a); instances of nasal vowels in stressed final syllables in (11b).

---

[16] As we can see in (6b), there is no raising in the post-stressed in antepenultimate stressed words (*cérebro* [séɾebɾu] 'mind').

[17] There are some exceptional cases, in EP, in which non-high vowels are maintained in the pre-stressed position: [a] *invasor* [ĩvazóɾ] 'invader'; [ɛ] *objecção* [ɔbʒɛséw̃] 'objection'; [ɔ] *adopção* [ɐdɔséw̃] 'adoption'.

(11) a. Stressed nasal vowels

Non-final

[ẽ] *canto* [kẽtu] 'song'
[ẽ] *entre* [ẽtɾɨ] 'between'
[ĩ] *cinco* [sĩku] 'five'
[õ] *ponto* [põtu] 'point'
[ũ] *fundo* [fũdu] 'deep'

Final

[ẽ] *irmã* [iɾmẽ] 'sister'

[ĩ] *fim* [fĩ] 'end'
[õ] *som* [sõ] 'sound'
[ũ] *comum* [kumũ] 'common'

b. Pre-stressed

[ɐ̃)] *cantar* [kɐ̃táɾ] 'to sing'
[ẽ] *entrar* [ẽtɾáɾ] 'to come in'
[ĩ] *findar* [fĩdáɾ] 'to end'
[õ] *apontar* [ɐpõtáɾ] 'to point'
[ũ] *untar* [ũtáɾ] 'to oil'

We assume that, *underlyingly, there are no nasal vowels in Portuguese*. At the underlying level, we will treat them as sequences of oral vowel plus nasal segment. The arguments in favour of this hypothesis are as follows:

(i) As we said above in 2.2.1.2.(3), as far as intervocalic rhotics ([R] and [ɾ]) are concerned, only [R] occurs in EP after a syllable-final consonant (*palrar* [paɫRár] 'chatter', *desregrado* [diʒRɨgɾádu] 'unruly'). The pronunciation of ⟨r⟩ after a nasal vowel follows a similar pattern to its pronunciation after a syllable-final consonant: only [R] is allowed in this case. See examples in (12).

(12) Rhotics after nasal and non-nasal vowels

a. Nasal vowels

[ẽ] *tenro* [tẽRu] 'tender'

[ẽ] *enrolo* [ẽRólu] 'confusion'

[õ] *honra* [õRɐ] 'honour'

[õ] *ronronar* [RõRunáɾ] 'to purr'

b. Non-nasal vowels

[é] *pera* [péɾɐ] 'pear'
[é] *perra* [péRɐ] 'hardy' (fem.)
[ɨ] *encerar* [ẽsɨɾáɾ] 'to wax'
[ɨ] *encerrar* [ẽsɨRáɾ] 'to enclose'
[ó] *coro* [kóɾu] 'coir'
[ó] *corro* [kóRu] 'I run'
[u] *coral* [kuɾáɫ] 'choral'
[u] *curral* [kuRáɫ] 'stable'

Examples in (12) illustrate the diverse behaviour of nasal and oral vowels. This diversity is due to the presence of an underlying nasal segment that is phonetically realized as the nasal feature of the vowel.

(ii) Let us consider the distribution of the nasal vowels and consonants in the following examples.[18]

---

[18] Phonetic transcriptions of the examples are in accordance with the EP realization, namely for the unstressed vowels (see (6) above).

(13) a. *intenção* [ĩtẽsẽ̃w̃] 'intention'
      incapaz [ĩkɐpáʃ] 'unable'
      imposto [ĩpóʃtu] 'tax'

   b. *inacabado* [inɐkɐbádu] 'unfinished'
      inoportuno [inopuɾtúnu] 'inopportune'
      inaceitável [inɐsɐjtávɛɫ] 'unacceptable'

(13a and b) include examples of derivations from base words which have the same prefix (spelled ⟨in⟩ or ⟨im⟩): *tenção* 'intention' / *intenção* 'intention'; *capaz* 'able'/*incapaz* 'unable'; *posto* 'put in place'/*imposto* 'forced'; *acabado* 'finished' / *inacabado* 'unfinished'; *oportuno* 'opportune' / *inoportuno* 'inopportune'; *aceitável* 'acceptable' / *inaceitável* 'unacceptable'. When placed before a conson-ant, the prefix is pronounced [ĩ], while before a vowel it is realized as an oral vowel and a nasal consonant—the sequence [in]. We propose that this particular prefix has a single underlying representation, but is phonetically realized as a nasal vowel before a consonant, or as a vowel followed by a nasal consonant, when the following context is a vowel. Compare the examples which we gave in (11a) (final stressed vowels), transcribed again below with the derived forms in (14):

(11a) [ẽ̃] *irmã* [iɾmẽ̃] 'sister'   (14) *irmanar* [iɾmɐnáɾ] 'fraternize'
      [ĩ] *fim* [fĩ] 'end'   *final* [fináɫ] 'end'
      [õ] *som* [sõ] 'sound'   *sonoro* [sunɔɾu] 'sonorous'
      [ũ] *comum* [kumũ] 'common'   *comunal* [kumunáɫ] 'communal'

The sequences of vowel plus nasal consonant in (14) correspond to the word-final nasal vowels in (11a).

Now, take the examples of EP nasal diphthongs. When we compare (15a) with the derivations from these examples given in (15b), we find the same alternation: nasal vowel/vowel plus nasal consonant (the occurrence of the nasal glide is dealt with in Chapter 7).

(15) a. *pão* [pẽ̃w̃] 'bread'   b. *panito* [pɐnítu] 'small bread'
      leão [ljẽ̃w̃] 'lion'   *leonino* [liunínu] 'leonine'
      irmão [iɾmẽ̃w̃] 'brother'   *irmanar* [iɾmɐnáɾ] 'unite, match'

The examples in (15b) reflect a distribution gap with respect to nasal conson-ants: they occur syllable-initially (e.g. [pɐ-nítu]) but they do not occur syllable-finally (e.g. *[pɐn-zítu]). Thus words like *[pin], *[bam] and *[saɲ] are not allowed in Portuguese.[19]

(iii) We may add another argument in favour of our proposition with regard to the 'nasal' vowels. It is not possible to have an antepenultimate stressed syllable if the penultimate has a nasal vowel, as shown in (16).

---

[19] There are a few exceptions ending in [ɛn] like *abdómen* [ɐbdɔmɛn] or *sémen* [sémɛn]. In BP these words have a final nasal diphthong (e.g. [abdɔmẽj̃]).

(16) *rápido* [Rápidu] 'quick' but *[Rápĩdu]
      cómodo [kɔ́mudu] 'suitable' but *[kɔ́mõdu]
      estômago [ʃtómɐgu] 'stomach' but *[ʃtómẽgu]

These examples show that nasalized vowels in penultimate position are never skipped by stress. The same occurs when the penultimate syllable is closed by a consonant or if there is a diphthong (e.g. *[Rápɐjdu] or *[Rápiʃdu], *[kɔ́mojdu] or *[kɔ́muʃdu]; cf. also Chapter 6).[20] This is due to the fact that prefinal heavy syllables cannot be unstressed. In the case of nasal vowels, the syllable is heavy because there is a nasal segment underlyingly.

Thus there seems to be enough evidence to support the idea that, underlyingly, Portuguese nasal vowels receive their nasality from a nasal segment that is deleted at the phonetic level. This problem has been dealt with in different frameworks. From a structuralist point of view, see Lüdtke (1953) and Head (1965) who are of the opinion both oral and nasal vowels are phonemic, and Câmara (1953 and 1970) and Barbosa (1965), who take the view that nasalized vowels correspond to 'oral vowels followed by a nasal consonantal archiphoneme', phonologically. An account of the nasalization process according to the SPE model can be seen in Mateus (1975). In Wetzels (1997) nasal diphthongs are represented as such at the level of lexical representation. With regards to nasality in Brazilian Portuguese, see also Callou and Leite (1990) and Cagliari (1977). Morales-Front and Holt (1997) treat problems concerning pluralization of words ending in nasal vowels in terms of optimality theory.

In the present work vowel nasality is treated within a non-linear theoretical framework. The nasalization process will be discussed in greater detail in Chapter 7.

2.3. THE ORGANIZATION OF PHONOLOGICAL FEATURES

In this book we assume that segments are made up of distinctive features. Even though most of the features we use coincide with those that have been proposed in *The Sound Pattern of English*, we do not consider segments as feature bundles; rather, we assume the componential dimension of segments, and take the view that features are organized in a geometrical way and that certain sets of features are interdependent.[21] This view, usually called *feature geometry*, allows for the possibility of grouping features into larger sets that can act together in certain processes.

Accordingly, we do not accept a bijective relation between the segment and the features that identify it, but see the latter as autosegments, i.e. entities which may

---

[20] See further arguments in Morales-Front and Holt (1997, 401–2).

[21] It is worth noting that Chomsky and Halle (1968: 300) have already pointed out in SPE 'that ultimately, the features themselves will be seen to be organized in a hierarchical structure which may resemble the structure that we have imposed on them for purely expository reasons.' On the geometrical organization of features see Clements (1985), Sagey (1986), Clements (1988), Halle (1991) and, more recently, Clements and Hume (1995).

spread over more than one segment, and may stay on even when the segment they are associated with is deleted. Autosegments correspond to sets of features or to single features, and function independently from one another.

Autosegmental phonology is, therefore, more suited to the identification of phonological processes involving feature spreading, and of processes such as the deletion of a segment combined with the persistence of one or more of its features. This is what happens, for instance, in vowel harmony in Portuguese (see Chapter 4).

The geometrical organization of features (represented in (17) below) implies that:
• terminal features are grouped into *class nodes*;
• these nodes are located in separate *tiers* which, at the upper level, are directly linked to a *root node*;
• each root node is connected to a position in a separate tier, called *skeleton*, which consists of a sequence of abstract time units; positions on this skeleton are marked by an X.[22]

(17)

Skeleton	X
Root	R
Class nodes	B C
Class nodes	D E F G
Terminal feature nodes	a b c d e f g h

The class nodes are independent of each other, but features of the same class, which belong to the same node, are also independent but behave as a functional unit in certain phonological processes. In this sense they define a 'natural class' of segments.

We subscribe to the claim that feature organization is universally determined, and agree with Clements and Hume (1995: 300–1) that 'feature organization may reflect functional aspects of vocal tract organization in which independent (or partly independent) articulators, determining vocal tract constrictions, are assigned to independent, interacting tiers'; we believe, furthermore, with these authors, that 'a hierarchical approach to feature organization promises both to allow a substantially constrained account of phonological organization at the most

[22] We have adopted the X notation, here, and not the CV notation. About this question, see 3.3.

abstract level, satisfying the requirements of formal linguistic theory, and to offer a bridge between phonological structure and phonetic interpretation.'

The representation of features, therefore, does not correspond to a bi-dimensional matrix, but rather to a multi-dimensional hierarchical structure or *geometry*. An autosegment is said to be *floating* when it is not linked to the tier immediately above it, or has become detached (see 7.2). Floating autosegments which remain non-associated at the end of phonological derivations are not realized phonetically.

There are a number of different proposals regarding the specific hierarchical organization of the features for consonants and vowels, as can be seen, for instance, in Goldsmith (1990), Kenstowicz (1994) and Clements and Hume (1995). In the present analysis of Portuguese phonological processes, we adopt the feature organization proposed by the latter: the *Constriction-based Model*. This is based on the assumption that 'any segment produced in the oral tract has a characteristic constriction, defined by two parameters, constriction degree and constriction location' (1995:275). Constriction degree is represented by the *continuant* node and location by the *place* node. So, continuant and place both depend on the oral cavity.

In (18a and b), we present the feature organization we have adopted in this book. As we said above, features that belong to the same class node are independent but they behave as a functional unit. For example, the laryngeal and the C-place nodes depend on the root node and function separately. As far as the place node is concerned, it dominates articulatory nodes which rely on the presence of an active articulator such as the lips, the blade and the dorsum of the tongue, and which are interrelated in many phonological processes.

One of the major class features included in (18), [sonorant], agrees with the organization proposed by Clements and Hume. They also propose [approximant] and [vocoid]. We do not use these two features for the following reasons:

• The feature [approximant] is not needed to identify liquids among the sonorants (see below what is said about [laterals]);
• The feature [vocoid], defined by Clements and Hume (1995: 269) as 'the terminological converse of [consonantal]' is proposed because of the need to group together vowels and glides. In the present book we assume there are no underlying glides in Portuguese (see discussion of Tables 2.4 and 2.5), and so we have used the traditional feature [consonantal], considering it to be adequate for the identification of Portuguese phonological segments.

Thus in (18) the root node is represented in terms of the two features [consonant] and [sonorant] that clearly distinguish obstruents from sonorants (consonants and vowels). Nasal consonants have their own feature, as do laterals: nasality and laterality evidence a peculiar behaviour in the languages of the world, which justifies a position of direct dependency on the root.[23]

---

[23] Another proposal for the placement of the [nasal] feature is, for example, Sagey (1986) and Halle (1991), who consider that this feature depends on the soft palate node, which is directly related to the root or is linked by means of the supralaryngeal class tier.

(18) a.

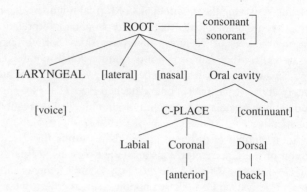

(18) b.

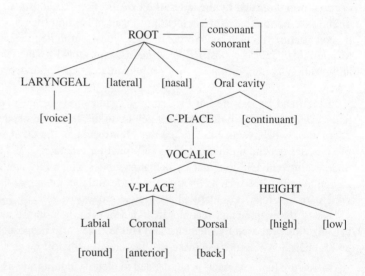

Due to the phonetic characteristics of consonants and vowels, this model makes a distinction between consonant place and vowel place, namely with respect to the class node of height features that is restricted to vowels (compare (18a) with (18b)). One of the arguments in favour of this position has to do with the fact that height features play an important role in processes vowels are subject to, in many languages (cf. Clements, 1991). In Portuguese, for example, both unstressed vowel specification and vowel harmony involve vowel height features.

It is worth noting that, in hierarchical organization of features presented in (18), two main class nodes—the *laryngeal* node and the *oral cavity* node—depend on the root node. These, in turn, dominate other class nodes (or features). Some authors propose the existence of further nodes but such extra nodes are not necessary in the case of Portuguese.[24]

[24] McCarthy (1988), for instance, suggests that there is a pharyngeal node (or feature) that is a sister node of the oral place. See Kenstowicz (1994) and Clements and Hume (1995) on these proposals.

As for the laryngeal node, it is motivated by the fact the features it dominates may not only behave individually, but also as a unit. Given that in Portuguese there are no aspirated or ejective consonants, we only use the [voice] feature to identify consonants. This feature depends on the functioning of the vocal cords (stiff or slack).

The following points should be taken into consideration:

(i) We assume that features are binary. Class nodes are unary. Formally, their presence is marked with a dot [•] in the definition of a segment.

(ii) The definition of Portuguese sound classes only requires the features indicated above.[25] Therefore, other features, such as [strident], will not be used in this book. Furthermore, unlike the features included in (18), [strident] does not depend on a specific articulator, but is connected with an acoustic property. While it is true that Portuguese fricatives and affricates are usually described as [strident], it is also the case that fricatives are the only consonants that can be identified as [+continuant] and [–sonorant], so that stridency becomes redundant. This feature does not play a distinctive role, either, in the case of affricates. Unlike other consonants (see 7.4), the latter involve two specifications for continuancy.

(iii) The feature [continuant] differentiates plosives (or stops) and nasals from all the other consonants, vowels and glides: in the production of plosives and nasals, such as [b], [m] or [n], the air flow passage is blocked in the vocal tract, and so they are [–continuant].

The classification of laterals with respect to this feature is somewhat problematic and depends, to a certain extent, on the behaviour of the sounds in the individual languages. If we establish that [–continuant] sounds are those produced with the blocking of the air passage at the place of constriction, then laterals are [–continuant]. On the other hand, we may consider laterals to be [+continuant] if the relevant property is the presence/absence of a total obstruction of the air flow.

The examination of the phonological behaviour of laterals /l/ and /ʎ/ in Portuguese has led some authors to classify them as [–continuant] while other authors classify them as [+continuant]. For example, /l/ may be interpreted as [–continuant] on the grounds of the following historical argument: during the early stages of the language, /l/ underwent a process of deletion in intervocalic position, together with /n/ and /d/, both [–continuant]. In the view of Andrade (1977), the behaviour of the three consonants as a single natural class is captured by their definition as [–continuant]. It should be stressed that this process of intervocalic deletion has had an enormously significant role in the history of the language. Finally, the classification of laterals as [–continuant] allows us to distinguish them from the rhotics, that are [+continuant] but are, as the laterals, [+ consonantal] and [+sonorant].

On the other hand, /l/ is classified as [+continuant] specially by its behaviour

---

[25] This concerns the dialects under study. Other dialects (like northern EP dialects) would need complementary features. In fact, the distinction between apical and dental sibilants ([ʂ], [ʐ], and [s], [z]) that still exists in some EP dialects is only captured if we use a supplementary feature as [distributed]: [ʂ] and [ʐ] are [-distributed] while [s] [z] are [+distributed].

in syllable coda: as it happens in many languages, it velarizes in EP and, in BP, it is subject to a gliding rule (see, for example, Callou and Leite, 1990; and Cagliari, 1997). Yet, we can argue that the fact that /l/ alternates with a glide syllable finally, in modern BP, can be interpreted as a positional phenomenon that does not require us to classify the lateral in question as [+continuant]. We have to admit, however, that none of these arguments provides a clear solution. In any event, codas in Portuguese seem to license only [+continuant] (see Chapter 3 on syllable codas). Therefore, laterals should be classified as such.

(iv) In Clements and Hume's proposal, the place feature [anterior] is negatively specified with respect to vowels, while its value specification is absent with respect to consonants. In fact, anterior sounds are realized with an obstruction located in front of the palato-alveolar region (see, for instance, SPE (1969: 304)), and so the definition of vowels as [−anterior] reflects the fact that vowel constrictions, front ones included, are produced further back in the vocal tract. Therefore, we prefer not to specify the value for this feature. We will see later that, for consonants, it is important to keep the binarity of this feature (see 2.4.2, where we deal with the concept of underspecification) even though for vowels the feature is not pertinent.

(v) Vowels in Portuguese are identified on the basis of the oral cavity features, as they do not involve differences in duration or tenseness. For their classification, we use the vocalic node dominating V-place and height. We strongly support the separate treatment of vowel height (or 'aperture' in Clements and Hume, op. cit.) and V-place through the establishment of two separate nodes. As we said above, we consider that this separation provides a better explanation for certain phonological processes that vowels undergo (see for instance, in 4.2.2.2, vowel harmony in verbs that involve only vowel height features).

Moreover, vowels are often subject to processes involving more than V-place dependent features (see, for example, the discussion of vowel assimilation in 4.2.2.1.2).[26]

Some proposals about vowel features assume scalar values for vowel height resulting from the interrelation of the [open] feature with two or more tiers, arguing that distinctions along this dimension cannot be adequately described by traditional [high] and [low] binary features. Authors such as Clements, Hume and Wetzels (e.g. Clements,1991; Clements and Hume, 1995; for Brazilian Portuguese, Wetzels,1992) state that the scalar aperture feature is specific to vowels (given the stricture characteristics of consonants) and they propose [open 1, 2, . . .] to classify different vocalic systems. According to them, Portuguese vowels show three degrees of aperture and then they can be identified with [+/−open 1], [+/−open 2] and [+/−open 3].

Nevertheless, Portuguese phonological processes do not warrant [open 1, 2, . . .] instead of [high] and [low], and so we keep the traditional [high] and [low]

---

[26] See de Jong (1995) for the discussion of the interrelated features [back] and [round] in English and for the presentation of different proposals in the geometrical organization of the features in order to match this interrelation.

features that adequately identify vocalic segments in both varieties, and also make it possible to classify vocalic systems with different degrees of height (cf. Clements, 1991; Clements and Hume, 1995).

We disagree with some authors who have argued in favour of the need for another feature, usually known as ATR (advanced tongue root), to define the Portuguese vowel system (e.g. Redenbarger, 1981; A. Andrade, 1992). As will be shown in the course of our analysis, V-place and height features are sufficient to represent the phonological processes of this language.[27]

So, we assume that groups of features function separately with respect to vowels and consonants which is confirmed by the analysis of Portuguese phonological processes. It is worth noting that this separation is precisely a consequence of the values showed by vowels with respect to the height parameter.

(vi) Processes involving consonants frequently reflect an interdependency between the features dominated by the C-place node, which provides support for the organization included in (18) (see the analysis of the palatalization processes, in 7.4.1.2, where the realization of the fricatives implies the interdependency of dorsal and coronal nodes, both dominated by the C-place node).

Table 2.2 presents the identification of the Portuguese consonants we have been dealing with at the phonetic level, based on the geometry proposed in (18a). Alternative realizations of [R] and [ɾ] either syllable-initially or syllable-finally— that is, [ʁ] and [χ], see 2.2.1.2—are given in Table 2.3, as well as velarized [ɫ]. Monovalent nodes are marked with a dot when they are present (otherwise, they are left blank). Terminal binary features dependent on the class nodes are specified positively or negatively. Redundant values (as, for instance, [+sonorant] or [–continuant] for [+nasal]) have not been included in Table 2.2. Since all the consonants are [+consonantal].

TABLE 2.2.

	p	b	t	d	k	g	m	n	ɲ	f	v	s	z	ʃ	ʒ	tʃ	dʒ	l	ɫ	λ	ɾ	R	ʁ	χ
[sonorant]	–		–		–					–		–		–		–					+	+	–	
[continuant]	–	–	–	–	–	–				+	+	+	+	+	+	–	–						+	+
[nasal]							+	+	+															
[lateral]																		+	+	+				
Laryngeal	•	•	•	•	•	•				•	•	•	•	•	•	•	•						•	•
[voice]	–	+	–	+	–	+				–	+	–	+	–	+	–	+						+	–
Labial	•	•					•			•	•													
Coronal			•	•				•	•			•	•	•	•	•	•	•	•	•	•			
[anterior]			+	+				+	–			+	+	–	–	–	–	+	+	–	+			
Dorsal					•	•													•			•	•	•
[back]					+	+													+			+	+	+

[27] Portuguese vowels have been widely discussed in the literature. Phonetic and phonological discussions of Portuguese vowels can be found in Vasconcellos (1901), Viana (1883), Sá Nogueira (1938), Mateus (1975), d'Andrade (1977) and A. Andrade (1987).

Tables 2.3 and 2.4 include the phonetic vowels and glides previously presented. Specification above the vocalic node has been left out, as all vowels and glides are [−consonantal, +sonorant]; moreover, they are all [+continuant] and [+voice]. V-place nodes—dorsal and labial—are monovalent, so that their specification is restricted to the sound classes they define positively. Due to their binary nature, the terminal features [round], [back], [high] and [low] are specified as [+] or [−]. Redundant values are not included.

TABLE 2.3

Vowels	i	e	ɛ	a	ɐ	ɔ	o	u	ɨ
Height	•	•	•	•	•	•	•	•	•
[high]	+	−		−			−	+	+
[low]		−	+	+	−	+	−		
Dorsal					•	•			•
[back]					+	+			+
Labial						•	•	•	
[round]						+	+	+	

TABLE 2.4

Glides	j	w
Height	•	•
[high]	+	+
[low]		
Labial		•
[round]		+

We can observe that the glides [j] and [w] and the high vowels [i] and [u] have the same feature specification. Underlyingly, glides are high vowels. When they are not stressed and when they are preceded by another vowel, these high vowels become glides and constitute a falling diphthong with the preceding vowel (see 3.2.2.2). This proposal is basically motivated by the fact that Portuguese does not contrast vowels and glides. For instance, contrasts involving diphthongs and two-vowel sequences do not occur in the language (e.g. of the type *pai* [páj] 'father' vs. *[pái]); on the other hand, there are oppositions based on diphthongs versus single vowels as in words like *laudo* [láwdu] 'report' vs. *lado* [ládu] 'side' and *pai* [páj] 'father' or *pau* [páw] 'stick' vs. *pá* [pá] 'spade'. Moreover, pairs like *pais* [pájʃ] 'parents' and *país* [pɐíʃ] 'country' are not counter-examples, for the first vowel is not the same and the alternation vowel/glide is actually dependent on word stress (high vowels cannot become glides when they are stressed).

Finally, it is worth noting the following: glides and vowels evidence a significantly different behaviour with respect to the syllable and stress; unlike vowels, glides cannot be the only element of syllable nuclei, as they cannot bear stress.

Some authors take the option of differentiating glides from vowels on the basis of syllable constituency, and propose the binary feature [± syllabic] to represent the distinction: glides are [–syllabic] and vowels are [+syllabic] (see for instance Roca, 1994: 133). We consider that the inclusion of syllabic in the universal inventory of features is unnecessary as this feature merely has the function of distinguishing vowels from glides. Moreover, as at the phonetic level glides result from a gliding rule (see Chapter 5), and the difference between vowels and glides consists in glides not being the head of a syllable nucleus, the feature [syllabic] is, in our view, useless.

On the contrary, if the focus is centred on stress, we have to mark the vowels that become glides as 'unstressable', in the lexical representations. This is also the way antepenultimate stressed words are handled, like *dúvida* [dúvidɐ] 'doubt' or *estômago* [ʃtómɐgu] 'stomach'. When an 'unstressable' vowel is high and preceded by another vowel, it becomes a phonetic glide by the application of a gliding rule.[28]

2.4. UNDERSPECIFICATION

In this book, we assume radical underspecification with regard to the underlying representation of segments.[29] To argue in favour of this assumption, we start from the fully specified phonetic vowels of the dialects under study (see Table 2.3). On the assumption that some feature specifications are absent in the underlying representation and get filled during the derivation, the question is to know *which* features are not specified and *when* they become so. It can also be the case that some identifying features of a segment will be specified at one point of the derivation and other features at another, until the segment is fully specified for its phonetic realization.

Radical underspecification is based on the evidence that in all languages there is at least one segment, usually a vowel, that behaves asymmetrically with respect to the other members of the system. This vowel is often subject to neutralization, epenthesis and deletion. Due to its specific functioning, the asymmetrical segment is the least marked in the lexical representation. According to the radical underspecification view, once the unmarked features of the asymmetrical segment are determined we may proceed to establish the representation of the remaining segments: in this case, features will be left blank in the matrix, whenever they correspond to the unmarked features of the asymmetrical segment and share the same values. The underspecification of the lexical representation of segments results from the application of this algorithm.

In order to establish which is the most unmarked of the vowels in Portuguese, we need to examine the characteristics listed in Table 2.3 (see Table 2.5).

[28] See 3.3. and Chapter 6 for a discussion of this question.
[29] On Radical Underspecification see Kiparsky (1982) and Archangeli (1988). For an overview of the question, see Kenstowicz (1994).

TABLE 2.5

Vowels	i	e	ɛ	a	ɐ	ɔ	o	u	ɨ
Height	•	•	•	•	•	•	•	•	•
[high]	+	−		−			−	+	+
[low]		−	+	+	−	+	−		
Dorsal					•	•			•
[back]					+	+			+
Labial						•	•	•	
[round]						+	+	+	

Let us first examine the behaviour of [a] and [ɐ]. Previously we argued that these two vocalic sounds had to be considered alternations of the same segment. In fact, in 2.2.2.2, we pointed out that stressed [ɐ] is context-determined, whereas unstressed [ɐ] always corresponds to /a/ or to a /e/ before a [j]. It results from the application of specification rules to unstressed vowels (see also 2.2.2.3). So, both vowels correspond to an underlying /a/.

With respect to the choice of the unmarked vowel, we could consider /a/ as the asymmetrical segment—it is the only 'central' vowel at the phonological level. However, it does not have the other characteristics of the unmarked segment (i.e. it is not subject to neutralization, epenthesis and deletion). In fact:

- Word-final unstressed [ɨ] and [u] are frequently deleted in colloquial speech while [ɐ] is never deleted (e.g. *bato* [bátu] / [bát] 'I beat'; *bate* [bátɨ] / [bát] 's/he beats'; *bata* [bátɐ] / *[bát] 'I beat' (subj.));

- [e] and [ɛ] are neutralized in unstressed position (EP [ɨ]: *devo* [dévu] 'I owe', *deve* [dévɨ] 's/he owes', *dever* [dɨvéɾ] 'to owe'; BP [e]: *dever* [devéɾ]); in certain circumstances, stressed [e], [ɛ] and [i] alternate with unstressed [ɨ] or [i]; the same happens with [o] and [ɔ] (EP [u]: *movo* [móvu] 'I move', *move* [mɔ́vɨ] 's/he moves', *mover* [muvéɾ]'; BP [o]: *mover* [movéɾ]); in certain circumstances stressed [o], [ɔ] and [u] alternate with unstressed [u] in EP. Thus, these vowels are all subject to clear neutralizations (see 2.2.2.2). On the contrary, /a/ never converges with other vowels when unstressed: it is always realized as [ɐ].

- [a] never occurs as an epenthetic vowel.[30]

Let us see now, with respect to the behaviour of the other vowels included in Table 2.5, which can be considered the unmarked segment. Epenthesis of [ɛ] or [ɔ] in Portuguese is not attested. Furthermore, when unstressed they converge with [e] and [o]: they are all realized as [+high] in EP, that is [ɨ] and [u], and they are mid vowels in BP, that is [e] and [o] respectively. Thus, none of these four vowels, [e], [ɛ], [o], [ɔ], can be the unmarked segment.

There are three vowels left: [i], [ɨ] and [u]. Among these vowels, [i] and [ɨ] are the most common epenthetic vowels in both varieties (e.g. *captar* [kapitáɾ] 'to

---

[30] There are a few words in EP where we can find an epenthetic [ɐ], as in *cancro* [kɛ̃kɾu] pronounced [kɛ̃kɐɾu] 'cancer', mostly by illiterate people, but this does not represent a regular process of epenthesis.

capture' in BP, *pneu* [pnéw] / [pɨnéw] 'tyre'). On the other hand, they alternate frequently in European Portuguese (e.g. *pequeno* [pɨkénu] / [pikénu] 'small', *ministro* [mɨníʃtɾu] / [miníʃtɾu] 'minister') and [ɨ] is the vowel that is most often deleted in this variety.[31] As phonetic [ɨ] does not occur in lexical representations because it results from neutralization of phonological vowels in unstressed position, we consider that there is enough evidence to state that, in Portuguese as in many languages, /i/ is the unmarked vowel at the lexical representation level.

2.4.1. Underspecified vowels

Having identified the asymmetrical segment, we can now establish the features that are not specified in the lexicon. According to the radical underspecification view, as indicated above, the distinctive features of the unmarked segment are left blank in the lexical representation. The features in question are also left blank in the representation of other segments, whenever the corresponding value specification is identical to that of the unmarked segment (/i/ in this case). Blanks are filled in during the course of derivation, by means of specific rules (known as complementary rules). See Table 2.6, where only the underlying vowels are included ([ɐ] and [ɨ] being left out).

TABLE 2.6

Vowels	i	e	ε	a	ɔ	o	u
[high]		−				−	
[low]			+	+	+		
[back]				+			
[round]					+	+	+

Table 2.6 contains other feature blanks besides those coinciding with [i] features, namely those that are redundant in the Portuguese system (e.g. [+back], for [+round] vowels).

We have so far established *which* features are not specified, underlyingly, in Portuguese; let us now see *when* are they filled and look at *how* the progress from underspecified segment to surface realization occurs.

One of the most impressive processes in EP Portuguese is the raising of unstressed vowels. We recall in (19) the set of unstressed vowels presented earlier (2.2.2.1,6a,b).

(19) EP unstressed vowels

    [i] *mirar* [miɾáɾ] 'to look at'   *dúvida* [dúviɖɐ] 'doubt'

    [u] *morar* [muɾáɾ] 'to live'   *pérola* [péɾulɐ] 'pearl'

    [u] *murar* [muɾáɾ] 'to enclose'   *báculo* [bákulu] 'stick'

    [ɐ] *pagar* [pɐgáɾ] 'to pay'   *ágape* [ágɐpɨ] 'agape'

    [ɨ] *pegar* [pɨgáɾ] 'to take'   *cérebro* [séɾɨbɾu] 'brain'

---

[31] As indicated in 2.2.2, unstressed [u] can also be deleted in EP, but this is not a regular process. Thus, it is not as strong a candidate to be the unmarked vowel as [i] or [ɨ].

The vowels [i], [u], [ɐ] and [ɨ] correspond to the contrastive vowels /i/, /e/, /ɛ/, /a/, /ɔ/, /o/ and /u/. As we have seen, these vowels are not fully specified, under-lyingly. As a consequence of stress assignment, the vowels that have not received stress are subject to a raising rule that fills the values of [high] and [low] features in accordance with the phonological process of unstressed vowels; the latter con-sists in the raising of vowels to the highest point they can reach, in the different varieties. Thus, in EP, /e, ɛ, o, ɔ/ when unstressed are specified [+high], but /a/ is specified [–low], whereas unstressed /e, ɛ, o, ɔ/ in BP are specified [–high, –low], and /a/ is not raised (see Chapter 7). Values for [back], in turn, are filled at the post-lexical level by complementary rules.

This proposal as to *when* the unspecified values are filled is represented by the organization of features presented above (see (18)): the features [high] and [low] are dominated by height, and the feature [back] is dependent from the dorsal node and dominated by V-place.

Let us now present our second example: the spreading of the features from the person suffix over the stressed theme vowel in certain verb forms. First and third persons of the perfect indicative in BP have the internal structure and phonetic realization presented in (20).

(20) /fal a]$_{St}$i/ [faléj] (1st person)
      /fal a]$_{St}$u/ [falów] (3rd person)

As is explained in greater detail in Chapter 4, the assimilation of the theme vowel (TV) /a/ by the suffix /i/ and by the suffix /u/ is a single spreading process, involving dorsal and labial features on one hand, and height features on the other hand. It should be noted that the gliding of the suffix vowel results from a gliding rule that is triggered whenever unstressed high vowels are preceded by another vowel. In other words: /i/ and /u/ are specified for the dorsal feature [back] and for the labial feature [round]; then they assimilate underspecified /a/ with respect to the features depending on the two nodes in question (dorsal and labial). This assimilation is followed by a raising process to which the unstressed vowel rule is subject. Thus, the whole vocalic nodes (V-place and height) of the suffix vowels /i/ and /u/ spread onto the TV (see the configuration of the process in Chapter 4).

To summarize, we have stated that we share Archangeli's view about the underspecified lexical representations: 'underspecification is preferred over full representation from a theoretical standpoint because it makes the theory of repre-sentations consistent with the concept of an evaluation metric: only idiosyncratic information is included in the most basic representations and all predictable infor-mation is encoded in rules' (1988: 203). Given that radical underspecification starts from the empirical analysis of the functioning of the least marked segments, 'the phonological primitives of a particular language can be expressed as feature specification' (Archangeli, 1988: 203). Finally, and to the benefit of theoretical explanation, phonological rules triggered by underspecified segments in phono-logical processes are filling-rules and not changing-rules. We will come back to these issues later when we discuss phonological processes.

Table 2.7 contains the underspecified vowels at the lexical level. Only the vocalic node dominating class nodes and features has been included (for the representation of feature geometry see (18a and b). The dots in the rows corresponding to V-place and height indicate that the segments have to be marked for the dependent nodes and features.

TABLE 2.7

	i	e	ɛ	a	ɔ	o	u
V-PLACE							
Labial					•	•	•
[round]					+	+	+
Dorsal				•			
[back]				+			
HEIGHT	•	•	•	•	•		
[high]	−				−		
[low]			+	+	+		

2.4.2. Underspecified consonants

Let us now see what happens with consonants. Table 2.8 contains the list of the underlying Portuguese consonants (phonetic affricates in BP, alternative realizations of [ʀ] and velarized [ɫ] are excluded). All of these consonants are underspecified in lexical representations. The proposed underspecification is determined by the following conditions:

(i) Consonants that alternate, i.e. those that occupy the syllable coda position and are frequently subject to neutralization or even deletion (see Chapter 7 for detailed discussion), are less marked than those that have a single realization; these consonants are mostly coronals.

(ii) Coronal consonants have a special status concerning the features depending on the C-place node: as they are the most frequent consonants in all languages, we may consider them as the unmarked consonants. The most frequently occurring coronals are [+anterior]; these consonants (/t/, /d/, /s/, /z/, /l/ and /ɾ/), therefore, are not specified for C-place, and the values for the features dominated by this node are filled at the post-lexical level, in accordance with the position the segment occupies in the syllable structure. If the consonant is in the onset, it is specified by default rules that specify it as coronal [+anterior]; if the consonant is in the coda, it triggers the specific rules for Portuguese codas (it should be noted that only coronals may occur in coda position in Portuguese).

With respect to /ɾ/, we pointed out above that it behaves differently, depending on its position in the syllable and in the word. When it is in the coda, it is specified by default rules as a [+anterior] coronal; when it is word-initial or when it is an onset preceded by a filled coda, it is subject to a specific rule (see Chapter 7).

(iii) [–anterior] coronals, that is, /ɲ/, /ʎ/, /ʃ/ and /ʒ/ (e.g. *chá* [ʃá] 'tea', *acha* [áʃɐ] 's/he finds', *já* [ʒá] 'already', *haja* [áʒɐ] 's/he has' (subj.), *malha* [máʎɐ] 'mesh', *manha* [méɲɐ] 'slyness') have to be specified for C-place as they are not characterized by unmarked features. For the same reason, non-coronal consonants also have to be specified for place: /p/, /b/, /m/ and /f/, /v/ are labial; /k/, /g/ and /R/ are dorsal.

This assumption follows from our view of lexical representations. We consider that only unpredictable information is specified at the underlying level; this applies to unmarked segments, that is, [+anterior] segments. The other segments have, therefore, to be specified underlyingly.

(iv) Feature values are also unspecified when they cannot co-occur and when they are redundant in the language in question, or when they are predictable by universal principles. For instance, [+sonorant] consonants are always [+voice]. Since nasal consonants are [+sonorant] they are also [+voice]. Thus nasal consonants do not need to be specified with respect to the features [sonorant] and [voice]; it is enough to specify them as [nasal].

Finally, features that are left unspecified until the end of the derivation will be specified by default rules.

A few points about Table 2.8:

- The feature [consonantal] is not included since all consonants are specified [+] for this feature.
- With respect to the features [sonorant] and [continuant], plosives and fricatives have to be specified; the same should be said about the laryngeal node, as the obstruents that are voiced have to be filled with a [+] for this feature.
- Liquids must also be specified with respect to the features [sonorant], [continuant] and [lateral]: both classes are [+sonorant], but rhotics are [+continuant] and laterals are [+lateral].
- As for vowels, dots in the lines corresponding to laryngeal and C-place indicate that the segments have to be marked for the dependent nodes and features.

TABLE 2.8

	p	b	t	d	k	g	m	n	ɲ	f	v	s	z	ʃ	ʒ	l	ʎ	ɾ
[sonor]	−		−		−					−		−		−				+
[cont]	−	−	−	−	−	−	−	−	−	+	+	+	+	+	+			+
[lateral]																+	+	
[nas]							+	+	+									
Laryngeal		•		•		•					•		•		•			
[voice]		+		+		+					+		+		+			
Labial	•	•					•			•	•							
Coronal									•					•	•			•
[anterior]									−					−	−			−
Dorsal					•	•												
[back]					+	+												

If we compare Table 2.8 with Table 2.2, we notice that some features are not specified due to our assumptions regarding underspecification. Besides the unspecified feature values that are redundant by universal principles (e.g. [sonorant] or [voice] for nasal and [approximant] for [−sonorant] obstruents), or those that are redundant within the Portuguese system (e.g. only velar plosives and the uvular trill [R] are [+back]), the most important implication of the radical underspecification assumption is the fact that [+anterior] coronal consonants (as /t/, /d/ or /l/) are not specified underlyingly for C-place, and have these values filled-in during the phonological processes.

In order to enable the reader to clearly grasp the proposed relation between filling-in the unspecified feature values and specific and default rules triggered by the segments, we exemplify below the derivations of consonants in the Portuguese grammar. In (21a and b) one can see the derivation of /ɾ/ in onset position (in words like *rato* [ʀátu] 'mouse') and in the coda (in words like *par* [páɾ] 'pair') from the underspecified segment till the full specification at the phonetic level; the same can be observed in (22a and b) for /s/ in onset (e.g. *sapo* [sápu] 'toad') and in coda (e.g. *pás* [páʃ] 'spades'). Only the C-place features are represented. (For the proposed formulation of these rules, see 7.4.1.2).

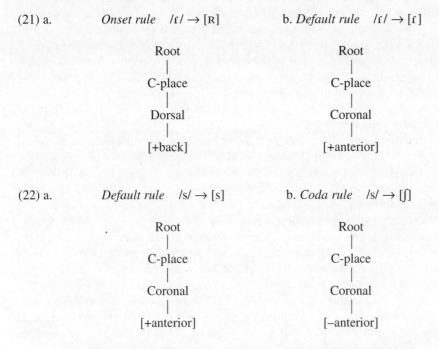

(21) a.   *Onset rule* /ɾ/ → [R]   b. *Default rule* /ɾ/ → [ɾ]

Root   Root
| |
C-place   C-place
| |
Dorsal   Coronal
| |
[+back]   [+anterior]

(22) a.   *Default rule* /s/ → [s]   b. *Coda rule* /s/ → [ʃ]

Root   Root
| |
C-place   C-place
| |
Coronal   Coronal
| |
[+anterior]   [−anterior]

We repeat what we have already said about the underspecified vowels: phonological rules triggered by underspecified segments in phonological processes are filling-rules and not changing-rules, which represents a significant theoretical improvement.

3

SYLLABLE STRUCTURE

3. 1. INTRODUCTION

This chapter deals with the Portuguese syllable. We assume, as Ohala (1996), that 'syllabicity is a perceptual construct, i.e., created in the mind of the listener'. In fact, speakers intuitively 'feel' the real existence of syllables and this feeling is evident in some kind of *lapsi linguae*. Among these, a very common one is a metathesis of syllables (e.g. in English [aminál] instead of [animál] for *animal* or, in Portuguese, [zɐgulínɐ] instead of [gɐzulínɐ] for *gasolina* 'gas'). Furthermore, syllable-based word games can be found in many languages. In Portuguese, for instance, there is a word game based on the syllable that consists in the duplication of each syllable with the same vowel preceded by a [p] (e.g. *casa* [kázɐ] 'home': [kapázɐpɐ]; *figo* [fígu] 'fig': [fipígupu]). Syllables are also the basis of secret languages like the one used by dockers in a very popular Lisbon's quarter (Alfama). In this language the onset of the stressed syllable is moved to the end of the word with all the segments preceding it, and the vowel [i] is added to this onset thus creating a new syllable (e.g. *pedra* [pédɾɐ] 'stone': [édɾɐ-pi]; *fujam* [fúʒẽw̃] 'you run': [úʒẽw̃-fi]).[1]

Standard generative phonology didn't consider the syllable to be a phonological unit or a domain of rule application. The identification of vowels with the feature [+syllabic] in a number of SPE-like works had nothing to do with the consideration of its role as the nucleus of a specific unit; this feature is only used within a classificatory scheme to identify the segment.

On the contrary, to multilinear generative phonology the syllable is an important linguistic unit and it has an internal hierarchical structure.[2] In this framework, the syllable is a multidimensional object with an internal structure that has a hierarchical organization where the onset and the rhyme constitute a branching structure. These syllable constituents behave independently, as we will see below (for instance, the number of the segments included in the onset is irrelevant with respect to the maximum number of segments allowed in the rhyme). Moreover, the concept of a branching structure is also supported by the cohesion between the elements belonging to each one of the constituents.

[1] See other word games with similar characteristics in Vago (1988).
[2] According to Paradis (1993), the Phonological Level Hierarchy (PLH) has the following organization: metrical > syllabic > skeletal > root node > non-terminal feature (class node and articultor with a dependent) > terminal feature (articulator without a dependent and binary feature).

In Portuguese, reference to the existence of a syllabic unit has been made since the sixteenth century by Oliveira (1536) and Barros (1540), and also by Barbosa (1822). But it is only in Viana (1883) that a list of all the elements that possibly constitute a syllable in European Portuguese appears for the first time.[3] The experimental work undertaken by Lacerda (1975) relates the syllable to articulatory-acoustic units of intonation, whose phonetic properties are analysed in great detail. Câmara (1953) refers very briefly to the relationship between stressed and unstressed syllables, his goal being the study of the occurring vowels in each kind of syllables. Barbosa (1965), working within Martinet's functionalist model, laid down the phonological schemes of the Portuguese syllables by using distributional criteria.[4] Following the standard generative perspective, Callou and Leite (1990) make a study of the segments and their place in the syllable. Using the same model, Mateus (1975) and Andrade (1977) discuss the properties of the segments that can be syllable-final.

3.2. THE PORTUGUESE SYLLABLE

In the first part of this chapter we will describe the phonetic distribution of the segments that constitute the possible syllables in Portuguese and their constituents: onsets and rhymes. Bearing in mind some general principles and phonotactic arguments, we will discuss phonetic glides and consonants with respect to their status as syllable constituents. This discussion raises some problems such as the existence of empty nuclei (see 3.2.1.2), the restrictions on the occurrence of diphthongs in certain positions (see 3.2.2.1) and the relation between underlying vowels and the corresponding phonetic glides (see 3.2.2.1 and 3.2.2.2). These problems are analysed in the second part of this chapter in conection with the syllable internal structure, whose constituents have to be filled in the base syllabification. Conventions for base syllabification are proposed in the third part of the chapter.[5]

3.2.1. Onsets

3.2.1.1. *Single consonants*

As we saw in 2.2.1, all single consonants can occur word-initially ([ɲ] and [ʎ] in a very few cases) and between vowels, and therefore they all can be onset (O) of the syllable in Portuguese. Some examples are given in (1).

---

[3] The work dedicated to the syllable by Sá Nogueira (1942) is a critical overview of the existing theories of the syllable, namely about the phonetic properties.

[4] This led him to establish that the glides preceding or following the nucleus could be viewed as consonants (e.g. CCVCC: *quais* [kwájʃ] 'which' (pl.); see Barbosa, 1965: 210).

[5] We do not deal with the difference between light and heavy syllables because this is only pertinent for languages that have long and short vowels, i.e. for quantity-sensitive languages, not for Portuguese. So, in general there is a coincidence between light and open syllables (syllables ending in a vowel), and heavy and closed syllables (ending in a consonant). Even so, the weight of the syllable shall be taken into account for the study of diphthongs (see 3.2.2.).

(1) a. Word-initial single onsets

pala [pálɐ] 'visor'
bom [bố] 'good'
fala [fálɐ] 'speech'
som [số] 'sound'
zelo [zélu] 'zeal'
chá [ʃá] 'tea'
lá [lá] 'there'
lhano [ʎénu] 'plain'
nata [nátɐ] 'cream'
mãe [mɐ̃ĵ)] 'mother'

b. Word-medial single onsets

mapa [mápɐ] 'map'
vaga [vágɐ] 'wave'
rato [ʀátu] 'mouse'
caça [kásɐ] 'hunting'
cola [kɔlɐ] 'glue'
malha [máʎɐ] 'mesh'
sumo [súmu] 'juice'
carro [káʀu] 'car'
vinho [víɲu] 'wine'
dúvida [dúvidɐ] 'doubt'

3.2.1.2. *Consonant clusters*

In common with other languages, Portuguese does not accept all consonant clusters as onsets. Typically, complex syllable onsets in Portuguese include plosive-plus-liquid, although the clusters ending with a lateral are much less frequent than those ending with a tap (see examples in (2a) and (2b)).

(2) Word-initial clusters   Word-medial clusters

a. Plosive-plus-tap

[pɾ] prato 'dish'   [pɾ] comprar 'to buy'
[bɾ] branco 'white'   [bɾ] abraço 'embrace'
[tɾ] trapo 'rug'   [tɾ] retrato 'photo'
[dɾ] droga 'drug'   [dɾ] sindroma 'syndrome'
[kɾ] cravo 'carnation'   [kɾ] acre 'biting'
[gɾ] graça 'grace'   [gɾ] regra 'rule'

b. Plosive-plus-lateral

[pl] plano 'plan'   [pl] repleto 'full'
[bl] bloco 'block'   [bl] ablução 'ablution'
*[tl][6]   [tl] atleta 'athlete'
*[dl][7]   *[dl]
[kl] claro 'bright'   [kl] recluso 'prisoner'
[gl] glande 'glans'   [gl] aglomerar 'to agglomerate'

These clusters are in accordance with the Sonority Principle (SP) which states that the sonority of the segments that constitute the syllable increases from the beginning till the nucleus and decreases till the end (concerning this principle, also called the Sonority Sequencing Generalization, see for instance Selkirk, 1984b). The proposals for the hierarchy of the segments that constitute the sonority scale are broadly consensual in establishing the following decreasing

---

[6] The only word beginning with [tl], *tlim* 'tinkle', is onomatopoeic.
[7] There is only one word with [dl], *adligar*, a technical term in botany: 'to adhere to the host by means of suckers'.

sonority: *vowels (low, medium, high)* > *glides* > *liquids* > *nasals* > *fricatives* > *plosives*. There is a discussion concerning the placement of plosives and fricatives in the scale, due to the fact that voicing is perhaps more important than continuity, and thus voiced plosives would be placed higher than voiceless fricatives (see Basbøll, 1988: 203). This is most probably due to language peculiarities, but in Portuguese we don't have enough evidence to reach a decision on this question.

The statement of the SP and its interrelation with the sonority scale are not enough to establish the possible sequences in Portuguese syllable onsets. We see in (3a and b) that, normally, fricative-plus-liquid constitutes an impossible onset—even though the combination should be an acceptable onset according to the SP. The exceptions are sequences of a non-coronal fricative ([f] or [v]) and a liquid, but even those are not frequent.

(3) Word-initial clusters   Word-medial clusters
  a. Fricative-plus-tap
     [fɾ] *fr*io 'cold'   [fɾ] – re*fr*escar 'to refresh'
     *[vɾ][8]   [vɾ] – pala*vr*a 'word'
     *[sɾ], *[zɾ], *[ʃɾ], *[ʒɾ]

  b. Fricative-plus-lateral
     [fl] *fl*or 'flower'   [fl] – a*fl*orar 'to emerge'
     *[vl], *[sl], *[zl], *[ʃl], *[ʒl]

Outside this kind of cluster—plosive and fricative plus liquid—any other sequence is impossible in both varieties of Portuguese. Yet these clusters would be acceptable if we only took into account the Sonority Principle (for instance, we do not find plosive-plus-fricative sequences like *[tf] or *[ts] either word-initially or word-medially). Such restrictions to the appearance of some consonant clusters in onset position occur in all languages: they are language-specific and they depend mostly on the distance between the members of the sonority scale.

This assumption is the basis of the Dissimilarity Condition, which states that it is necessary to stipulate, for each language, the value of the permitted sonority difference between two segments in sequence belonging to the same syllable. The quantification of this difference implies the indexation of the sonority scale, as proposed by Selkirk (1984b).[9] In Portuguese, for instance, onset clusters do not include consonants with the same degree of sonority, like sequences of two plosives or two fricatives (e.g.*[tb], *[pt], *[sf], *[vʃ], etc.). Also, the impossible onset clusters plosive-plus-fricative (e.g. *[tf], *[bʃ], *[pʒ], *[ts] etc.) and fricative-plus-nasals (e.g. *[fn], *[sn], *[ʃm], *[vɲ], etc.) point to the unacceptability of sequences including elements of two adjacent members in the sonority scale. The same happens with other adjacent members, as, for instance, nasal-plus-liquid

---

[8] There is one word beginning with this cluster: *vrancelhas* [vrɐ̃sɐ́ʎɐʃ], which refers to a 'type of grape'. We do not consider it because of its exceptionality.
[9] Vigário and Falé (1993) have presented a tentative indexation for Portuguese.

(e.g. *[ɲl], *[mʎ], *[mɾ], *[nɾ] etc.). Following Harris (1983), the non-adjacency statement of the two segments represents the universally unmarked case for syllable constituency and thus Portuguese grammar has no additional costs in this specific case.

Recalling that plosive-plus-liquid is the most common onset cluster in Portuguese (see (2) above), it is very likely that it has the preferred distance between onset elements, even though a smaller distance can also be acceptable, as between fricatives and liquids. In the latter case, however, only non-coronal fricatives are licensed as the first element of regular onsets. Moreover, the second element in all regular clusters is always coronal and [+anterior].[10]

We should bear in mind that the Sonority Principle and the Dissimilarity Condition are intended primarily as applying to base syllabification, as shown by many violations of these principles at the phonetic level in different languages including Portuguese, as we shall see below.

Apart from the sequences in (2) and (3), other consonant clusters can begin a word in European Portuguese phonetic level and seem to be the onsets of their respective syllables. Some examples are given in (4).

(4)   *Word-initial*   *Word-medial*
      a. *Plosive-plus-plosive*
      [pt] *pt*ério 'pterion'   ca*pt*ar 'to capture'
      [bt]   o*bt*er 'to obtain'
      [bd] *bd*délio 'bdellium'   a*bd*ómen 'abdomen'
      [dk]   a*dq*uirir 'to acquire'
      [kt] *ct*enóforo 'ctenophore'   pa*ct*o 'pact'

      b. *Plosive-plus-fricative*
      [ps]   *ps*icologia 'psychology'
      [bs]   a*bs*urdo 'absurd'
      [bv]   ó*bv*io 'obvious'
      [bʒ]   a*bj*urar 'to abjurate'
      [tz]   quar*tz*o 'quartz'
      [dv]   a*dv*ertir 'to advert'
      [ks]   a*x*ioma 'axiom'

      c. *Plosive-plus-nasal*
      [pn] *pn*eu 'tyre'   a*pn*eia 'apnea'
      [bn]   o*bn*óxio 'obnoxious'
      [tm] *tm*ese 'tmesis'   ri*tm*o 'rhythm'
      [tn]   é*tn*ico 'ethnic'
      [dm]   a*dm*irar 'to admire'

---

[10] Facing this preference for [−coronal] consonants, Vigário and Falé (1993) conclude that [−coronal] fricatives are closer to the plosives than the [+coronal] fricatives in the sonority scale. As a consequence of this licensing, the decreasing sonority in the last degrees of the scale for Portuguese would be: [+coronal] fricatives > [−coronal] fricatives > plosives.

[dn]	*adn*ominal 'paronomastic'
[gm]	esti*gm*a 'stigma'
[gn] *gn*omo 'gnome'	dia*gn*ose 'diagnosis'

d. *Fricative-plus-plosive*

[ft]	a*ft*a 'aphthae'

e. *Nasal-plus-nasal*

[mn] *mn*emónics 'mnemonic'	am*n*ésia 'amnesia'

These clusters clearly violate the Sonority Principle and the set of conditions following the definition above (e.g. (4a and e), where both consonants have the same degree of sonority, or (4b and c), showing two adjacent consonants in sequence). Due to the fact that some of the clusters are word-initial (e.g. [pn] in *pneu* or [ps] in *psicologia*), we could postulate that these sequences (and not only plosive-plus-liquid sequences) are possible onsets in Portuguese.

Let us now look at other phonetic clusters in colloquial EP. They give rise to still more onsets violating the Sonority Principle and the Dissimilarity Condition. (See examples below, in (5)).

(5) *Phonetic consonant clusters in EP*

   a. *esp*aço [ʃpásu] 'space'
      *esb*irro [ʒbíʀu] 'constable'
      *est*ar [ʃtáɾ] 'to be'
      *esdr*úxula [ʒdɾúʃulɐ] 'dactyl'
      *esc*uta [ʃkútɐ] 'listening'
      *esg*ana [ʒgénɐ] 'strangulation'
      *esf*inge [ʃfĩʒ] 'sphynx'
      *esv*air [ʒvɐíɾ] 'to dissipate'
      *esc*indir [ʃsĩdíɾ] 'to cancel'
      *esl*avo [ʒlávu] 'Slav'
      *esm*agar [ʒmɐgáɾ] 'to crush'

   b. *peq*ueno [pkénu] 'small'
      *dep*ender [dpẽdéɾ] 'to depend'
      *dec*ifrar [dsifɾáɾ] 'to decode'
      *terr*eno [tʀénu] 'ground'
      *sep*arar [spɐɾáɾ] 'to divide'
      *seg*uro [sgúɾu] 'sure'
      *met*er [mtéɾ] 'to put in'

   c. so*terr*ar [sutʀáɾ] 'to bury'
      so*ss*egar [susgáɾ] 'to calm'
      co*met*er [kumtéɾ] 'to commit'

We could hypothesize that in these cases odd consonant sequences are also onsets at the phonetic level, word-initially (cf. (5a and b)) and word-medially (cf.

(5c)). However, it is much more difficult to accept this solution in view of the examples included in (6a to d).

(6) *Phonetic consonant clusters in EP*

    a. *telef*one [tlfɔ́n] 'telephone'
       *merec*er [mɾséɾ] 'to deserve'
       *deved*or [dvdóɾ] 'debtor'
       *depen*icar [dpnikáɾ] 'to pull at'
       *rememo*rar [ʀmmuɾáɾ] 'to remember'

    b. *despeg*ar [dʃpgáɾ] 'to unstick'
       *deper*ecer [dpɾséɾ] 'to decline'
       *empeder*nir [ẽpdɾníɾ] 'to petrify'

    c. *despreg*ar [dʃpɾgáɾ] 'to unfasten'
       *desperdi*çar [dʃpɾdisáɾ] 'to waste'

    d. *despreven*ir [dʃpɾvníɾ] 'to fail to provide'
       *desprest*igiar [dʃpɾʃtiʒjáɾ] 'to depreciate'

Examples in (6a to d) show sequences of three consonants (e.g. *devedor* [dvdóɾ]: plosive+fricative+plosive), four consonants (e.g. *despegar* [dʃpgáɾ]: plosive+fricative+plosive+plosive), five consonants (e.g. *despregar* [dʃpɾgáɾ]: plosive+fricative+plosive+tap+plosive) and even six consonants (e.g. *desprestigiar* [dʃpɾʃtiʒjáɾ]: plosive+fricative+plosive+tap+fricative+plosive), and thus the number of sequences violating the Sonority Principle and the Dissimilarity Condition increases.

In fact we are facing two different sets of data: in (4) and (5a) there is no underlying vowel; but clusters in the words included in (5b), (5c) and (6) result from the deletion of an underlying vowel, and in these cases a vowel has been deleted because there is an alternation in morphological related words (e.g. *devo* [dévu] 'I owe' / *dever* [dvéɾ] 'to owe' and *devedor* [dvdóɾ] 'debtor'). In (4) and (5a) there is no evidence for an underlying vowel.

The conclusion of all this is that we need to postulate *empty nuclei* in Portuguese for words like those of (4) and (5a). In fact, in order to explain these consonant clusters it is necessary to assume that they are not onsets of a single syllable but that they are onsets of different syllables whose nuclei are empty. This assumption is justified by empirical arguments:

(i) It is worth noting, for instance, that speakers have some difficulties in assigning, either one or both of the consonants in (4), to the coda of the first syllable or to the onset of the second one. This is true when speakers have to spell out a word (see Andrade and Viana, 1993b), as for instance when they hesitate between *ad-mirar* and *a-dmirar*.

(ii) Furthermore, child productions during language acquisition show an inserted vowel between the consonants (e.g. *pneu* [pɨnéw] instead of [pnéw] 'tire' or *afta* [áfɨtɐ] instead of [áftɐ] 'aphthae'). Moreover, in child language we often find the deletion of the second consonant in allowed onset clusters (e.g. [pátu] for *prato* 'dish' or [bẽku] for *branco* 'white'). Nevertheless, we never find the deletion of the second element in disallowed sequences like those included in (4); on the contrary, in other languages we have the loss of the first segment in this last kind of sequences, like in *neumático* (Spanish 'tire') or in the pronunciation of *psychology* [sajkɒlədʒi] in English. This fact may confirm that plosive-plus-liquid sequences are really allowed onset clusters in Portuguese, while the other sequences are not.

(iii) Another argument is of a phonetic nature: words included in (4) like *obter* [obtéɾ] 'to obtain', *adquirir* [ɐdkɾiɾ] 'to acquire', *absurdo* [ɐbsúɾdu] 'absurd', *quartzo* [kwáɾtzu] 'quartz', the sequences [bt], [dk], [bs] and [tz] do not show an assimilation in voicing of the first consonant, as it happens in the examples in (5a), for instance (e.g. *espaço* [ʃpásu] 'space' vs. *esbirro* [ʒbíʀu] 'constable'). This is due precisely to the fact that there is an empty nucleus between the two consonants that prevents the consonant triggering the assimilation rule. In (5a), /s/ in coda position assimilates the voicing of the following consonant.

(iv) Finally, an argument that reinforces our statement that the consonant clusters in (4) and (5a) do not belong to the same syllable is the fact that, in most dialects of Brazilian Portuguese, the empty nucleus is filled with a vowel, mostly [i], as exemplified in (7) and (8).

(7) [pi-néw] *p*neu 'tyre'
     [gi-nɔ́mu] *g*nomo 'gnome'
     [pi-sikoloʒíɐ] *p*sicologia 'psychology'
     [abi-súɾdu] a*b*surdo 'absurd'
     [kapi-táɾ] ca*p*tar 'to capture'
     [páki-tu] pa*c*to 'pact'
     [áfi-tɐ] a*f*ta 'aphthae'

(8) *espaço* [iʃ-pásu] 'space'
     esbirro [iʒ-bíʀu] 'constable'
     estar [iʃ-táɾ] 'to be'
     esdrúxula [iʒ-drúʃulɐ] 'dactyl'
     escuta [iʃ-kútɐ] 'listening'
     esgana [iʒ-génɐ] 'strangulation'
     esfinge [iʃ-fĩʒ] 'sphynx'
     esvair [iʒ-vɐíɾ] 'to dissipate'
     escindir [iʃ-sĩdíɾ] 'to cancel'
     eslavo [iʒ-lávu] 'Slav'
     esmagar [iʒ-mɐgáɾ] 'to crush'

Notice that consonant clusters in (1), which are allowed onset clusters in Portuguese, never show this inserted vowel in BP. So, for instance, *[pi-ɾátu] (*prato* 'dish'), *[bi-ɾẽku] (*branco* 'white'), *[palá-vi-ɾɐ] (*palavra* 'word') are unacceptable.

All the phonetic consonant clusters included in (4) to (6) are specific to EP and some are due to phonological processes that do not apply in BP (namely [ɨ] deletion). The differences observed at the phonetic level between EP and BP caused by the existence of these consonant clusters have an obvious bearing on the distinct rhythm of each of the two varieties.

In sum: to explain this apparent violation of the Sonority Principle and the Dissimilarity Condition, we hypothesize the existence of an *empty nucleus* and we propose that this nucleus is not filled at the EP phonetic level (see 3.2.3). This means that, in base syllabification, only the consonant clusters included in (2) and in (3) are licensed as onset syllable.[11]

3.2.2. Rhymes

In Portuguese there are no syllabic consonants. The rhymes (R) of Portuguese syllables always have a nuclear vowel and all vowels can be syllable nuclei (N). They are the only indispensable elements in the syllabic parsing.

(9)   *Single vowel rhymes*
       ví [ví] 'I saw'   *tu* [tú] 'you'
       lê [lé] 's/he reads'   *casa* [ká-ɐ] 'house'
       é [ɛ́] 's/he is'   *bote* [bɔ́-tɨ] / [bɔ́-ti] 'boat'
       pá [pá] 'spade'   *irmã* [iɾ-mɐ̃́] 'sister'
       mó [mɔ́] 'millstone'   *assim* [ɐ-sĩ́] 'so'
       vou [vó] 'I go'   *ponte* [pṍ- tɨ] / [pṍ- ti] 'bridge'

3.2.2.1. *Complex nuclei*

Single vowels may be followed by glides at the phonetic level, thus nuclei can include falling diphthongs. See the representation of the phonetic monosyllabic word *boi* [bój], whose nucleus has a diphthong.[12]

(10) *boi*

These diphthongs are traditionally called in Portuguese 'true diphthongs' and they may occur in stressed, pre-stressed and post-stressed syllables at the phonetic level (oral diphthongs from EP and BP are included in (11a, b and c)).

---

[11] In the sense of Goldsmith (1990) syllable licensing.

[12] Representations of syllables show one stress on the vowel since stress assignement has already applied.

(11) a. *Stressed diphthongs*
   queixa [kéj-ʃɐ] (EP)[13]
      [kéj-ʃɐ]] (BP) 'complaint'
   papéis [pɐ-péjʃ] 'papers'
   ensaio [ẽ-sáj-u] 'essay'
   herói [e-ɾɔ́j] 'hero'
   boi [bój] 'ox'
   azúis [ɐ-zújʃ] 'blue (pl.)'
   viu [víw] 's/he saw'
   silvo [síw-vu](BP) 'whistle'
   deus [déwʃ] 'god'
   véu [vέw] 'veil'
   pauta [páw-tɐ] 'register'
   volta [vɔ́w-tɐ] (BP) 'turn'
   solta [sów-tɐ] (BP) 'free'

b. *Pre-stressed*
   queixume [kɐj-ʃú-mɨ] (EP)
      [kej-ʃú-mi] (BP) 'complaint'
   ensaiar [ẽ-saj-aɾ] 'to rehearse'

   boiada [boj-á-dɐ] 'drove'
   cuidado [kuj-dá-du] 'care'

   silvar [siw-váɾ] (BP) 'to whistle'
   endeusar [ẽ-dew-záɾ] 'to divinize'

   pautar [paw-táɾ] 'to rule'

   voltar [vow-táɾ] (BP) 'to turn'

c. *Post-stressed*
fáceis [fá-sɐjʃ] (EP)
      [fá-sejʃ] (BP) 'easy'
estéril [iʃ-té-ɾiw] (BP) 'sterile'
terrível [te-ʀí-vew] (BP) 'terrible'

As we can see in (11), the stressed diphthongs [ɔ́w], [ów] and the unstressed [ow], [iw] only occur in BP due to the realization of syllable-final /l/ as a glide.[14] Except for these cases, all vowels can combine with the two glides in stressed syllable but in pre- and post-stressed positions there are fewer possibilities. Besides that, we cannot find phonetic sequences of vowel and glide that coincide in place of articulation and height (*[ij], *[uw]). In EP, [ɨ] never occurs in diphthongs.

Nasal diphthongs are quite frequent in Portuguese at the phonetic level due to the fact, among others, that they appear in every third person plural of verb forms. Nevertheless, they only occur in word-final syllables, either stressed or post-stressed.[15]

---

[13] We should recall that, except in word-final position, there is no [ɐ] in BP. EP [ɐj], stressed or unstressed, corresponds generally to BP [ej].

[14] [ow] can also be due to the occurrence of a phonetic glide, as in *pouco* [pówku], 'few', which is the normal pronunciation in BP and in some northern dialects of EP.

[15] There is a small number of words in Portuguese which have a diphthong in the penultimate syllable: *cãibra* [kɐ́jbrɐ] 'crump' and dialectal *cãibo, cãibas, cãibeiro* 'different pieces of the oxen-cart'. As for their exceptionality, *cãibra* is often pronounced as [kέbrɐ], without the diphthong, and the others have alternating forms without the glide. The word *muito* [mṹjtu] 'many' is the only one with the [ṹj] diphthong—due to the spreading of the nasality of the initial nasal consonant—and the diphthong occurs exceptionally in the penultimate syllable. Also, derived words with the prefix *bem+*, as *bendito* 'blessed', and the very frequent word *também* 'also' have alternated pronunciations of the penultimate syllable, either with a nasal vowel or with a diphthong (e. g. [bẽdítu]/[bẽj+dítu]; [tẽbéj̃]/[tẽ w̃béj̃]).

(12) a. *Stressed*

   mãe [mɐ̃ĵ] 'mother'
   refém [ʀɨféĵ] (EP)
         [ʀeféĵ] (BP) 'hostage'
   compõe [kõpóĵ] 's/he composes'
   mão [mɐ̃w̃] 'hand'

   b. *Post-stressed*

   prendem [pɾɐ̃́dẽĵ] (EP)
            [pɾɐ̃́dẽĵ] (BP) 'they fasten'
   falam [fálẽw̃] 'they talk'
   homem [ɔ́mẽĵ] (EP)
          [ɔ́mẽĵ] (BP) 'man'
   sótão [sɔ́tẽw̃] 'garret'

Nasal diphthongs argue in favour of considering the diphthongs as part of the syllable nucleus, as both elements, vowel and glide, are nasalized. Thus, in all the words mentioned above, the syllable nucleus includes *at most two segments* at the phonetic level.

Recall that in 2.3. we assumed that phonetic glides are high vowels underlyingly: they are underspecified, as all vowels, and get full specification in accordance with specific rules, complementary rules and default rules. Furthermore, high vowels that integrate falling diphthongs at the phonetic level cannot receive the stress, that is, they are marked in the lexical representation as not being able to be stressed—like non-stressable vowels in ante-penultimate stressed words (e.g. *dúvida* [dúvidɐ] 'doubt' or *árvore* [áɾvuɾɨ] 'tree' whose penultimate vowel cannot be stressed and so it is underlyingly marked). Thus, if a high vowel is marked and if it is preceded by another vowel, it becomes a glide at the phonetic level and it is integrated in the syllable nucleus with the preceding vowel (see in Chapter 6 what is said about these vowels being a 'trough' for the rhythmic wave, in the treatment of the main stress). In the following diagrams for syllable structure representation we use a capital letter to indicate these lexically marked vowels.

It is worth noting that high vowels which do not have a lexical mark can be stressed and are realized as vowels at the phonetic level, even though they are preceded by other vowels (e.g. *país* [pɐíʃ] 'country' or verb forms as *sair* [sɐíɾ] 'to leave' where [i] is the theme vowel). We will see in 3.4. the consequences of this fact for the application of the base syllabification conventions.

3.2.2.2. *Sequences of glide-plus-vowel at the phonetic level*

Let us see now what happens with the sequences of glide-plus-vowel. If these glides also integrate the nucleus and if they can be followed by a diphthong, then the statement made above—the syllable nucleus includes at most two segments at the phonetic level—is wrong, and a three-segment nucleus can occur.

Glides before vowels pose some difficult problems, even simply in describing them phonetically. When we spell words like *viés* 'bias band', *suor* 'perspiration', *farmácia* 'pharmacy', the segment preceding the vowel can be perceived by Portuguese speakers as syllabic, that is, as being a vowel and not a glide. This is confirmed, for instance, by the classification of the word *farmácia* as a proparoxytone, which indicates that two syllables are counted following stress.

Within a structuralist approach, these segments are also considered to form a syllabic nucleus. Barbosa (1965) takes this view when he describes the syllable from an auditory perspective (except for the sequences *qu* and *gu* (see footnote 4, this chapter). In the SPE framework, the underlying representations can integrate glides but only when they occur after vowels (cf. Mateus, 1975); otherwise—if the unstressed high vowels precede other vowels—they are integrated as vowels in the underlying representations. We can argue in favour of this proposal given the fact that the stress may fall on these high vowels in words that are morphophonologically related (e.g. *pio* [píw] 'chirp' / *piar* [piáɾ] 'to chirp'; *suo* [súw] 'I sweat' / *suar* [suáɾ] 'to sweat').

In colloquial Portuguese, however, these two vowels—[i] and [u] when unstressed and followed by another vowel, as in the examples given above—have a reduced duration and intensity. They can be perceived by the speakers as belonging to the same syllable as the following vowel (e.g. it is possible to have the realizations [pjáɾ] and [swáɾ]). We can find this interpretation, among others, in Viana (1883). He considers unstressed [i] and [u], either before or after a vowel, as 'subjunctive' of a diphthong and integrated in the syllable to which the vowel belongs: for example (1883: 5/87) he describes *maior* [majɔ́ɾ] 'bigger' as having two syllables: *mai-or*). Yet, [i] and [u] adjacent to a vowel are identified by this author as glides (traditionally, 'semivowels') in the chart of the Portuguese consonants, and their occurrence is exemplified in *faia* [fájɐ] 'beech-tree', *fiar* [fjáɾ] 'to spin', *qual* [kwáɫ]'which' and *soar* [swáɾ] 'to sound'. Callou and Leite (1990: 92) also point to the existence of diphthongs formed by a glide followed by a vowel in BP. However, they say that the pronunciation of the first element varies and it is realized sometimes as a vowel, sometimes as a glide. This variation is common to a wide number of languages.

In casual speech we find sequences of glides followed by any vowel (with the same restrictions of the falling diphthongs). See examples of this in (13a and b).

(13) Glides + vowels (casual speech)

a. *Stressed*

frieza [fɾjézɐ] 'cold'	*suíno* [swínu] 'pig'
viés [vjéʃ] 'bias band'	*roer* [ʀwéɾ] 'to gnaw'
real [ʀjáɫ] 'royal'	*cuecas* [kwékɐʃ] 'pants'
pior [pjɔ́ɾ] 'worst'	*voar* [vwáɾ] 'to fly'
mioma [mjómɐ] 'myoma'	*suor* [swɔ́ɾ] 'sweat'
miúdo [mjúdu] 'kid'	*voou* [vwó] 's/he flew'
criança [kɾjɐ̃sɐ] 'child'	*coentros* [kwɐ̃tɾuʃ] 'coriander'

b. *Unstressed*
realeza [ʀjɐléze] (EP)
        [ʀjalézɐ] (BP) 'royalty'
miudeza [mjudézɐʃ] 'minuteness'
suinicultura [swinikułtúɾe] 'pig breeding'
voador [vwɐdóɾ] (EP)
        [vwadóɾ] (BP) 'flying'
criançada [kɾjẽsádɐ] 'bunch of children'

The same glides can precede diphthongs:

(14) *criais* [kɾjájʃ] 'you create'   *suais* [swájʃ] 'you sweat'
      fiéis [fjɛ́jʃ] 'faithful'   *cruéis* [kɾwɛ́jʃ] 'cruel (pl.)'
      pião [pjẽ́w̃] '(toy) top'   *voei* [vwɛ́j] (EP)
                                           [vwéj](BP) 'I flew'

We propose that these phonetic glides are vowels underlyingly, and they are
nuclei of independent syllables as we can see in the representation of *pião*.

(15) *pião*

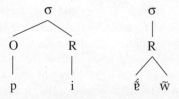

However, as they are perceived as glides by the speakers and constitute a rising diphthong, it is worth discussing if, at the phonetic level, they are integrated
in the rhyme with the following vowel or if they belong to another syllable constituent. The examples in (13) and (14) above show that, when these glides occur
before a nasal vowel or a nasal diphthong, they are not nasalized, contrary to what
happens with falling diphthongs (cf. *criança* [kɾjẽ́se] 'child' and *pião* [pjẽ́w̃]).
This is enough evidence to consider that they are not integrated in the phonetic
rhyme (on this question see Andrade and Viana, 1993a; Mateus, 1993). These
phonetic sequences of glide and vowel in Portuguese are thus clearly different
from the true rising diphthongs existing in other languages, whose glides are associated with the following vowel and integrate the rhyme.

In Spanish, for instance, according to Harris (1983) these glides are part of the
rhyme. To make clear the difference between the two languages and, at the same
time, to reinforce our statement that Portuguese glides are underlying vowels, it
is relevant to discuss Harris's argument. He postulates that the Spanish rhyme
may include up to three elements (nucleus and coda), and the glide preceding the
vowel is part of the rhyme (e.g. *buei* [bwéj] 'ox'). In the second syllable of words
like *lim-piais* 'you clean' there are four elements after the onset, which appears

to contradict the previous statement. Yet, there is no contradiction because final /s/ pertains to the person morpheme and is considered extrametrical (that is, it is not counted for the segments of the rhyme). Therefore, the maximal number of segments in the rhyme is not violated.

In Portuguese we find parallel cases in corresponding morphemes which can also be considered extrametrical (e.g. *criais* [krjájʃ] 'you create', *suais* [swájʃ] 'you sweat'). On the other hand, it has been established that the syllable nucleus in Portuguese can have two segments, maximally, which means that the rhyme has at most three elements including the coda. We might think, therefore, that Harris's argument in favour of including the glide in the rhyme would also be valid for Portuguese.

This is not so, however. In fact, there are rhymes with falling diphthongs and an /s/ in the coda, in which the consonant is not a morpheme. Such is the case of *aus-cultar* [awʃkuɫtáɾ] 'to auscultate', where the pre-stressed syllable has a falling diphthong, [aw], and a [ʃ] in the coda. When words like this start with the prefix *re-*, for instance, a new syllable—that is, a different syllable— is created (*reaus-cultar* [ʀjawʃkuɫtáɾ]). In this example, where the new syllable contains consonant + glide + vowel + glide + [ʃ], this [ʃ] cannot be considered a morpheme and is not therefore predictably extrametrical. In this case, then, the inclusion of the glide in the rhyme would entail one rhyme with four elements. Thus, Harris's argument for Spanish is not valid for Portuguese. Consequently since the glide is included in the onset, there is no reason to consider that the Portuguese rhyme can have more than three elements.

We can conclude that the syllable constituent which the glide integrates, at the Portuguese phonetic level, must be the onset, as the number of the elements in the onset is irrelevant for the maximum number of elements in the rhyme (the assumption that glides of rising diphthongs belong to the onset of the syllable is defended in Mateus (1993) and Andrade and Viana (1993a)).

To summarize, glides preceding vowels are vowels in underlying structure. In colloquial speech this configuration triggers a gliding rule that causes the glide to integrate the syllable whose nucleus is the following vowel. It fills the empty onset of this syllable (together with the preceding consonant(s)) and becomes part of the onset in the new syllabic parsing. See the representation of this process in the word *criais*.

(16) *criais*

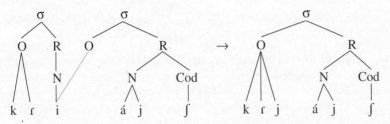

3.2.3. Codas

We pointed out (2.1.1.1) that only the underspecified consonants /l/, /ɾ/ and /s/, with different realizations, are possible codas in Portuguese. Some examples are given in (17).

(17) Realizations of consonants in coda

a. EP	BP
par [páɾ]	[páʀ] / [páx] / [páh] 'pair'
mal [máɫ]	[máw] (BP) 'evil'
más [máʃ]	[máʃ] 'bad' (fem.pl.)
b. *parte* [páɾ-tɨ]	[páʀ-tʃi] / [páx t͡ʃi] / [páh-t͡ʃi] 'part'
falta [fáɫ-tɐ]	[fáw-tɐ] 'fault'
peste [péʃ-tɨ]	[péʃ-tʃi] 'plague'
mesmo [méʒ-mu]	[méʒ-mu] 'same'

Besides the occurrence exemplified in (17), it is worth noting also that:

(i) They are the only consonants that can occur in word-final position in Portuguese.

(ii) Moreover, [ɾ] is not allowed word-initially and [l] never begins a word if followed by another consonant (needless to say that the velarized lateral, [ɫ], never occurs word-initially). Thus, in the middle of the word, when sequences of consonants like [ɾt] (as in *parta* [páɾtɐ] 's/he leaves') or [ɫm] (as in *calma* [káɫmɐ] 'calm') happens to occur, we have to separate [ɾ] from [t] and [ɫ] from [m] as they never occur in sequence in initial position.

(iii) Concerning the fricative represented by /s/, its phonetic realizations included in (17) show that this consonant triggers a palatalization rule and the voice assimilation of the following consonant (e.g. *peste* [péʃ-tɨ] 'plague', *mesmo* [méʒ-mu] 'same'). This voice assimilation also occurs when the fricative is in word-initial position at the phonetic level (see (18) for examples).

(18) a. *esvaído*   [ʒvɐídu] 'faint'
      esbelto   [ʒbéɫtu] 'slender'
      esperado [ʃpɨɾádu] 'expected'
      estar   [ʃtáɾ] 'to be'

      b. *esperado* [ʃpɨɾádu] 'expected' / *inesperado* [iniʃpɨɾádu] 'unexpected'
      feliz [fɨlíʃ] 'happy' / *infeliz* [ĩfɨlíʃ] 'unhappy'

Apparently, at least in the cases exemplified in (18a), the fricative would be in onset position, not in coda. Nevertheless, [ʃ] and [ʒ] are codas of the syllable, as they are preceded, at the underlying level, by an empty nucleus. The existence of this empty nucleus is attested by the examples in (18b) like *inesperado*, resulting from the syllabification of the word *esperado* with the prefix /in/: the empty nucleus is filled by [ɨ]; the nasal autosegment of the prefix that precedes the vowel fills the onset of this syllable and is phonetically manifested as a nasal consonant (*in+esperado* /in+esperado/ → [iniʃpɨrádu]) and the consonant [ʃ] (or [ʒ]) is syllabified as the coda of the syllable. This analysis shows that empty nuclei can occur at the right side of the non-syllabified consonant, as in the clusters presented in 3.2.1.2, e.g. *afta*, between [f] and [t], or at the left side of the consonant, as in the beginning of the words exemplified in (18), such as *estar* [ʃtáɾ].

On the other hand, if the word begins with a consonant, like *feliz*, the nasal autosegment of the prefix will be associated with its own nucleus and the nasality will spread over the vowel (*in+feliz* /in+felis/ → [ĩfɨlíʃ]).

In words where sequences of three (or four) consonants occur in pre-stressed syllable at the phonetic level (as in *perspectiva* [pɨrʃ-pɛtíve] 'perspective' or *abstrair* [ebʃ-tɾeíɾ] 'to abstract') the consonants belong to two different syllables. In these examples, the first syllable seems to have a coda with two consonants ([ebʃ]-trair, [pɨrʃ]-pectiva) where the /s/ is the second element; in fact, this is not so because, under this analysis, there is an empty nucleus between the two consonants as in the consonant clusters included in (4). Therefore, the only underlying consonant in coda in the first syllable of these words is /s/. See the representation of *abstrair* in (19).

(19) *abstrair*

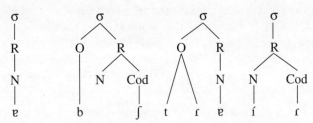

In BP, namely in colloquial speech, the introduction of an [i] to occupy the position of the empty nucleus creates a new syllable, and the first of the two consonants is moved into the onset of this syllable (e.g. *a-bis-trair* [abiʃ-tɾaíɾ]).[16]

In sum, the three underlying segments, /ɾ/, /l/ and /s/, are the only consonants that are licensed in Portuguese codas. As in most languages, consonants licensed in the coda are fewer than those that are licensed in the onset are; in Portuguese their number is restricted to three.

Due to the fact that Portuguese rhyme can only have one consonant in coda and, if this consonant is /s/,[17] the nucleus may also include a diphthong (e.g. *pois* [pójʃ] 'so', *aus-cultar* 'to auscultate'). In the syllables we have analysed so far the

---

[16] A sequence of two consonants also occurs in EP in final position, in a post-stressed syllable, although only with [ks] and [ps] in a very small number of words (*índex* [ídɛks], *forceps* [fɔ́rsɛps] and a few more). Again there is an empty nucleus between them that is filled in BP by an epenthetic [i] (e.g. *for-ce-pis* [fɔ́rsɛpis]).

[17] This consonant has a special status in many languages.

rhyme may have up to three segments, normally three positions,[18] independently of how many segments there are in the onset. This fact shows that the relation between the internal segments of the rhyme is closer than that between the rhyme and the onset.

3.3. THE SKELETON

Syllable constituents are associated with the *skeletal tier*: each syllable constituent is associated with a position (or more if it branches) of the skeleton.

In the process of syllabification exemplified in (20), the first vowel is associated with the nucleus and the second vowel is also assigned to the same nucleus (see section 3.4 on base syllabification). Thus, this segment is no longer a vowel but it is not a consonant, either. This segmental change, and other segment alternations due to syllabic processes that are found in many languages (including Portuguese), makes us think it is preferable to represent the positions occupied in the skeleton by each syllable segment with an X, instead of using the CV representation.[19] The roots of the underlying segments are thus associated with these X nodes. See the representation of the one-syllable words *pai* [páj] 'father' and *mãe* [mḗj̃] 'mother', where the nucleus branches into two vowels. The second vowel is lexically marked as not being able to get the stress and thus it cannot be a nucleus *per se* but it is integrated in the nucleus leftwards. At the phonetic level it is realized as a glide and is included in the syllable nucleus (see 3.2.2.1). In (20b) the nasal autosegment projects the nasal feature over the whole nucleus. We represent this autosegment as [+nasal]—and not as a consonant like the coda autosegments /l/ or /s/—because the realization of this segment may only consist

(20) a. *pai*   b. *mãe*

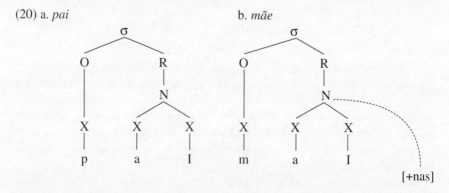

<hr>

[18] We will see further on that in some cases the phonetic diphthong included in the nucleus is created during the derivation of the word.

[19] In studying the BP syllable, Albano (1992) prefers the CV tier, as she takes the position that C and V elements are 'rule-governed projections of certain distinctive feature configurations'. We agree with Basbøll who argues that 'CV model fails to express the high degree of predictability of the feature [syllabic] from the sonority of the segments in question' (1988: 205).

in the nasalization of the vowel at the phonetic level. Its representation with a feature thus seems more appropriate, even though, under certain circumstances, the realization of the segment can be a coronal consonant (cf. 7.2).

This model allows us to maintain the number of positions in the skeleton. Yet there also exist skeletal positions that are not associated with any segment. This statement allowed us to assume the existence of empty syllable nuclei (see 3.2.1.2). If the position corresponding to one constituent is not filled, this fact can have a significant consequence at the phonetic level (see 3.3.2 and the proposal about empty onsets). Furthermore, some segments may have an ambisyllabic status and can be associated with two syllables (see 3.4).

3.3.1. Segments without skeletal positions

As there are skeletal positions that are not associated with a segment, there are also segments that do not have a proper position in the skeleton (for instance, the nasal autosegment), and others that have a phonetic realization but do not represent an independent position in the skeleton.

In Portuguese there is no phonological difference between long and short vowels. Diphthongs, however, seem to have different weights, which produces some interesting consequences in respect of the number of skeletal positions they occupy. We consider that the number of positions occupied by the diphthongs should be analysed in relation to the word-stressed syllable, in order to establish their different 'weights', if there are any. This is what we shall do next.

We observed in 3.2.2.1 that, in Portuguese, there are strong restrictions on the occurrence of diphthongs in post-stressed position either oral or nasal. Thus, it is very likely that the number of positions corresponding to diphthongs is interconnected with their position with respect to the placing of the word's stressed syllable. (21) repeats the examples given above in (11c) and (12b) and adds some more).[20]

(21) Diphthongs in post-stressed position

    a. *fáceis* [fásejʃ] 'easy' (BP)
       estéril [iʃtɛɾiw] 'sterile' (BP)
       terrível [tɛɾívew] 'terrible' (BP)
       sótão [sɔ́tẽw̃] 'garret'
       órfão [ɔ́ɾfẽw̃] 'orphan'

    b. *prendem* [pɾɛ́dẽj̃)] 'they fasten' (EP)
       prenderam [pɾẽdérẽw̃] 'they have fastened'
       falam [fálẽw̃] 'they talk'
       falariam [fɐlɐɾíẽw̃] 'they would talk'
       pairam [pájɾẽw̃] 'they hover'
       homem [ɔ́mẽj̃] 'man' (BP)
       paisagem [pajzáʒẽj̃] 'landscape' (BP)

[20] We do not present the different pronunciations of each diphthong in both varieties because what

All these words are stressed on the penultimate syllable. In (21b), the glide of final unstressed diphthongs, either in words like *homem* or in verbal endings, is epenthetic: in the lexical representation of these phonetic nasal diphthongs, as we saw above, there is a phonological floating nasal autosegment that, when it is associated with the rhyme, spreads its nasality over the syllable nucleus. The glide does not exist in the underlying representation; it is introduced after the spreading of the nasalization by a diphthongization rule. As this glide is part of the nucleus, the nasality also spreads over it. In this situation the diphthong is light and may occupy one position in the skeleton.

In (21a) the glide is the result of the coda vocalization (e.g. *terrível*), or it is the phonetic realization of a class marker (e.g. *sótão*). This kind of diphthong is heavy and may occupy two positions in the skeleton.

Syllabic representation of *pairam* and *sótão* is given in (22a and b). The difference between the two representations lies in the number of skeletal positions held by the diphthong in the last syllable.

(22)

a. *pairam*   b. *sótão*

There is another kind of diphthong that can be viewed as light. See in (23) the morphological alternations between the lexical representations of *passear* /pase+ar/ [pɐsiáɾ][21] 'to walk' and *passeio* /pase+o/ [pɐséju] 'walk', or between *areal* /are+al/ [ɐɾiál] 'beach' and *areia* /are+a/ [ɐɾéjɐ] 'sand'.

(23) /pase+ar/ [pɐsiáɾ] 'to walk'
      /pase+o/ [pɐséju] 'walk'
      /are+al/ [ɐɾiál] 'beach'
      /are+a/ [ɐɾéjɐ] 'sand'

matters here is the occurrence of the diphthong, not the differences in the realization of the vowel. So, we include examples in BP pronunciation because in this variety we find all the diphthongs belonging to EP and also the phonetic diphthongs like in *estéril* [iʃtériw], resulting from the gliding of the [ɫ].

[21] As it happens with *piar*, these words are pronounced with a rising diphthong in casual speech (e.g. *passear* [pɐsjáɾ])

Portuguese shows the same alternation 'light diphthongs'/'single vowel' related to morphological alternation as do some other languages (e.g. French: *voir* 'to see' / *verrons* 'we shall see'; Spanish: *poder* 'can' / *puedo* 'I can'). The glide is introduced in the segmental tier as a consequence of the word-formation, when the morphemic vowel is added to the root. In this case, the resulting diphthong occupies a single position in the skeleton. See the representation of *areia* in (24).

(24) *areia*

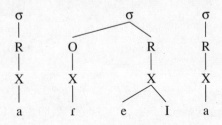

In order to relate the occurrence of diphthongs to the stressed syllable, it is worth noting that, in Portuguese, if the penultimate stressed syllable has a diphthong, restrictions are stronger and the only diphthong that can occur in post-stressed position is the nasal suffix of the verb third person plural (25). In this case, the rhyme has no coda.

(25) ´VG–... ṼG̃ #   *pairam* [pájɾẽw̃] 'they hover'
       *´VG–... ṼG̃ C #   _____
       *´VG...–...VG (non nasal)#   _____

The fact that this specific nasal diphthong is the only one occurring in post-stressed position following a stressed diphthong is due to the non-existence of an underlying vowel corresponding to the phonetic glide. In fact, this glide is inserted during the derivation. Therefore, to postulate the weight of the diphthongs, it is important to relate them to the stressed syllable—or to the alternation diphthong/single vowel in morphologically related words.[22] The restrictions mentioned above concerning the occurrence of unstressed diphthongs in post-stressed syllable(s) argue in favour of our previous assumption that the rhymes can have in total up to three positions in the skeleton: one or two in the stressed position and two or one in the post-stressed, respectively (/s/ in coda does not count for the weight of the syllable).

On the other hand, words stressed on the antepenultimate cannot have post-stressed diphthongs. The non-existence of post-stressed diphthongs in these words also supports our prior analysis: the antepenultimate syllable cannot be stressed if there is another diphthong in any of the following syllables. This means that, after the stressed syllable, all nuclei have one single position, that is, two positions in total. See in (26) the representation of the antepenultimate stressed word *dúvida* [dúvidɐ] 'doubt'.

---

[22] See Bisol (1989) and (1994a) for an alternative explanation.

(26) *dúvida*

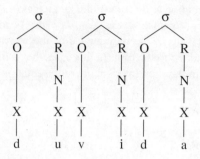

3.3.2. Empty positions

As stated above, we assume that it is possible for skeletal positions not to be associated with a segment. This view allowed us to propose the existence of empty
syllable nuclei. We also assume that, in Portuguese, a syllable obligatorily consists of a an onset and a rhyme. If a position corresponding to a constituent is not
filled, this fact can have consequences at the phonetic level.

It is generally recognized that syllables always possess a rhyme (with its
nucleus). Concerning the onset, we assume that its presence in Portuguese is also
obligatory, i.e. every base syllable in Portuguese consists of an onset and a rhyme
even though any of them (but not both) may be empty. There is interesting evidence that can support our assumption about empty onset positions.

This evidence comes from words beginning with some unstressed vowels.
Examples are given in (27) and (28).

(27) a. *Elvira* [ɛ]lvira 'Elvire'
          Eldorado [ɛ]ldorado 'El Dorado'

      b. *elefante* [i]lefante 'elephant'
          ermida [i] / [e]rmida 'chapel'
          evidente [i] / [e]vidente 'evident'
          economia [i] / [e]conomia 'economics'

As we saw above, unstressed underlying vowels /e/ and /ɛ/ are phonetically [ɨ]
in EP in word-final and word-internal position. However, in word-initial position,
[ɨ] does not exist. In this position, underlying /e/ and /ɛ/:

• occur as [ɛ] when the coda is /l/ (27a);
• show some variation between [i] and [e] in the remaining cases (27b).

The same happens with unstressed underlying /o/ and /ɔ/ that are [u] in every
context except word-initially, where there is a variation between [o] and [ɔ]
(examples given in (28)).

(28) *ornar* [o] / [ɔ]rnar 'to adorn'
    organizar [o] / [ɔ]rganizar 'to organize'
    hospital [o] / [ɔ]spital 'hospital'
    hospedaria [o] / [ɔ]spedaria 'guest house'
    olhar [o] / [ɔ]lhar 'to look'
    ovelha [o] / [ɔ]velha 'ewe'
    operário [o] / [ɔ]perário 'worker'

This exceptional behaviour is probably due to the fact that these word-initial syllables have an empty onset: the empty position doesn't allow the presence of [ɨ] and [u] resulting from the application of the rules for unstressed vowels (that is, unstressed [u] can appear word-initially if it is an /u/ underlyingly, as in *ufania* [ufɐníɐ] 'boasting').[23]

In the representation of *ermida* the empty onset position can be seen clearly.

(29) *ermida*

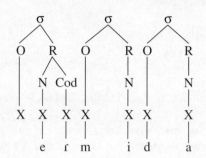

The existence of this empty position has other consequences at the phonetic level. It allows, for instance, the phonetic realization of some consonants that occupy the empty onset position in certain circumstances such as:

(a) the realization of the nasal autosegment [+nas] as an [n] in derived words like *irmanar* /iɾma[+nas]+a+ɾ/ [iɾmɐnáɾ] 'to match' vs. its realization only as the nasalization of the nucleus such as in *irmão* /iɾma[+nas]+o/ [iɾmɐ̃w̃] 'brother';

(b) the specification of the underspecified fricative /s/ as [z] before a vowel (e.g. *desiludir* /des+iludiɾ/ [dɨziludíɾ] 'to disappoint') instead of its specification as a palatal before a consonant (e.g. *descrer* /des+kɾéɾ/ [dɨʃkɾéɾ] 'to disbelieve').

On the basis of these arguments, we propose that, in Portuguese, an onset and a rhyme obligatorily constitute any syllable.

3.4. THE BASE SYLLABIFICATION: CONVENTIONS

We assume that syllables are not parsed in the lexical representation: parsing and internal structure result from the base syllabification. By application of the base syllabification conventions, each syllable is associated with the skeleton through

---

[23] For a different analysis see Vigário (1997).

'association lines' and they fill this tier with a certain number of timing units or positions.

After having considered the syllable from a phonotactic point of view and having discussed a few questions related to the syllable internal structure, we are now in a position to make some statements about base syllabification in Portuguese.

The considerations made above show the restrictions on determining syllable onsets and codas. Bearing in mind the referred theoretical principles and restrictions, the appropriate way to build up syllable structure in Portuguese seems to be the approach usually called 'all-nuclei-first', starting with the construction of the rhymes in accordance with the language's restrictions. (See Goldsmith (1990) on different proposals for base syllabification.) This means that we consider the rule-based algorithm more appropriate than the template-matching algorithm (see Blevins, 1995). Thus it is necessary to formulate an algorithm to be applied in base syllabification. This algorithm functions on the basis of the application of the conventions presented below.

(30) *Nucleus Association Convention*

(a) Associate with a Nucleus all X [-cons] that are simultaneously not lexically marked and preceded by a [–cons].
(b) Adjoin the remainder X [–cons] to the Nucleus leftwards.

The first part of Nucleus Association Convention associates with a nucleus all X assigned to a [-cons] segment if not lexically marked (which is indicated by a capital letter, as we said above) and if they are not preceded by a vowel. This means that underlying vowels that are lexically marked as not stressable but that are not preceded by another vowel are nuclei *per se*.

The second part of this convention integrates the remainder [–consonant] in the created nuclei. The creation of the syllable nucleus automatically builds up the rhyme.

The application of the Nucleus Association Convention is exemplified in (31) with the words *preitos* 'homage', *pneu* 'tire', *afta* 'aphthae' and *país* 'country'.

(31)

The high vowels included in the nuclei leftwards (31a–b) are subject to a gliding rule and both vowels become a falling diphthong.

The next convention, that of Onset Association, syllabifies the consonants followed by a vowel (a nucleus) in assigning them to an onset.

(32) Onset Association Convention

(a) Associate all X [+cons] immediately preceding a Nucleus with an Onset.
(b) Adjoin to the same Onset a preceding X [+cons] if it is in accordance with the Sonority Principle and the Dissimilarity Condition.

Each X [+cons] that precedes a vowel is associated with an onset. A sequence of two [+cons] is assigned to the same onset if the consonants are in accordance with the Sonority Principle and the Dissimilarity Condition. The application of (32) is illustrated in (33a–e).

(33)

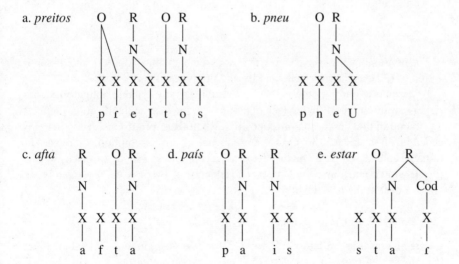

Conventions (30) and (32) are considered to be persistent in the sense that they apply every time the requirements for their application are present.

After the application of (32), the remaining X [+cons] preceding an onset that are not associated with any constituent of the syllable, either word-initially (as /p/ in *pneu*) or word-internally (as /f/ in *afta*), are not integrated in the syllabic structure. The existence of a 'non-associated' consonant gives rise to the introduction of an empty nucleus position through the application of the Empty Nucleus Creation Convention.

(34) *Empty Nucleus Creation Convention*

Create a Nucleus to the left of an Onset, with the corresponding skeletal position, if in the skeleton tier this Onset is preceded by a non-associated position specified for voicing. Otherwise, create a Nucleus to the left of that non-associated position.

In (35) the convention for the creation of empty nuclei is applied in *pneu* and *afta* words that kept non-associated X [+cons] after the application of (32).

(35)

a. *pneu*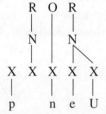   b. *afta*

The non-associated consonants can now associate with an onset by the re-application of (32), as they are followed by an (empty) nucleus.

According to our hypothesis that, in Portuguese, any syllable obligatorily consists in an onset and a rhyme (see above 3.3.2), the base syllabification includes a convention that creates an onset position when there is a rhyme that is not preceded by an onset (see (36)). As a consequence of this assumption, what is traditionally considered as a 'hiatus' (two adjacent vowels as, for instance, in *boa* [bóɐ] 'good' (fem.) or *país*) is in fact a sequence of two vowels separated by an empty onset at the base level.

(36) *Empty Onset Creation Convention*

Create an Onset to the left of a Rhyme, with the corresponding skeletal position, if in the skeleton tier this Rhyme is not preceded by an Onset.

In (37a and b) the application of the Empty Onset Creation Convention in the base syllabification of *afta* and *país* is demonstrated.

(37)

a. *afta*    b. *país*

At this point of the base syllabification, the only consonants left non-associated are consonants that follow the nuclei, that is, they are in codas. They remain non-associated and, in the post-lexical level, they are assigned to the codas of the preceding rhyme through the application of the Coda Association Convention.

(38) *Coda Association Convention*

Assign the non-associated X [+cons] to the coda of the preceding rhyme.

The application of the Coda Association Convention is represented in (39) for the words *preitos* and *país*. This application is preceded by all the processes and rules that apply in the lexical level. So, the stress and the result of the unstressed vowel rules are included in (39a) and (39b).

(39)

a. *preitos* 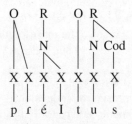   b. *país*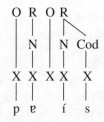

The application of (38) ends the syllabification of the words presented above. Postlexical rules and default rules apply to the syllable constituents.

It is worth noting that, when there is a diphthong followed by a vowel at the phonetic level (e.g. *areia* [ɐɾéjɐ] 'sand', see (24), or *saia* [sájɐ] 'skirt'), after the application of the Empty Onset Creation Convention, the glide can associate with the onset of the following syllable (an empty onset) and it becomes then ambi-syllabic (see the representation of *areia* and *saia* in (40) below).

(40)

a. *areia*

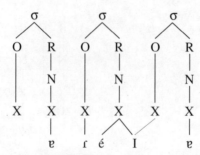

b. *saia*

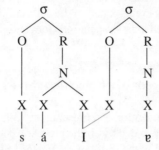

Thus, base syllables in Portuguese are CV syllables, despite the apparent violations of European Portuguese at the phonetic level. Consequently, the underlying syllables differ crucially from those on the phonetic level, namely for EP, as the number of CV syllables is obviously higher underlyingly. It is worth noting, on account of our proposal, that CV syllables are also the most frequent ones in Portuguese at the phonetic level (see Andrade and Viana, 1993a; Vigário and Falé, 1993).

We consider that our approach, involving rules of syllabification that apply in an ordered fashion, is better than any other approach so far developed for syllable with respect to Portuguese. Empirically, it accounts satisfactorily for the oral and nasal falling diphthongs and the consonant clusters in European Portuguese. Moreover, it is in accordance with our proposal of floating codas.

4

PORTUGUESE MORPHOLOGY: INFLECTION

4.1. INTRODUCTION

The understanding of Portuguese phonology,requires some degree of familiarity with its morphology. As in other languages, a number of phonological rules are interrelated with word-formation rules. The present chapter and the following one are concerned with the most relevant and basic morphological aspects and with the morpho-phonological processes involved in Portuguese word inflection (this chapter) and derivation (Chapter 5).

Morphologically, EP and BP do not diverge. There are a few interesting differences with respect to morphologically triggered phonological rules, however, which call for a comparison between the two varieties. Except in such cases, the phonetic transcriptions of the two chapters correspond to an EP pronunciation; for comparison with a BP pronunciation, however, the information given in Chapters 2 and 3 is relevant.

Akin to what has been observed in most European languages, Portuguese inflectional processes involve suffix alternations; these are associated, in nouns and adjectives, with number (singular/plural), and, in verbs, with tense–mood–aspect, and person–number. Besides suffixation, derivational processes also involve prefixation.

We assume, in accordance with lexical phonology, that word-formation rules may operate at the lexical level of representation. It has been claimed by some of the proponents of this theory that derivational and inflectional rules operate at distinct levels: the former apply at the lexical level and generate the lexical representation, whereas the latter occur post-lexically, thus generating the word. In Portuguese, the available evidence does not support this view; rather, we propose that derivation and inflection both apply at the lexical level.[1] However, as will be shown in due course (5.2), there are some exceptional cases, which have interesting implications for this claim.

In characterizing inflectional versus derivational suffixes, it is also important to point out that the former cannot apply recursively (they cannot co-occur in a word to identify a given grammatical category), while certain derivational suffixes, such as modifiers, can be subject to a recursive application (see Villalva (1994a) on this type of suffix).

[1] Regarding lexical phonology, see 5.2.1. By 'proponents of this theory' we mean Kiparsky (1982) and Mohanan (1986).

The study of Portuguese morphology has been made from different stances: historical (e.g. Nunes, 1919; Williams, 1938), structuralist (e.g. Mattoso Câmara, 1970a and b) and in the 1970s, standard generative (see Mateus, 1975 and Andrade, 1977). Villalva (1994a) discusses the configuration of the morphological and derivational structures (see 4.3.below) within a more recent generative approach. Her detailed discussion is commended to anyone who seeks a deeper understanding of the syntactic and semantic functions of inflectional and derivational suffixes in Portuguese.

4.2. INFLECTION

Inflection is an obligatory, systematic and productive morphological process, which creates paradigms encompassing all words in the language. In this chapter we outline the most relevant characteristics of noun and verb inflection.[2]

4.2.1. Nouns and adjectives

We may group Portuguese nouns and adjectives into three classes (see (1), (2) and (3)). The regular nouns and adjectives belonging to these classes differ with respect to stress distribution at the phonetic level. As we shall see in Chapter 6, Portuguese word stress generally tends to fall on the last vowel of the stem. At the phonetic level, this may correspond to the penultimate syllable of the word (class 1 nouns), or to the last one (classes 2 and 3). This phonetic difference is due to the fact that class 1 nominals end in an unstressable vowel, the class marker, whereas the final vowel of the nominals in the other two classes belongs to the root and is, therefore, stressable (see Chapter 6 and 4.2.1.2 on pluralization).

(1) Class 1: Word-final class markers (underlyingly /a/, /o/, /e/)

   a. Unstressed [ɐ] (/a/)
       chuva [ʃúvɐ] 'rain'
       casa [kázɐ] 'house'
       porta [pɔ́rtɐ] 'door'
       galinha [gɐlíɲɐ] 'hen'
       fantasma [fɐ̃táʒmɐ] 'ghost'

   b. Unstressed [u] (/o/)
       livro [lívɾu] 'book'
       barco [báɾku] 'boat'
       cesto [séʃtu] 'basket'
       galo [gálu] 'cock'
       sofrimento [sufɾimẽ́tu] 'suffering'

---

[2] In this chapter, affixes are represented in orthographic form and in italic.

c. Unstressed [ɨ]³ (/e/)
   pente [pétɨ] 'comb'
   sede [sédɨ] 'thirst'
   cidade [sidádɨ] 'town'
   gente [ʒétɨ] 'people'
   romance [ʀumẽsɨ] 'romance'
   fome [fɔmɨ] 'hungry'
   bote [bɔtɨ] 'boat'

(2) Class 2: Word-final root consonants (underlyingly /s/, /ɾ/, /l/)

   a. final [ʃ] (/s/)
      francês [fɾẽséʃ] 'French'
      arroz [ɐʀóʃ] 'rice'
      paz [páʃ] 'peace'
      xadrez [ʃɐdɾéʃ] 'chess'
      nariz [nɐɾíʃ] 'nose'

   b. final [ɾ] (/ɾ/)
      dor [dóɾ] 'pain'
      amor [ɐmóɾ] 'love'
      colher [kuʎéɾ] 'spoon'
      mulher [muʎéɾ] 'woman'
      flor [flóɾ] 'flower'

   c. final [ɫ] (/l/)
      catedral [kɐtɨdráɫ] 'cathedral'
      animal [ɐnimáɫ] 'animal'
      papel [pɐpéɫ] 'paper'
      barril [bɐʀíɫ] 'barrel'
      azul [ɐzúɫ] 'blue'

(3) Class 3: Word-final root vowel or diphthong⁴

   a. Stressed vowel oral and nasal⁵

rajá [ʀaʒá] 'raja'	*manhã* [mɐɲẽ] 'morning'
café [kɐfé] 'coffee'	*mandarim* [mẽdɐɾí] 'mandarin'
rubi [ʀubí] 'ruby'	*som* [sṍ] 'sound'
avó [ɐvɔ] 'grandmother'	*atum* [ɐtṹ] 'tuna'
caju [kaʒú] 'cashew fruit'	

³ As it is said before, in EP, unstressed final [ɨ] is usually deleted in colloquial speech (see 2.1.2.1 and 3.2.1.2.). Thus words in (1c) normally end in the root consonant at the phonetic level.

⁴ Final graphic *-m* indicates nasalization. Nouns spelled with this final graphic consonant are included in the set of nouns characterized by final nasal vowel nouns. It may be recalled from Chapters 2 and 3 that, underlyingly, they have a nasal floating segment.

⁵ A few words like *taxi* [táksi] 'taxi' and *juri* [ʒúɾi] 'jury' end in unstressed [i] and constitute a special group. The same happens with *viagem* [viáʒẽj] 'travel' and the words ending in the unstressed diphthong [ẽj]. All these words are borrowings.

b. Stressed oral and nasal diphthongs
  calhau [keʎáw] 'stone'
  judeu [ʒudéw] 'jew'
  chapéu [ʃɐpéw] 'hat'[6]
  acção [asẽ́w̃] 'action'
  irmão [iɾmẽ́w̃] 'brother'

The unstressed final vowel that follows the root of class 1 nouns and adjectives is the 'class marker'. In the verb paradigm, the vowel that follows the root, /a/, /e/ or /i/, is the 'theme vowel' (see 4.2.2). The distinction between these two kinds of morphemes is made thus:

(i) The theme vowel is an idiosyncratic property of the verb. It is added at the lexical level as a result of the application of word-formation rules; moreover, it gets its full specification in the sequence of its adjunction (see, for instance, 4.2.2.1.2). The class marker is also an idiosyncratic property of lexical items, but it only acquires its segmental specification following the application of all word-formation rules (see 5.2).

(ii) Due to the characteristics referred to in (i), theme vowels may be either deleted as in some forms of the present tenses (see in 4.2.2.1.1) or stressed, as in all past tense verb forms (see 4.2.2.1.2). The first case has implications from the point of view of vowel harmony, as will be shown in 4.2.2.2. Class markers, in turn, are never stressed and their deletion does not have any grammatical consequences.

(iii) The adjunction of the theme vowel does not obligatorily generate the word, for theme vowels are most of the time followed by other (verb) suffixes. On the other hand, the adjunction of class markers (as well as the number suffix) does generate the word.

(iv) At the phonetic level, theme vowels precede tense suffixes, for instance, /fal+a+va/ [feláve] 'I was speaking' where the TV /a/ precedes the suffix of the imperfect tense; except in a very special kind of derived words discussed in 5.2.1, class markers always occupy the word-final position.

In sum: theme vowels are part of the word stem and are submitted to morphological processes; class markers are not part of the word stem, in fact they may even not occur at all, as in classes 2 and 3, and are not subject to morphological rules, at the lexical level.

Besides stress-related differences, the three classes of nouns and adjectives also behave differently with respect to their derivation with morphological modifiers, i.e. evaluative suffixes such as *–inho, -ico-, -ito*, and *z*-evaluative suffixes such as *-zinho, -zico, -zito*. We shall address this subject in Chapter 5.

---

[6] Recall that unlike EP, BP has diphthongs resulting from coda lateral gliding (e.g. *lençol* [lẽsɔw] 'bed sheet', *nível* [nívew] 'level').

4.2.1.1. *Gender*

Gender is an intrinsic property of nouns and can have a referential content. It is an inherent property of the base-form of the word and, thus, it cannot be considered as an inflectional category. The inclusion of this section under a discussion of inflexion is justified, however, as it is a requisite for studying the interaction between nasalization and gender alternations in a subset of [+animate] nouns.

Portuguese nouns may be either masculine or feminine independently of the classes they belong to. Gender in adjectives, on the other hand, results from the agreement with the noun and is only grammatical. Moreover, adjectives may not always change, even though they always agree with the noun's gender.

Normally, nouns ending in unstressed [ɐ] are feminine and those ending in [u] are masculine. Only [+animate] nouns can have gender contrasts and alternate final [ɐ] for feminine [+animate] with final [u] for masculine ((4a)). Nouns that have final /e/, as in (4b), can be either masculine or feminine. Nouns ending in a consonant, /l/, /s/ or /ɾ/, are usually masculine with a few exceptions: (4c).

(4) Masculine

a. *menino* [mɨnínu] 'little boy'
   gato [gátu] 'male cat'

b. *romance* [ʀumɐ̃sɨ] 'novel'

c. *capital* [kɐpitáɫ] 'funds'
   mês [méʃ] 'month'
   nariz [nɐɾíʃ] 'nose'
   talher [tɐʎéɾ] 'cutlery'
   amor [ɐmóɾ] 'love'

Feminine

a. *menina* [mɨnínɐ] 'little girl'
   gata [gátɐ] 'female cat'

b. *fome* [fómɨ] 'hunger'

c. *capital* [kɐpitáɫ] 'capital'
   rês [ʀéʃ] 'cattle'
   raiz [ʀɐíʃ] 'root'
   mulher [muʎéɾ] 'woman'
   flor [flóɾ] 'flower'

Gender alternations for [+animate] nouns ending in nasal diphthongs will be discussed fully in Chapter 7, together with the nasalization process, as they show the regular behaviour of phonetic nasal vowels. For the moment, some examples are given below: (5).

5. Masculine

[ẽw̃]
folgazão [fɔɫgɐzẽw̃]
comilão [kumilẽw̃]

[ẽw̃]
leão [liẽw̃]
patrão [pɐtɾẽw̃]

[ẽw̃]
irmão [irmẽw̃]
anão [ɐnẽw̃]

Feminine

[onɐ]
folgazona [fɔɫgɐzónɐ] 'merry fellow'
comilona [kumilónɐ] 'glutton'

[oɐ]
leoa [lióɐ] 'lion'
patroa [pɐtróɐ] 'master'

[ẽ]
irmã [irmẽ] 'brother and sister'
anã [ɐnẽ] 'dwarf'

4.2.1.2. *Number*

Number in Portuguese is an inflectional category of nouns and adjectives: it is obligatory and functions in a systematic manner. Number specification for nouns results from the speaker's choice; adjectives draw their specification from their agreement with nouns. Thus, they all present an alternation between the two values of the morphological category 'number'. The latter is not conditioned by any information: it only depends on syntactic and semantic information.

4.2.1.2.1. *Number in nouns and adjectives from classes 1 and 2*

The plural morpheme is /s/, an underspecified segment for voice and place.[7] Class 1 nouns and adjectives trigger the word-formation rule that adjoins this suffix to the class markers. The complete specification of plural morpheme /s/ results from the application of post-lexical phonological rules.

Nouns and adjectives belonging to class 2, with root final /s/ and /ɾ/ and lacking class markers (see (2)), evidence an epenthetic vowel preceding the suffix— the unmarked EP vowel [ɨ]—at the phonetic level:[8] *francês* [fɾẽséʃ] 'French man', *franceses* [fɾẽsézɨʃ] 'French men'; *mar* [máɾ] 'sea', *mares* [máɾɨʃ] 'seas'. In fact, when the plural suffix /s/ is added, a new syllabic parsing gives way to a new final syllable with an empty nucleus by the application of the Empty Nucleus Creation Convention (see 3.4 above). This nucleus is filled with the mentioned epenthetic vowel.

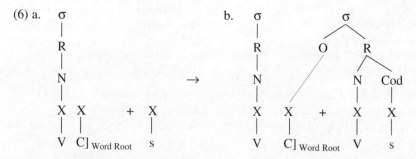

As may be seen in (6a), the root final /s/ or /ɾ/ fill a non-associated position that becomes a syllable onset in (6b). Both /s/ and /ɾ/ are underspecified segments. They are specified for place by a default rule that is triggered by the application of the morphology suffixation rule (see 2.4.2). Specification of the laryngeal node in case of the fricative final root (*franceses* [fɾẽsézɨʃ]), results from the spreading of the [+voice] vowel feature over the non-associated consonant. (7) below represents the application of the default and voicing rules.

---

[7] There are a few exceptions of words ending in /s/ that are invariant for number (*lápis* [lápɨʃ] 'pencil', *simples* [sĩplɨʃ] 'easy', *ourives* [oɾívɨʃ] 'goldsmith' sg. and pl.). There is also a small set of forms that are lexicalized and can only be used in the plural (like *pêsames* [pézɐmɨʃ] 'condolences'): they are lexicalized plurals.

[8] [i] in BP.

(7)   /s/ → [z]

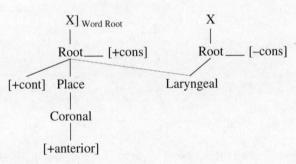

The plural suffix is associated with the coda of the new syllable and triggers the coda rule at the end of the derivation.

Number alternation in nouns and adjectives ending in /l/ raises somewhat different problems from what we have just described. The following word pairs exemplify the alternation between [ł] and [jʃ].

(8)   Singular
       animal [ɐnimáł] 'animal'
       nível [nívɛł] 'level'
       lençol [lẽsɔ́ł] 'sheet'

       Plural
       animais [ɐnimájʃ] 'animals'
       níveis [nívɐjʃ] 'levels'
       lençóis [lẽsɔ́jʃ] 'sheets'

This alternation is the result of the application of morphology-sensitive phonological rules. Let us see what happens.

Similarly to what has been shown for the other class 2 words, when the plural suffix /s/ is added, the creation of a new syllable with an empty nucleus should give rise to the insertion of an epenthetic vowel. However, this does not occur. Instead, when the number suffix /s/ is added to /l/, the lateral is 'forced' into the nucleus leftwards because there is no place for it to be a coda. This syllabification implies the gliding of the lateral; in fact, this happens in BP whenever this consonant is in coda position (e.g. *mal* [máw], see 3.2.3). If we adopt the view that the velarization of /l/ is also a manifestation of its nuclearization (as does Girelli (1988), for instance), we can see an interrelation between these different realizations of the post-vocalic /l/.

This change of value of the feature [lateral] 'turns out to be the least marked option' to explain the plural forms of these words (Morales-Front and Holt, 1997), instead of the deletion of the /l/ when the suffix /s/ is added. See the following configuration.

(9) a.

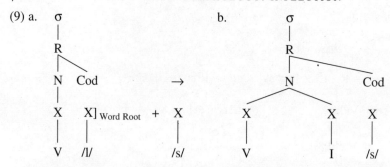

In accordance with Girelli (1988), the features that distinguish both glides resulting from the vocalization of the /l/ ([w] in coda in BP and [j] before /s/) are underspecified; their values depend on the application of specific rules as the one represented in (9).[9]

4.2.1.2.2. *Number in words ending in stressed nasal diphthong*

Class 3 nouns and adjectives simply add the plural suffix /s/ to the final vowels or diphthongs, except for words ending in the stressed nasal diphthong [ḗw̃] at the phonetic level. These words may have a regular plural form as, for instance, *mão* [mḗw̃] 'hand'/*mãos* [mḗw̃ʃ] 'hands', *cidadão* [sidɐdḗw̃] 'citizen'/*cidadãos* [sidɐdḗw̃ʃ] 'citizens'. In these nouns and adjectives the glide results from the class marker /o/ that integrates the nucleus.

Besides these regular forms, there are others exemplified in (10), which also exhibit alternations.

(10) Singular   Plural

a.   *acção* [asḗw̃]   *acções* [asṍjʃ] 'actions'
     leão [ljḗw̃]   *leões* [ljṍjʃ] 'lions'
     sermão [sɨɾmḗw̃]   *sermões* [sɨɾmṍjʃ] 'sermons'

b.   *pão* [pḗw̃]   *pães* [pḗjʃ] 'bread'
     cão [kḗw̃]   *cães* [kḗjʃ] 'dogs'
     capitão [kɐpitḗw̃]   *capitães* [kɐpitḗjʃ] 'captains'

The difference between (10a) and (10b) can be explained as follows. In (10a), *leão* is related to *leonino* [ljunínu] 'leonine', from /leo[+nasal]/, *acção* is the base-form of *accionar* [asjunáɾ] 'to put in action', from /asio[+nasal]/. We may thus infer that the root of the two nouns includes the vowel /o/ and the nasal auto-segment. When the plural suffix /s/ is added, the nasal autosegment spreads its feature over the root vowel, that is, the nucleus of the stressed syllable. In this case, in final position, the stressed nasal nucleus has a tendency to branch. So, the existence of the floating nasal segment implies the introduction of a glide into the nucleus.

[9] Morales-Front and Holt (1997) present an interesting interpretation of the lateral nuclearization within the framework of the Optimality Theory.

The fact that the nasal glide is a front one (cf. *leões* [ljõĵʃ]) and does not agree with the vowel of the nucleus reflects historical facts. Morales-Front and Holt (1997: 424) view this 'as an indication that assimilation to the consonant (palatal [ʃ]) has a higher ranking than V-Agr', as established within the OT framework. We do not agree with this interpretation. In fact, V-Agr—that is, place agreement between the two elements of the diphthong—is very general. Furthermore, there are a number of BP dialects where the plural suffix is not a palatal [ʃ] but rather a dental [s] (e.g. *liões* [ljõĵs]), and in these cases we would not be able to justify the palatal glide as resulting from an agreement with the consonant.[10]

In (10b), *cão* is related to *canídeos* [kɐnídjuʃ] 'canidae', from /ka[+nasal]/, *capitão* is related to *capitania* [kɐpitɐníɐ] 'captainship', from /kapita[+nasal]/. In these words, the root vowel is /a/ and the phonological process is the same as that characterizing the words in (10a).

The difference between the two diphthongs in the plural ([õĵ]/[ẽĵ], *liões/pães*) is caused by different underlying vowels: in *lião*, [ẽ] results from an /o/ and in *pão* from an /a/. The glide results from the branching of a nasal nucleus in the final syllable.

4.2.2. Verb inflection

One of the most striking aspects of the Portuguese language is the diversity of inflection in verb forms. Five different persons are used in a great number of tenses: 1st (I), 2nd (you) and 3rd (s/he) singular, 1st (we) and 3rd (they) plural. The 2nd person plural is restricted to some dialects that are not under study here; thus, its forms are not given in the data presented below.[11] 3rd person plural forms usually replace 2nd person plural ones. The 3rd person singular is also used to address someone; the corresponding pronoun is *você* (you, sg.). The person–number suffixes are characteristic of both varieties of Portuguese. Sentences may present no subject pronouns: Portuguese is a null-subject language.

We may group the Portuguese verbs into three paradigms depending on the stressed vowel which precedes the infinitive morpheme: the first paradigm in /a/ (like *falar* [fɐlár] 'to speak'), the second one in /e/ (like *bater* [bɐtér] 'to beat') and the third one in /i/ (like *partir* [pɐrtír] 'to leave'). Verbs like *pôr* [pór] 'to put' and its related derived verbs (e.g. *compor* [kõpór] 'to compound', *dispor* [diʃpór] 'to dispose' etc.) are irregular and they conform with the /e/ paradigm for most of their forms. Some remarks about irregular verbs are made in 4.2.2.3. The first paradigm is still productive while the others are not, except for verbs in *-ecer* (like *anoitecer* [ɐnojtɨsér] 'to darken') that denote the inchoative aspect and can give rise to new words in modern Portuguese.

Verb forms include the *root* (R), the *theme vowel* (TV), the *tense–mood–aspect* (TMA) and the *person–number* (PN) morphemes. In the verb forms presented

---

[10] Regarding the lexical representation of nasality see also Wetzels (1997).

[11] The second person plural corresponds to the pronoun *vós* 'you' (pl.). It is only used in the north of Portugal and in the north of Brazil.

below, [+] symbolizes the morpheme boundary. The R and the TV morphemes constitute the Stem (St).

The morphological structure of the infinitive, whose stem forms in verbs *falar*, *bater*, *partir* is phonemically /fal+**a**/, /bat+**e**/, /part+**i**/, includes one of the three TVs, /a/, /e/ and /i/; these are stressed, and are thus surface unchanged realizations. Besides the infinitive stem, verbs also have the past participle stem—*falado* /fal+**a**/, *batido* /bat+**i**/ and *partido* /part+**i**/—that differs from the infinitive stem in the 2nd paradigm, for the theme vowel is /i/ and not /e/.

The three verb tenses, *present*, *past* and *future*, diverge with respect to stress placement as we will see in 6.2. There is also a difference in the morphological structure of the forms of the future tenses with respect to the other two groups, as will be seen in 4.2.2.1.3. These facts, and some other peculiarities that will be mentioned in the present section, motivate the classification of verb tenses into these three groups.

4.2.2.1. *Regular verbs*

When the last root vowel is /a/ there is no alternation in any of the verb forms. This class of verbs, therefore, is appropriate to exemplify the Portuguese verb forms belonging to the three paradigms. Examples are from the verbs *falar* [fɐlár] 'to speak', *bater* [bɐtér] 'to beat' and *partir* [pɐɾtír] 'to leave'.

4.2.2.1.1. *Present Tenses:* Present Indicative and Subjunctive, and Infinitive[12]

Present Indicative and Subjunctive
Present indicative forms only have person–number morphemes. They all present the theme vowel at the phonetic level, with the exception of the 1st person singular (see (11)). Tense morphemes of the present subjunctive are /e/ for the /a/ paradigm, and /a/ for the other two paradigms. The forms of this tense never exhibit the TV at the phonetic level (see (12) and (13)). Underlyingly, the PN morphemes for both tenses are the following ones:

1st sing.	/o/ (Pres.Ind.)	1st plur. /mos/;
	ø (Pres.Subj.)	
2nd sing.	/s/	
3rd sing.	ø	3rd plur. /N/ (nasal autosegment)[13]

Tense morphemes and person–number morphemes are added to the item and they get full specification following the application of all word-formation rules.

---

[12] The imperative and the gerund are also present tenses. We do not mention them in this chapter because they are not subject to specific phonological rules, but to the regular processes of the language. They will be considered with respect to stress placement in Chapter 6.

[13] The realization of the nasal autosegment in verb forms is included in the whole process of nasalization and will be dealt with in Chapter 7.

(11) Present Indicative[14]

/fal+a]$_{St}$ o/ [fálu] /bat+e]$_{St}$ o/ [bátu] /paɾt+i]$_{St}$ o/ [páɾtu]

/fal+a]$_{St}$ s/ [fáleʃ] /bat+e]$_{St}$ s/ [bátiʃ] /paɾt+i]$_{St}$ s/ [páɾtiʃ]

/fal+a]$_{St}$ / [fále] /bat+e]$_{St}$ / [báti] /paɾt+i]$_{St}$ / [páɾti]

/fal+a]$_{St}$ mos/ [felémuʃ] /bat+e]$_{St}$ mos/ [betémuʃ] /paɾt+i]$_{St}$ mos/ [peɾtímuʃ]

/fal+a]$_{St}$ N/ [fálẽw̃] /bat+e]$_{St}$ N/ [bátẽj̃] /paɾt+i]$_{St}$ N/ [páɾtẽj̃]

(12) Present Subjunctive

/fal+a]$_{St}$ e/ [fáli] /bat+e]$_{St}$ a/ [báte] /paɾt+i]$_{St}$ a/ [páɾte]

/fal+a]$_{St}$ e+s/ [fáliʃ] /bat+e]$_{St}$ a+s/ [báteʃ] /paɾt+i]$_{St}$ a+s/ [páɾteʃ]

/fal+a]$_{St}$ e/ [fáli] /bat+e]$_{St}$ a/ [báte] /paɾt+i]$_{St}$ a/ [páɾte]

/fal+a]$_{St}$ e+mos/ [felémuʃ] /bat+e]$_{St}$ a+mos/ [betémuʃ] /paɾt+i]$_{St}$ a+mos/[peɾtémuʃ]

/fal+a]$_{St}$ e+N/ [fálẽj̃] /bat+e]$_{St}$ a+N/ [bátẽw̃] /paɾt+i]$_{St}$ a+N/ [páɾtẽw̃]

In both present tenses, the theme vowel is deleted when another vowel is added. The added vowel is the person–number morpheme /o/ in the indicative, the tense–mood–aspect morphemes /e/ (first paradigm) and /a/ (second and third paradigms) in the subjunctive. Theme vowel deletion occurs in many languages; since it is morphologically conditioned, it takes place at the lexical level. In Portuguese this deletion is restricted to the present tenses: in fact, the theme vowel is not suppressed in the past tenses.

The theme vowel deletion process entails the deletion of the skeleton slot, (X), with which it is associated (see (13)). However, if this node is delinked when the skeleton unit is deleted, this deletion may leave the vowel height node as a *floating autosegment*.

(13) TV Deletion (Present Tenses)

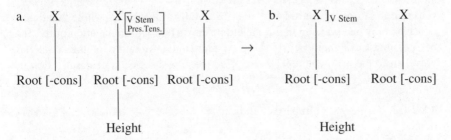

The phonetic realization of this floating segment consists on the spreading of its height features over the root vowel, as we shall see in our discussion of vowel harmony (see 4.2.2.2).

In the 2nd and 3rd person singular and in the 3rd person plural, the TV takes the word-final position, and stress falls in the last root vowel, as similarly happens

---

[14] The internal structure of the verb forms included in (11) and (12) distinguish the stem (St)—including the root (R) and the theme vowel (TV)—from the tense–mood–aspect (TMA) and person–number (PN) suffixes. The nasalization of the last part of these verb forms will be dealt with in Chapter 7.

in the 1st person singular.[15] As to the 1st person plural, it is stressed in the theme vowel (present indicative /fal á]$_{St}$ mos/) or in the tense–mood vowel that occupies the TV place (present subjunctive /bat á]$_{St}$ mos/).

Infinitive

For historical reasons, Portuguese has inflected forms in the infinitive that have the same person morphemes as the other present tenses (1st and 3rd persons singular have no morpheme). Inflected forms are obligatory in some syntactic structures as, for instance, with verbs of compulsion like *mandar* 'order' in sentences like *eu mandei os alunos falarem* (and not **falar*), 'I ordered the students to speak', or in nominal complement clauses such as *é possível as crianças falarem* (and not **falar*), 'it is possible for the children to speak'. This is one of the most striking peculiarities of the Portuguese among all the Romance languages. See (14) and (15) as an example for the regular verbs.

(14) Inflected Infinitive   (15) Uninflected Infinitive
/fal+a]$_{St}$ ɾ/ [fɐláɾ]   /fal+a]$_{St}$ ɾ/ [fɐláɾ]
/fal+a]$_{St}$ ɾ +s/ [fɐláɾiʃ]
/fal+a]$_{St}$ ɾ/ [fɐláɾ]
/fal+a]$_{St}$ ɾ +mos/ [fɐláɾmuʃ]
/fal+a]$_{St}$ ɾ +N/ [fɐláɾẽj̃]

The morpheme of the infinitive is /ɾ/. When the 2nd person singular suffix, /s/, is added to the tense morpheme, an epenthetic vowel, [ɨ], occurs at the phonetic level.[16]

Similarly, in the 3rd person plural (e.g. *falarem* [fɐláɾẽj̃]), where the person suffix is the nasal segment: the epenthetic vowel is syllabified and the nasal autosegment spreads its nasality over the vowel ([ẽ]). As in the remaining 3rd persons plural, the glide is introduced after the nasalization, and the whole diphthong occupies only one position in the skeleton ([ẽj̃]). The EP pronunciation of the 3rd person plural diphthong ([ẽj̃]) shows a regular dissimilation of the nasalized vowel from the following epenthetic glide (see the discussion of nasalization in Chapter 7).

4.2.2.1.2. *Past tenses*: Imperfect Indicative, Past Perfect Indicative, Past Participle[17]

Imperfect Indicative

Morphemes in the Imperfect Indicative distinguish the 1st paradigm from the other two (/e/ and /i/), as in the present subjunctive: the tense morpheme in /a/ verbs is /va/ and in /e/, /i/ verbs is /ia/.

---

[15] These forms are traditionally called in Portuguese 'rizotónicas', 'stressed in the root'. About this stress see also Chapter 6.

[16] See in 4.2.1.2 a similar process, when the number suffix /s/ is added to the final root consonant /ɾ/.

[17] Portuguese verbs have other past tenses—pluperfect indicative, and imperfect and future

(16) Imperfect Indicative

/fal+a]$_{St}$ va/ [feláve]	/bat+e]$_{St}$ ia/ [betíe]	/paɾt+i]$_{St}$ ia/ [peɾtíe]
/fal+a]$_{St}$ va+s/ [feláveʃ]	/bat+e]$_{St}$ ia+s/ [betíeʃ]	/paɾt+i]$_{St}$ ia+s/ [petíeʃ]
/fal+a]$_{St}$ va/ [feláve]	/bat+e]$_{St}$ ia/ [betíe]	/paɾt+i]$_{St}$ ia/ [peɾtíe]
/fal+a]$_{St}$ va+mos/	/bat+e]$_{St}$ ia+mos/	/paɾt+i]$_{St}$ ia+mos/
[felávemuʃ]	[betíemuʃ]	[peɾtíemuʃ]
/fal+a]$_{St}$ va+N/ [felávẽw̃]	/bat+e]$_{St}$ ia+N/ [betíẽw̃]	/paɾt+i]$_{St}$ ia+N/ [peɾtíẽw̃]

In this tense, as in the other past tenses, the TV is always stressed. In the second and third verb paradigms, the theme vowel is followed by the vowel of the suffix. As this last vowel is a lexical trough,[18] that is, unstressable in past tenses, the TV is not deleted and gets the stress. In the second paradigm the stressed theme vowel /e/ becomes [i]. The two adjacent high vowels fuse: /bat+**e** + **i**a/ → [betíe]; /paɾt+**i** + **i**a/→ [peɾtíe]. The same process takes place in the past perfect indicative.

Past Perfect Indicative
The past perfect indicative has no tense morpheme; moreover, its person–number morphemes are different from those in the other tenses, except for the 1st plural (see (17)):

1st sing. /i/   1st plur. /mos/;
2nd sing. /ste/
3rd sing. /u/   3rd plur. /ɾaN/ (nasal autosegment)

(17) Past Perfect Indicative

/fal+a]$_{St}$i/ [feléj][19]	/bat+e]$_{St}$i/ [betí]	/paɾt+i]$_{St}$i/ [peɾtí]
/fal+a]$_{St}$ste/ [feláʃtɨ]	/bat+e]$_{St}$ste/ betéʃtɨ]	/paɾt+i]$_{St}$ste/ [peɾtíʃtɨ]
/fal+a]$_{St}$u/ [feló]	/bat+e]$_{St}$u/ [betéw]	/paɾt+i]$_{St}$u/ [peɾtíw]
/fal+a]$_{St}$mos/ [felámuʃ]	/bat+e]$_{St}$mos/ [betémuʃ]	/paɾt+i]$_{St}$mos/ [peɾtímuʃ]
/fal+a]$_{St}$raN/ [felárẽw̃]	/bat+e]$_{St}$raN/ [betérẽw̃]	/paɾt+i]$_{St}$raN/ [peɾtírẽw̃]

Again, as in the imperfect, the stressed theme vowel of the /e/ verbs becomes [i], and the two adjacent vowels fuse (cf. /bat+é+i/ → [betí]). In the /a/ verbs, at the phonetic level, the TV /a/ shows an alternation between 1st and 3rd person singular due to the spreading of the V-place and the height features of the person suffix (see (18)). This assimilation is better understood when we compare EP dialects under study with other dialects (European and Brazilian).

---

subjunctive—that are not subject to specific rules but to the regular phonological processes of the language. Thus, we do not analyse them in this chapter but we present their characteristics with respect to stress (see Chapter 6). Nevertheless, it is worth noting that the future subjunctive is also a striking aspect of the verb system in Portuguese that has no correspondence in the other Romance languages that simply do not have this tense. In regular verbs, this tense has exactly the same forms as the inflected infinitive. In irregular verbs, it has the stem of the past tenses.

[18] See later, in Chapter 6, what is said about a lexical 'trough' in the treatment of main stress.

[19] This stressed [e] doesn't exist in BP, as we saw earlier on; the corresponding verb form is [faléj].

(18) Theme vowel alternation: 1st and 3rd person singular

/fal+a]$_{St}$i/ fal[ɐ́j] (EP)   fal[éj] (other dialects)

/fal+a]$_{St}$u/ fal[ó] (EP)   fal[ów] (other dialects)

One should note that the sequences [áj] and [áw] are accepted within the root of nouns and verbs of all dialects in Portuguese: e.g. *paixão* [pajʃɐ̃́w̃] 'passion', *bairro* [bájʀu] 'quarter', *pairar* [pajɾáɾ] 'to hover', *pau* [páw] 'stick', *causar* [kawzáɾ] 'cause'. This fact shows that the domain of application of the spreading rule involved in the examples in (18) is restricted to the morphological boundary [VT + person suffix] in past tenses.

With respect to the first person, the phonetic sequence [ɐ́j] is specific to EP studied dialects; it corresponds to the sequence [éj] in BP and some southern dialects in Portugal.[20] In the EP dialects under study the sequence [ej] does not exist. The traditional analysis of the relation between underlying /ai/ and phonetic [ɐ́j], is to consider it as a process including two steps:[21] an assimilation by the TV of some features of the suffix /i/ (/ái/ → /éi/) for all dialects, followed by dissimilation in EP (/éi/ → [ɐ́j]); the gliding of the second vowel is the automatic result of the syllabification. This two-step interpretation is in accordance with the diachronic facts and is reflected in the orthography (*falei*).

With respect to the third person, the traditional analysis also proposes an assimilation by the TV of some features of the corresponding suffix, /u/: /áu/ → /óu/. This assimilation is followed, in EP, by the deletion of the glide resulting from syllabification: /ów/ → [ó]. Just like [ɐ́j], the sequence [ów] does not exist in the EP dialects under study; it occurs, however, in some northern dialects. Once more, the two-step interpretation accords with historical facts and with orthography (*falou*).

Even though we have described these two assimilations separately (/ái/ → /éi/ and /áu/ → /óu/), it is clear that they are manifestations of a single process. There are two important points to be clarified with respect to this interpretation.

(a) The morpheme vowels that spread the features over the theme vowel /a/ are fully specified (they get this specification after the word-formation rule), and they spread the features [−back] ([i]), and [+round] ([u]) over the /a/. The assimilation represented in (20) *is an example of the interaction between morphological and phonological rules*: the word-formation rule that adds the morphemes to the verb root and generates these verb forms is the one that is responsible for the application of the assimilation rule.

Thus, we can say that (19) is a lexical rule, for it has access to the morphological structure of the string.

(b) The underlying vowels in these assimilations are [−back, −round] (/i/) and [+back, +round] (/u/): /i/ spreads the [−back] feature while /u/ spreads the [+round] feature over the /a/. So, the assimilations in question involve features

---

[20] Regarding the relation between stressed [ɐ] and [e], see 2.2.2.1.

[21] Or between etymological ⟨ai⟩ and phonetic [ɐj], see for instance Williams (1938).

depending on the V-place node and the height node, both belonging to the vocalic node. We repeat in (19) part of the feature geometry represented in 2.3.

(19)

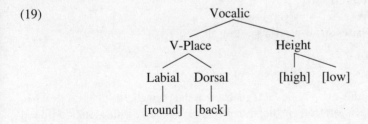

Due to the fact that there are only two vowels, /i/ and /u/, appearing in this morphological boundary, the features [back] and [round], depending on the V-place node, spread over the TV in both cases (/ái/ → /éi/ and /áu/ → /ou/).

With respect to the assimilation in height, things are different as /i/ and /u/ are high vowels and /a/ becomes, in both cases, [−low] but not [+high]. Thus, it is necessary to restrict (20) in this specific point.

(20)   /ái/ → /éi/   and   /áu/ → /ou/

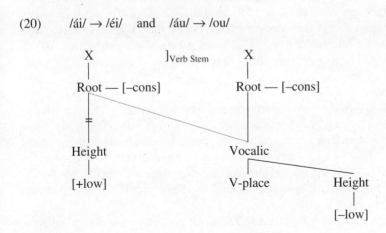

Therefore, it is the vocalic node itself that spreads over the TV.

Besides the rule presented in (20), the theme vowels in the first and second paradigms also trigger a height assimilation rule, namely the rule mentioned in the imperfect indicative.

With respect to the EP dissimilation /éi/ → [ɐj] mentioned above, affecting all /éi/ sequences resulting from /ai/, this is a process which is clearly related to the diachronic explanation of these verb forms. It is interesting to note that synchronic data provide us with the evidence in support of this explanation. In fact, many of the phonetic [ẽj] sequences alternate with the single vowel [i] when unstressed in related words:

(21) Alternation [ẽj] / [i]
      passeio /pase+o/ → pas[ẽj]o 'walk'
      passear /pase+ar/ → pas[i]ar][22] 'to walk'

      areia /are+a/ → ar[ẽj]a 'sand'
      areal /are+al/ → ar[i]al 'stretch of sand'

In our view, this underlying /e/ is realized at the phonetic level as an [i] when unstressed. When stressed, it diphthongizes, as happens with a stressed nasal vowel (see 4.2.1.2.2). An epenthetic glide is introduced in the syllable nucleus and the sequence [éj] is realized as [ẽj] by dissimilation.

Even though in nouns as *passeio* and *areia* the sequence [ẽj] does not result from the adjunction of the person suffix to the TV, the latter being realized as a glide (as it does in (18), /fal a]$_{Vb\ St}$ i/ → fal[ẽj]), there is a clear parallelism between these two groups of words: the sequence /éj/, where the [j] is the result of an epenthesis of the glide after the root vowel (e.g. /are]$_{N\ Root}$+a/), becomes [ẽj] because the sequence [éj] is not allowed in these dialects.[23]

In sum, it is evident from the above considerations that: (i) the morpheme features are fully specified when the verb form triggers the assimilation rule (19), and (ii) the spreading of the morpheme features over the TV is a lexical rule having access to the internal structure of the word, otherwise the assimilation should take place every time it gets the same sequence.

Past Participle

The *past participle* is an uninflected nominal form in Portuguese. Its corresponding tense morpheme is /do/. In the past participles of some strong verbs like *fazer* 'to do' (*feito* 'done') or *pôr* 'to put' (*posto* 'put') the morpheme of this nominal form is /to/; these past participles are lexicalized. Regular verbs may have /to/ as a second past participle form, besides /do/: e.g. *completo* 'completed', besides the regular *completado*, from *completar* 'complete'. See also 5.1.2.2 on the past participle suffix.

It is worth noting that the stressed TV of the past participle of the 2nd paradigm is similar to the TV in the 3rd paradigm: *batido* [bɐtídu] 'beaten' from *bater*, *partido* [pɐrtídu] 'left' from *partir*. This fact has consequences in the construction of derived words, as we shall see in 5.1.2.

4.2.2.1.3. *Future tenses*: Future Indicative and Conditional

In Portuguese, as in almost all of the Romance languages, except for Rumanian and some southern Italian dialects, the future indicative and the conditional

---

[22] Recall that in these kind of words, the unstressed high vowel can alternate with a glide at the phonetic level (e.g. [pɐsiáɾ] / [pɐsjáɾ]).
[23] See what is said about these stressed diphthongs in 3.2.2.1.

replace a periphrastic construction composed of the main verb and the Latin verb *habere* (e.g. *partire habeo* or *habebam*). In modern Portuguese, this periphrasis still exists but it expresses, as in English, a deontic modality: (*eu*) *hei-de partir* 'I must leave' or 'I have to leave'.[24]

The modality is not so evident in the future and the conditional, given the forms of *haver* ('to have') function as tense markers and constitute a single word with the main verb. However, this word must be viewed as a compound: infinitive of the verb + present indicative of *haver* (future) / infinitive of the verb + imperfect indicative of *haver* (conditional). Some forms of *haver* are completely integrated in the verb form (*hei* [éj] 'I have', *hás* [áʃ] 'you have', *há* [á] 's/he has'); others lose the segmental material preceding the stressed vowel (present indicative 1st person plural: *havemos* 'we have' [ɐvémuʃ] → [émuʃ]; all persons of the imperfect indicative: *havia* 'I had' [ɐvíɐ] → [íɐ], etc.). Examples in (22) and (23) are from the 1st paradigm.

(22) Future Indicative

/fal+a]$_{St}$ɾ # e+i/ [fɐlɐɾéj]
/fal+a]$_{St}$ɾ # a+s/ [fɐlɐɾáʃ]
/fal+a]$_{St}$ɾ # a/ [fɐlɐɾá]
/fal+a]$_{St}$ɾ # e+mos/ [fɐlɐɾémuʃ]
/fal+a]$_{St}$ɾ # a+N/ [fɐlɐɾéw̃]

(23) Conditional

/fal+a]$_{St}$ɾ # ia/ [fɐlɐɾíɐ]
/fal+a]$_{St}$ɾ # ia+s/ [fɐlɐɾíɐʃ]
/fal+a]$_{St}$ɾ # ia/ [fɐlɐɾíɐ]
/fal+a]$_{St}$ɾ # ia+mos/ [fɐlɐɾíɐmuʃ]
/fal+a]$_{St}$ɾ # ia+N/ [fɐlɐɾíɐw̃]

The proposal that the internal structure of these two tenses involves a word boundary is supported by a morphological process called tmesis, still preserved by modern EP but already lost by other Romance languages: the insertion of cliticized forms of personal pronouns inside the verb form, to the left of the stressed vowel of the tense morpheme.[25]

(24) Insertion of cliticized forms

falará 's/he will speak'   falar-*me*-á 's/he will speak *to me*'
falaremos 'we wil speak'   falar-*te*-emos 'we will speak *to you*'
falaria 's/he would speak'   falar-*te*-ia 's/he would speak *to you*'

4.2.2.2. *Vowel harmony in verbs*

One of the most striking features of verbs possessing /e/, /ɛ/, /o/ or /ɔ/ as the final root vowel is the pattern of alternation this vowel is subject to when stressed, if we compare the three paradigms. This alternation occurs in the 1st person singular of the present indicative and in the 1st, 2nd and 3rd persons singular and 3rd plural of the present subjunctive. Let us look at the verbs *levar* 'to take away' and *morar* 'to inhabit' (/a/ paradigm), *dever* 'to owe' and *mover* 'to move' (/e/ paradigm),

---

[24] About the relation between these two verb tenses and the main stress, see below Chapter 6.
[25] In Portuguese, this specific tmesis is named *mesóclisis*. We will say more about it in 6.2 with respect to stress placement.

ferir 'to hurt' and *dormir* 'to sleep' (/i/ paradigm). The alternation is exemplified in (25):

(25) Verbs *levar, morar* (TV /a/), *dever, mover* (TV /e/), *ferir, dormir* (TV /i/)

(a) Present Indicative (1st person singular)

l[ɛ́]vo   m[ɔ́]ro   d[é]vo   m[ó]vo   f[í]ro   d[ú]rmo

Present Subjunctive (1st, 2nd and 3rd person singular and 3rd plural)

l[ɛ́]ve	m[ɔ́]re	d[é]va	m[ó]va	f[í]ra	d[ú]rma
l[ɛ́]ves	m[ɔ́]res	d[é]vas	m[ó]vas	f[í]ras	d[ú]rmas
l[ɛ́]ve	m[ɔ́]re	d[é]va	m[ó]va	f[í]ra	d[ú]rma
l[ɛ́]vem	m[ɔ́]rem	d[é]vam	m[ó]vam	f[í]ram	d[ú]rmam

The verb forms included in (25) show that:
• /a/ verbs (first paradigm), have low vowels, [ɛ] and [ɔ];
• /e/ verbs (second paradigm), have mid vowels, [e] and [o];
• /i/ verbs, (third paradigm) have high vowels, [i] and [u].

As may be observed, low, mid and high vowels occur in the forms *where the TV has been deleted*, i.e. the 1st singular present indicative and in all persons of the present subjunctive.[26] In these cases, /a/ verbs like *levar* and *morar*, with a low TV, have a low vowel in the root; /e/ verbs like *dever* and *mover*, with a mid TV, have mid vowels in the root; /i/ verbs *ferir* and *dormir*, with a high TV, have high vowels in the root.

We are dealing with a clear case of assimilation conditioned by the theme vowel, usually known as *vowel harmony*. This consists in the spreading of theme vowel height features onto the stressed vowel. It is worth noting that root vowels only assimilate the height features and maintain the values of the features [back] and [round].

Vowel harmony does not occur in verbs with a high root vowel, /i/ or /u/, as *virar* 'to turn' and *furar* 'to pierce' or *viver* 'to live' and *iludir* 'to illude' (e.g. *furo* f[ú]ro 'I pierce', not *f[ɔ́]ro; *vivo* v[í]vo 'I live', not *[vé]vo, etc.).

Furthermore, verbs with final root /a/ do not show either vowel alternation. In fact, verbs like *falar* 'to speak', *bater* 'to beat' and *partir* 'to leave' maintain the low root vowel in the three paradigms, as may be observed in (26) (see also (11) and (12)).

(26) Verbs *falar, bater, partir*

Present Indicative	Present Subjunctive
f[á]lo	f[á]le
b[á]to	b[á]ta
p[á]rto	p[á]rta

[26] When the root vowel is unstressed the alternation does not occur due to the unstressed vowel system.

Thus, the target vowel, in the harmony process, suffers two strong restrictions: it cannot be [+high], /i/ or /u/, or [+back, –round], that is,/a/.

There is another peculiarity in the present indicative. In verbs with stressed root vowels /e/, /ɛ/, /o/, /ɔ/, in the forms where the TV is maintained (that is, 2nd and 3rd persons singular and 3rd plural) only low vowels occur. See (27).

(27) Verbs *levar, morar* (TV /a/), *dever, mover* (TV /e/), *ferir, dormir* (TV /i/)

Present Indicative

l[ɛ̃]vas	m[ɔ]ras	d[ɛ]ves	m[ɔ]ves	f[ɛ]res	d[ɔ]rmes
l[ɛ̃]va	m[ɔ]ra	d[ɛ]ve	m[ɔ]ve	f[ɛ]re	d[ɔ]rme
l[ɛ̃]vam	m[ɔ]ram	d[ɛ]vem	m[ɔ]vem	f[ɛ]rem	d[ɔ]rmem

These low vowels are the result of a lowering process that affects root vowels /e/, /ɛ/, /o/ or /ɔ/ in the three paradigms.The fact that in first conjugation the last root vowel is always [+low] is due to the vowel harmony in the 1st person singular, and to the general lowering effect in all other cases.

Verbs with high root vowels /i/ and /u/ do not show this kind of lowering as we see in (28).

(28) Verbs *viver* and *iludir*

Present Indicative

v[í]vo   il[ú]do
v[í]ves (*v[ɛ́]ves)[27]   il[ú]des (*il[ɔ́]des)
v[í]ve (*v[ɛ́]ve)   il[ú]de (*il[ɔ́]de)
v[í]vem (*v[ɛ́]vem)   il[ú]dem (*il[ɔ́]dem)

4.2.2.2.1. *More on vowel harmony*

Vowel harmony in Portuguese has been discussed in traditional grammar and within the SPE model (see, for instance, Harris, 1974; Mateus, 1975; Andrade, 1977 and 1981). In Wetzels (1991) there is a review of the SPE rules and a new proposal in the framework of autosegmental phonology.

The problems we are dealing with are:

(a) the relationship between the TV deletion and the assimilation of the root vowel, and

(b) the lexical specification of the phonetic low vowels in 2nd and 3rd persons singular and 3rd plural in the present indicative.

Let us discuss these two problems.

(i) Portuguese vowel harmony involves a floating segment, in this case, the theme vowel. In fact, when a vowel morpheme is added to the stem in the present tenses, the skeleton unit associated with the TV is deleted; its height features

---

[27] Although, this form exists in certain popular dialects.

become a floating segment and anchor on the preceding root vowel (see above the TV deletion rule represented in (13)). This assimilation has a parallel in vowel nasalization, as the latter is also a projection of a floating segment.

In our view, we are dealing with a two-step process. Accordingly, it is necessary to account for the fact that high vowels do not trigger the assimilation rule.

In Wetzels (1991) Portuguese vowel harmony is presented in support of Clements' (1991) proposal of a specific place node for vowels with different aperture degrees. Wetzels considers that the Portuguese vowel system has three degrees of aperture, and claims that only [open 1] and [open 2] (that is, only mid and mid-low vowels) are allowed in the representation of the root vowel. The fact that vowel harmony rule does not apply to high vowels is directly represented in Wetzels's proposal. His representation of vowel harmony is given in (29), where SL stands for Supralaryngeal.

(29) Vowel Harmony (Wetzels version)

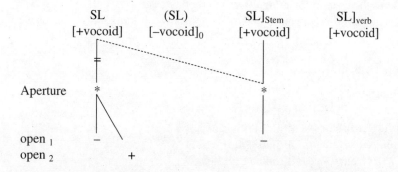

Apart from the fact that we do not use aperture features, Wetzels's harmony rule differs from the one we present below in (30) because he does not consider that the theme vowel /a/ also spreads its height features onto the root vowel. For Wetzel, vowel harmony is a rising rule, and therefore /a/ cannot be a source of the assimilation. We disagree with this interpretation. For us, vowel harmony in the Portuguese verb system is quite regular and it involves all theme vowels. So, in (30) the TV floating height segment that spreads onto the root vowel *has no restriction*: it anchors in the root vowel and its height node is delinked.

To show how vowel harmony works it is necessary to take account of the root vowels that are *not* subject to it (that is, /a/, /i/ and /u/).

First of all, only verbs with [–high] vowels trigger the rule. Concerning the root vowel /a/, we must use the features [back] and [round] to distinguish it from /ɛ/ and /ɔ/, as these three vowels are identified together as [+low] in our system. In fact, TV height features only spread onto the vowels that agree in backness and roundness (/e/, /ɛ/ [–back, –round], or /o/, /ɔ/ [+back, +round]). We represent this agreement with the variable α.

In (30a) we present the result of the theme vowel deletion, already given in (13b), to make the two steps of this phonological process clearer.

(30)

a. TV Deletion

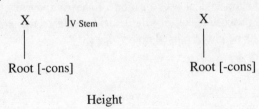

b. Root vowel harmony

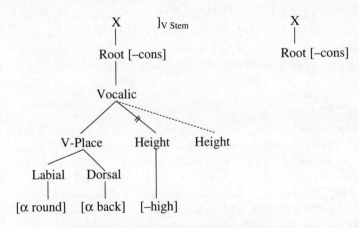

In sum: the vowel harmony is a two-step assimilation process that functions at the lexical level and has some restrictions. In the first step the theme vowel is deleted in a specific morphological context (the adjunction of a vowel morpheme in present tenses) and leaves its height node as a floating segment. In the second step, the floating segment spreads its features onto the root vowel (except if the root vowel is high, /i/ or /u/, or if it is an /a/).

2. We shall now discuss the question of low vowels in the remaining forms (see again (27) and (28)). There are different views on this from theorists of both the standard and the autosegmental position. In Harris (1974) these low vowels result from the application of a lowering rule. Harris considers this root vowel alternation evidence for the Elsewhere Condition: the context for the application of the lowering rule (LR) is more general than that of the vowel harmony (VH), as all root vowels would be lowered and only some of them would be assimilated. In this case, LR will be ordered after VH.

We do not agree with making the LR dependent on the VH and we accept Wetzels' arguments maintaining that LR interacts with the morphological rules and it applies at the lexical level, which is the domain of the verb stem's formation. This proposal allows the LR to be a filling-rule that fills the feature values of the root vowel that is not lexically specified.

With respect to the lexical specification of the root vowels, some authors, including Harris, propose to specify the lexical height of the stressed vowel in accordance with its height in related nouns: see (31).

(31)

Noun	*Verb*
escova esc[o]va 'brush'	esc[ɔ]ova 's/he brushes'
interesse inter[e]sse 'interest'	inter[ɛ]ssa 's/he interests'
conversa conv[ɛ]rsa 'talk'	conv[ɛ]rsa 's/he talks'
demora dem[ɔ]ra 'delay'	dem[ɔ]ra 's/he is late'

There are many verbs for which it is not possible to specify the root vowels in accordance with the above scheme, as they do not have related nouns. We therefore consider that this vowel is specified by the application of vowel harmony and lowering rules.

4.2.2.3. *Allomorphy in verbs*

The irregular verbs *perder* [pɨɾdéɾ] 'to lose', *poder* [pudéɾ] 'to be able to', *trazer* [tɾɐzéɾ] 'to bring', *fazer* [fɐzéɾ] 'to make', *valer* [vɐléɾ] 'to be worth', *dizer* [dizéɾ] 'to say', *medir* [mɨdíɾ] 'to measure', *pedir* [pɨdíɾ] 'to ask' and *ouvir* [ovíɾ] 'to listen' have allomorphy in the last root consonant in present indicative and present subjunctive. Once more, the verb forms that show a different consonant from the one of the infinitive are those where the TV has been deleted (see above 4.2.2.2). We can only account for this alternation on historical grounds. All of these verbs belong to the second and third paradigms.

This allomorphy is marked with a diacritic in the lexicon or, following Halle and Vergnaud's proposal, 'it is determined by rules of the allomorphy component' which 'is ordered before the first word-internal rule stratum' (1987: 77). Some data are given in (32).

(32)

Present Indicative	Present Subjunctive
a. *perder*	
per[k]o	per[k]a
per[d]es	per[k]as
per[d]e	per[k]a
per[d]em	per[k]am

b. *valer*

va[ʎ]o   va[ʎ]a
va[l]es   va[ʎ]as
va[l]e   va[ʎ]a
va[l]em   va[ʎ]am

c. *pedir*

pe[s]o   pe[s]a
pe[d]es   pe[s]as
pe[d]e   pe[s]a
pe[d]em   pe[s]am

Some irregular verbs also have allomorphy in the present vs. past tenses as, for instance, *ter* (*tenho* [téɲu] 'I have' / *tive* [tívɨ] 'I had') or *querer* (*quero* [kɛɾu] 'I want' / *quis* [kíʃ] 'I wanted').[28] Allomorphy in the last consonant of the past participle root is also marked in the lexicon.

---

[28] This allomorphy can be indicated in the lexicon by the diacritic [+past]. For the analysis of this question in the SPE model see Mateus (1975), 3.5.2.

5

PORTUGUESE MORPHOLOGY: DERIVATION

5.1. SOME BASIC ASSUMPTIONS[1]

5.1.1. What is the base-form of words?

In the previous section we presented the internal structure of verbs and non-verbs in Portuguese in respect to the inflectional suffixes and class markers. Besides these suffixes, words can also include derivational affixes.

In order to decompose the base-form of the word into its internal constituents, it is necessary to state which constituents can be considered to be the base of word-formation. As we will see in 5.1.2, there are several arguments showing that, in Portuguese, words (inflected forms), roots and stems can be chosen by derivational suffixes to provide the base of word-formation. In this sense, Villalva (1994a: 120) proposes the following *Condition upon the base*: 'All word-formation processes operate upon bases that are lexical variables.'[2] Word-formation processes seem to be language-specific and even in a particular language they may vary.

5.1.2. Roots, stems and words

5.1.2.1. Infinitive verb stems

Examples of a suffix that chooses infinitive verb stems, giving rise to nominal and adjectival forms, are included in (1), where [If Vb St] means Infinitive Verb Stem, [R], [N], [Adj] and [W] stand respectively for Root, Noun, Adjective and Word.[3]

---

[1] We thank A. Villalva for the discussion of some of the topics treated in this section.

[2] With regard to lexical variables, see Villalva (1994a: 120): 'Roots, stems and words can be characterized as lexical variables, while affixes can be characterized as lexical constants.'

Aronoff's first proposal for word-formation states, 'all regular word-formation processes are word-based' (1976: 21). Later on (1994) he gave an interpretation of this statement saying that the bases of word-formation are understood to be lexemes, not concrete words. See Villalva (1994) for the discussion of this problem. One of the main arguments sustaining the proposal of considering roots, stems and words as bases of word-formation is the fact that it avoids the need for truncation rules deleting the theme vowels or the inflectional suffixes in the derived words.

[3] The internal constituents of the words are separated by brackets avoiding the use of different boundaries as in SPE. All the morphemes inside the brackets are indicated in their orthographic forms to make it easier to present the problems under discussion in this section. For a complete list of Portuguese traditional suffixes and prefixes see, for instance, Cunha and Cintra (1984).

(1) *-dor*

  falador [feledóɾ] [[[[fal+a]$_{If Vb St}$ dor]$_{Adj R}$]$_{St}$]w 'speaker'
  aquecedor [ɐkɛsɨdóɾ] [[[aquec+e]$_{If Vb St}$ dor]$_{N R}$]$_{St}$]w 'heater'
  destruidor [diʃtruidóɾ] [[[[destru+i]$_{If Vb St}$ dor]$_{Adj R}$]$_{St}$]w 'destructive'

The identification of verb stems seems to present no problems in derived words such as those in (1) which have the TV in their surface forms. The theme vowels /a/, /e/ and /i/ occur respectively in *falador* (from the verb [[fal+a] r]), *aquecedor* (from the verb [[aquec+e]r]) and *destruidor* (from [[destru+i]r]).

The question raised by these words concerns the suffix. In fact, we can raise the hypothesis that the consonant [d] belongs to the base instead of being part of the suffix. In this case, the suffix would be *-or* and the base-word would not be the infinitive stem. However, we would be dealing with a past participle root, as [d] is the consonant of the past participle morpheme (see 4.2.2.1).

Due to the fact that this consonant alternates with [t] in other derived words (like *formatura* [forma+tura] 'formation', *dormitório* [dormi+tório] 'dormitory', *recreativo* [recrea+tivo] 'recreative', *acomodatício* [acomoda+tício] 'condescending'), if we state that in all cases the base-word is the past participle, we will have to establish an underlying /t/ for this tense. This should trigger off a voicing rule in certain derived words.

This hypothesis therefore entails:

(a) establishing an underlying /t/ (instead of a /d/) in the morpheme of the past participle, the evidence of which lies only in its occurrence in derived words with certain suffixes;
(b) the existence of a voicing rule that applies to the past participle forms of all regular verbs in Portuguese (e.g. *falador* /fala+t/ → [[[[fal a]d]or]]);
(c) the need to block the voicing rule in the formation of derived words with certain suffixes (e.g. *formatura* [[[[[form a]t]ur]a]]);
(d) the statement that the base-form of these derived words is the past participle root, whose evidence depends on the established consonant and the voicing rule (thus setting up a vicious circle).

Furthermore, there is lack of evidence that we are dealing with the past participle, for the theme vowel of the /e/ verbs does not occur as an [i], as it should do if we had a past participle of this paradigm (cf. in 4.2.2.1, *batido* from *bater*). This fact could be explained by the application of the unstressed vowel rule that would reduce the unstressed [i] to [ɨ] (e.g. *aquecedor*, from *aquecer*, would be [[aquec+i]dor] → [ɐkɛsɨdóɾ]). However, this reduction does not occur, for instance, in *aquecimento* [[aquec+i]mento] → [ɐkɛsimétu] (see (3), where the base-form is, in fact, the past participle stem).

Traditional Portuguese grammar lists these suffixes with the initial consonant in brackets (e.g. *-(d)or*) meaning that this consonant may or may not occur. In fact these suffixes are attached to past participles whose morpheme used to be *-tu* in Latin (e.g. *amatu*). The change /t/ → [d] is a well-known occurrence in the diachrony of western Romance languages, and thus Portuguese is no exception.

Nevertheless, words such as *formatura*, *dormitório*, *recreativo*, *acomodatício* are lexicalized in modern Portuguese because derivation resorting to these suffixes is no longer productive.

As we are not dealing with the history of the language, we have to base our proposal on the data we are discussing and back it up with theoretical arguments. Thus, on behalf of the synchronic data, choosing between the two proposals— underlying /t/ and change into [d] vs. storing the suffix beginning with a conson- ant and storing full derived words that no longer belong to productive word- formation—we prefer the latter because it does not require the application of a phonological voicing rule unwarranted by phonological or morphological con- texts.

This choice implies that the suffix *-dor* presented in (1) is stored in the lexicon, and the word-formation processes only establish domains for the application of productive phonological rules. In theoretical terms, this means that we prefer a minimal set of rules (a reduced grammar) and a heavier lexicon.[4] We will see fur- ther on that this proposal has consequences for the establishment of the word-for- mation levels.

It is worth noting that the infinitive stem is also chosen by a suffix beginning with the nasal auto-segment (represented here by the orthographic -n-), as we can see in the following examples.

(2) *-nte*

(Vb /a/)
amante [ɐmɐ̃ti] [[[am+a]$_{\text{If Vb St}}$ nt]$_{\text{N R}}$ e]$_{\text{St}}$]$_W$ 'lover'
negociante [nɨgusiɐ̃ti] [[[negoci+a]$_{\text{If Vb St}}$ nt]$_{\text{N R}}$ e]$_{\text{St}}$]$_W$ 'business-person'
falante [fɐlɐ̃ti] [[[fal+a]$_{\text{If Vb St}}$ nt]$_{\text{N R}}$ e]$_{\text{St}}$]$_W$ 'speaker'

(Vb /e/)
pendente [pẽdẽti] [[[pend+e]$_{\text{If Vb St}}$ nt]$_{\text{N R}}$ e]$_{\text{St}}$]$_W$ 'wall-hanging'
requerente [ʀikɨɾẽti] [[[requer+e]$_{\text{If Vb St}}$ nt]$_{\text{N R}}$ e]$_{\text{St}}$]$_W$ 'petitioner'
absorvente [ɐbsɔɾvẽti] [[[absorv+e]$_{\text{If Vb St}}$ nt]$_{\text{N R}}$ e]$_{\text{St}}$]$_W$ 'absorbent'

(Vb /i/)
pedinte [pɨdĩti] [[[ped+i]$_{\text{If Vb St}}$ nt]$_{\text{N R}}$ e]$_{\text{St}}$]$_W$ 'beggar'
ouvinte [ovĩti] [[[ouv+i]$_{\text{If Vb St}}$ nt]$_{\text{N R}}$ e]$_{\text{St}}$]$_W$ 'listener'

5.1.2.2. *Past Participle stem*

A second verbal base-form is the past participle stem in derived words where the TV /e/ occurs as [i], as mentioned above with regard to this tense. As Villalva (1994a) points out, certain suffixes choose the past participle's stem and not the infinitive stem. Evidence comes from the second paradigm, where the theme vowel /e/ is different in the two stems: [e] in the infinitive and [i] in the participle (see 4.2.2.1, and words with the *-mento* suffix, like *adormecimento* 'the state of

---

[4] See Kenstowicz (1994), 5.8.1 for discussion of a similar issue.

having fallen asleep', from *adormecer* 'to fall asleep', where the base-form is the past participle).

For the same reason, words with the *-ção* [sẽw̃] suffix (/sioN/) also have the past participle stem as the base-form (see *perdição* 'perdition' from *perder* 'to lose' and *demolição* 'demolition' from *demolir* 'to demolish'). As was stated above about the [t] / [d] initial consonants of the suffixes, the [s] of the *-ção* suffix is explained in traditional grammar as being the result of a spirantization of the past participle's consonant /t/ when placed before the /ioN/ suffix (cf. *demolitione → demolição, contradictione → contradição*). According to the arguments we presented above, we also consider this suffix to be stored in the lexicon as a lexical entry and, thus, there is no spirantization rule applied in this context.[5] Examples of derived words with different suffixes and with a past participle stem are included in (3), where [Pt Vb St] means [Past Participle Verb Stem].

(3) *-mento*

(Vb /a/)

saneamento [sɐnjɐmétu] [[[sane+a]$_{Pt Vb St}$ ment]$_{N R}$ o]$_{St}$]$_W$ 'sanitation'
andamento [ẽdɐmétu] [[[and+a]$_{Pt Vb St}$ ment]$_{N R}$ o]$_{St}$]$_W$ 'movement'
mandamento [mẽdɐmétu] [[[mand+a]$_{Pt Vb St}$ ment]$_{N R}$ o]$_{St}$]$_W$ 'commandment'

(Vb /e/)

movimento [muvimétu] [[[mov+i]$_{Pt Vb St}$ ment]$_{N R}$ o] $_{St}$]$_W$ 'movement'
entendimento [ẽtẽdimétu] [[[entend+i]$_{Pt Vb St}$ ment]$_{N R}$ o] $_{St}$]$_W$ 'understanding'
crescimento [kɾɨʃsimétu] [[[cresc+i]$_{Pt Vb St}$ ment]$_{N R}$ o] $_{St}$]$_W$ 'growth'

(Vb /i/)

entupimento [ẽtupimétu] [[[entup+i]$_{Pt Vb St}$ ment]$_{N R}$ o] $_{St}$]$_W$ 'clogging'
descobrimento [diʃkubrimétu] [[[descobr+i]$_{Pt Vb St}$ ment]$_{N R}$ o] $_{St}$]$_W$ 'discovery'
sentimento [sẽtimétu] [[[sent+i]$_{Pt Vb St}$ ment]$_{N R}$ o] $_{St}$]$_W$ 'feeling'

-vel

(Vb /a/)

amável [ɐmávɛɫ] [[[am+a]$_{Pt Vb St}$ vel]$_{Adj R}$]$_{St}$]$_W$ 'kind'
aceitável [ɐsɐjtávɛɫ] [[[aceit+a]$_{Pt Vb St}$ vel]$_{Adj R}$]$_{St}$]$_W$ 'acceptable'
respeitável [ʀiʃpɐjtávɛɫ] [[[respeit+a]$_{Pt Vb St}$ vel]$_{Adj R}$]$_{St}$]$_W$ 'respectable'

(Vb /e/)

temível [tɨmívɛɫ] [[[[tem+i]$_{Pt Vb St}$ vel]$_{Adj R}$]$_{St}$]$_W$ 'fearful'
comível [kumívɛɫ] [[[[com+i]$_{Pt Vb St}$ vel]$_{Adj R}$]$_{St}$]$_W$ 'edible'
invencível [ĩvẽsívɛɫ] [[[[invenc+i]$_{Pt Vb St}$ vel]$_{Adj R}$]$_{St}$]$_W$ 'invincible'

(Vb /i/)

punível [punívɛɫ] [[[[pun+i]$_{Pt Vb St}$ vel]$_{Adj R}$]$_{St}$]$_W$ 'punishable'
incorrigível [ĩkuʀiʒívɛɫ] [[[[incorrig+i]$_{Pt Vb St}$ vel]$_{Adj R}$]$_{St}$]$_W$ 'incorrigible'
transferível [tɾẽʃfɨrívɛɫ] [[[[tansfer+i]$_{Pt Vb St}$ vel]$_{Adj R}$]$_{St}$]$_W$ 'transferable'

[5] Nevertheless, there is a spirantization rule in the grammar of Portuguese. Words like *presidência, abundância* and similar words (see (7))—where some of them are derived from the N/Adj R emerging from the process in (2)—trigger off that rule when the *-ia* suffix is added. See 5.2.1 on this phonological rule, which is still productive in Portuguese.

-ção

(Vb /a/)

preparação [pɾɨpɐɾɐsẽ́w̃] [[[[prepar+a]$_{Pt\ Vb\ St}$ ção]$_{N\ R}$]$_{St}$]$_W$ 'preparation'
simbolização [sĩbulizɐsẽ́w̃] [[[[simboliz+a]$_{Pt\ Vb\ St}$ ção]$_{N\ R}$]$_{St}$]$_W$ 'symbolizing'
humanização [umɐnizɐsẽ́w̃] [[[[humaniz+a]$_{Pt\ Vb\ St}$ ção]$_{N\ R}$]$_{St}$]$_W$ 'humaniz-
  ation'

(Vb /e/)

rendição [R̃ẽdisẽ́w̃] [[[[rend+i]$_{Pt\ Vb\ St}$ ção]$_{N\ R}$]$_{St}$]$_W$ 'surrender'
aparição [ɐpɐɾisẽ́w̃] [[[[apar+i]$_{Pt\ Vb\ St}$ ção]$_{N\ R}$]$_{St}$]$_W$ 'appearance'
perdição [pɨɾdisẽ́w̃] [[[[perd+i]$_{Pt\ Vb\ St}$ ção]$_{N\ R}$]$_{St}$]$_W$ 'perdition'

(Vb /i/)

demolição [dɨmulisẽ́w̃] [[[[demol+i]$_{Pt\ Vb\ St}$ ção]$_{N\ R}$]$_{St}$]$_W$ 'demolition'
competição [kõpɨtisẽ́w̃] [[[[compet+i]$_{Pt\ Vb\ St}$ ção]$_{N\ R}$]$_{St}$]$_W$ 'competition'
definição [dɨfɨnisẽ́w̃] [[[[defin i]$_{Pt\ Vb\ St}$ ção]$_{N\ R}$]$_{St}$]$_W$ 'definition'

The *-vel* and *-ção* (/sioN/) suffixes have allomorphic forms (respectively, *-bil-*
and *-cion-*) when they do not occur at the end of the word (e.g. *amabilidade*
[[[[am+a]bil]idad]e] 'amiability' and *nacional* [[[nac]ion]al] 'national').

5.1.2.3. *Verb root*

Finally, there are suffixes that may choose the verb root because the theme vowel
does not occur in the phonetic form of the derived words where these suffixes
appear.[6]

(4) *-or*
  cantor [kɐ̃tóɾ] [[[[cant]$_{Vb\ R}$ or]$_{N\ R}$]$_{St}$]$_W$ 'singer'
  desertor [dɨzɨɾtóɾ] [[[[desert]$_{Vb\ R}$ or]$_{N\ R}$]$_{St}$]$_W$ 'deserter'
  injector [ĩʒetóɾ] [[[[inject]$_{Vb\ R}$ or]$_{N\ R}$]$_{St}$]$_W$ 'injector'

  -ão
  intrujão [ĩtɾuʒẽ́w̃] [[[[intruj]$_{Vb\ R}$ ão]$_{N/Adj\ R}$]$_{St}$]$_W$ 'imposter'
  saltão [sáɬtẽ́w̃] [[[[salt]$_{Vb\ R}$ ão]$_{N/Adj\ R}$]$_{St}$]$_W$ 'jumper'
  refilão [R̃ɨfilẽ́w̃] [[[[refil]$_{Vb\ R}$ ão]$_{N/Adj\ R}$]$_{St}$]$_W$ 'unruly'

  -ista
  determinista [dɨtɨɾminíʃtɐ] [[[[determin]$_{Vb\ R}$ ist]$_{N\ R}$ a]$_{St}$]$_W$ 'determinist'

These suffixes are also stored in the lexicon. They allow us to parse the word in
order to recognize a specific string—in this case a verb root and a derivational
suffix that establishes a nominal root.

Strong participles like *perverso* 'perverse' (from *perverter* 'to pervert') or *con-
verso* 'converted' (from *converter* 'to convert'), whose derived words are respectively *perversor* 'perverter', *perversão* 'perversion' and *conversor* 'converter',
conversão 'conversion', are also explained by traditional grammar through the
spirantization of the Latin /t/ of the root. According to the perspective we have

---

[6] The same suffixes can be added to noun/adjective roots.

already presented, the alternation in the last consonant of the root is marked in the lexicon (e.g. *pervert-* vs. *pervers-*). Words like *perversor* or *conversor* are independently stored in spite of the speaker being able to recognize the relationship between them and the regular forms of the corresponding verbs (*perverter* and *converter*). In fact, words like *cantor* and *intrujão*, where the suffixes choose the regular root of the verbs (see (4)), give the parser the possibility of separating the root from the suffix and setting up a mechanism to analyse alternating roots akin to those in the strong participles (see *pervert-* vs. *pervers-*).

To sum up: there are three verb word-formation bases for derived nouns and adjectives in Portuguese—verb roots and two types of verb stems (infinitive and past participle).

5.1.2.4. *Noun and adjective stems*

Identifying noun and adjective stems is more problematic. In fact, the phonetic form of their stems coincides with the singular form of the words when they end in class markers (the unstressed vowels [ɐ], [u], [ɨ], e.g. $[[[cas]_R a]_{St}]_W$), or when the stem coincides with the root where the word has no explicit class marker (e.g. $[[animal]_{R/St}]_W$; $[[café]_{R/St}]_W$). Given this occurrence, we can conclude that nouns and adjectives provide the evidence that suffixes are attached to the root. In fact, derived nouns and adjectives like the ones in (5), where the class marker is not present in the base, give us the chance to say that these suffixes are adjoined to roots.

(5) *livreiro* [livrɐ́jɾu] 'bookseller' $[[[livr]_{Base} eir]o]$ (from $[[livr]o]$)
   certeza [sɨɾtézɐ] 'certainty' $[[[cert]_{Base} ez]a]$ (from $[[cert]o/a]$)
   apologista [ɐpuluʒíʃtɐ] 'apologist' $[[[apolog]_{Base} ist]a]$ (from $[[apologi]a]$)
   semanal [sɨmɐnáɫ] 'weekly' $[[seman]_{Base} al]$ (from $[[seman]a]$)

On the other hand, if we raise the hypothesis that stems are the base, and the class marker is deleted by a truncation rule, in cases of words formed from adjectives, like *certeza*, it is not possible to learn whether the class marker is /o/ or /a/. In other words, we are not able to choose *certo* (masculine) or *certa* (feminine) as the base for the derived word.

Thus we propose that suffixes in (6) and (7) be attached to nominal roots to derive nouns and adjectives. Those included in (6) do not have any effect in demanding phonological rules. On the contrary, (7) presents a small set of suffixes where the attachment to the root calls for the application of specific phonological rules.

(6) *-al*
   natural $[[[[natur]_{N R} al]_{Adj R}]_{St}]_W$ 'natural'
   coqueiral $[[[[coqueir]_{N R} al]_{N R}]_{St}]_W$ 'cocoa-tree grove'
   semestral $[[[[semestr]_{N R} al]_{Adj R}]_{St}]_W$ 'semestrial'
   neutral $[[[[neutr]_{Adj R} al]_{Adj R}]_{St}]_W$ 'neutral'

-eza

tristeza [[[[trist]$_{Adj R}$ ez]$_{N R}$ a]$_{St}$]$_W$ 'sadness'

grandeza [[[[grand]$_{Adj R}$ ez]$_{N R}$ a]$_{St}$]$_W$ 'greatness'

beleza [[[[bel]$_{Adj R}$ ez]$_{N R}$ a]$_{St}$]$_W$ 'beauty'

-eir-

engenheiro [[[engenh]$_{N R}$ eir]$_{N R}$ o]$_{St}$]$_W$ 'engineer'

pedreiro [[[pedr]$_{N R}$ eir]$_{N R}$ o]$_{St}$]$_W$ 'mason'

parteira [[[part]$_{N R}$ eir]$_{N R}$ a]$_{St}$]$_W$ 'midwife'

interesseiro [[[[interess]$_{N R}$ eir]$_{Adj R}$ o]$_{St}$]$_W$ 'calculating'

-os-

espinhoso [[[[espinh]$_{N R}$ os]$_{Adj R}$ o]$_{St}$]$_W$ 'thorny'

volumoso [[[[volum]$_{N R}$ os]$_{Adj R}$ o]$_{St}$]$_W$ 'voluminous'

glorioso [[[[glori]$_{N R}$ os]$_{Adj R}$ o]$_{St}$]$_W$ 'glorious'

(7) *-ia*

presidência [prɨzidḗsiɐ] [[[[president]$_{N R}$ ia]$_{N R}$]$_{St}$]$_W$ 'presidency'

residência [ʀɨzidḗsiɐ] [[[[resident]$_{Adj R}$ ia]$_{N R}$]$_{St}$]$_W$ 'residence'

constância [kõʃtḗsiɐ] [[[[constant]$_{Adj R}$ ia]$_{N R}$]$_{St}$]$_W$ 'constancy'

-ia

democracia [dɨmukɾɐsíɐ] [[[[democrat]$_{Adj R}$ ia]$_{N R}$]$_{St}$]$_W$ 'democracy'

diplomacia [diplumɐsíɐ] [[[[diplomat]$_{Adj R}$ ia]$_{N R}$]$_{St}$]$_W$ 'diplomacy'

burocracia [buɾukɾɐsíɐ] [[[[burocrat]$_{Adj R}$ ia]$_{N R}$]$_{St}$]$_W$ 'bureaucracy'

psicologia [psikuluʒíɐ] [[[[psicolog]$_{Adj R}$ ia]$_{N R}$]$_{St}$]$_W$ 'psychology'

fonologia [funuluʒíɐ] [[[[fonolog]$_{Adj R}$ ia]$_{N R}$]$_{St}$]$_W$ 'phonology'

musicologia [muzikuluʒíɐ] [[[[musicolog]$_{Adj R}$ ia]$_{N R}$]$_{St}$]$_W$ 'musicology'

-ismo

catolicismo [kɐtulisíʃmu] [[[[catolic]$_{Adj R}$ ism]$_{N R}$ o]$_{St}$]$_W$ 'Catholicism'

logicismo [lɔʒisíʃmu] [[[[logic]$_{Adj R}$ ism]$_{N R}$ o]$_{St}$]$_W$ 'logicism'

laicismo [laisíʃmu] [[[[laic]$_{Adj R}$ ism]$_{N R}$ o]$_{St}$]$_W$ 'laicism'

-ista

electricista [ilɛtɾisíʃtɐ] [[[[electric]$_{Adj R}$ ist]$_{Adj R}$ a]$_{St}$]$_W$ 'electrician'

logicista [lɔʒisíʃtɐ] [[[[logic]$_{Adj R}$ ist]$_{N R}$ a]$_{St}$]$_W$ 'logician'

laicista [laisíʃtɐ] [[[[laic]$_{Adj R}$ ist]$_{N R}$ a]$_{St}$]$_W$ 'laic'

psicologista [psikuluʒíʃtɐ] [[[[psicolog]$_{Adj R}$ ist]$_{Adj R}$ a]$_{St}$]$_W$ 'psychologist'

biologista [biuluʒíʃtɐ] [[[[biolog]$_{Adj R}$ ist]$_{N R}$ a]$_{St}$]$_W$ 'biologist'

etimologista [etimuluʒíʃtɐ] [[[[etimolog]$_{Adj R}$ ist]$_{N R}$ a]$_{St}$]$_W$ 'etymologist'

-idade

electricidade [ilɛtrisidádɨ] [[[[electric]$_{Adj R}$ idad]$_{N R}$ e]$_{St}$]$_W$ 'electricity'

lubricidade [lubrisidádɨ] [[[[electric]$_{Adj R}$ idad]$_{N R}$ e]$_{St}$]$_W$ 'lubricity'

opacidade [opɐsidádɨ] [[[[opac]$_{Adj R}$ idad]$_{N R}$ e]$_{St}$]$_W$ 'opacity'

In the words included in (7), the last consonants of the root present the following alternation, discussed below in 5.2.1:

- /t/ and /k/ trigger off a spirantization rule when the suffixes are added (e.g. *presidente* [prɨzidḗt-ɨ] 'president' / *presidência* [prɨzidḗs-iɐ] 'presidency'; *eléctrico* [ilḗtrik-u] 'electric' / *electricista* [ilɛtris-íʃtɐ] 'electrician' / *electricidade* [ilɛtris-idádɨ] 'electricity')
- /g/ gives rise to a velar softening rule (e.g. *psicólogo* [psikɔlug-u] 'psychologist'/ *psicolog-ia* [psikuluʒ-íɐ] 'psychology').

Suffixes in (8) are attached to noun and adjective roots to derive verb roots.

(8) *-iz-*
    organizar [orgɐnizár] [[[[organ]$_{N\ R}$ iz]$_{Vb\ R}$ a]$_{St}$ r]$_W$ 'to organize'
    europeizar [ewropɐizár] [[[[europe]$_{Adj\ R}$ iz]$_{Vb\ R}$ a]$_{St}$ r]$_W$ 'to Europeanize'
    fiscalizar [fiʃkɐlizár] [[[[fiscal]$_{N\ R}$ iz]$_{Vb\ R}$ a]$_{St}$ r]$_W$ 'to superintend'

    -ific-
    dignificar [dignifikár] [[[[dign]$_{Adj\ R}$ ific]$_{Vb\ R}$ a]$_{St}$ r]$_W$ 'to dignify'
    bonificar [bunifikár] [[[[bon]$_{Adj\ R}$ ific]$_{Vb\ R}$ a]$_{St}$ r]$_W$ 'to improve'
    gratificar [grɐtifikár] [[[[grat]$_{Adj\ R}$ ific]$_{Vb\ R}$ a]$_{St}$ r]$_W$ 'to gratify'

5.1.2.5. *Words as base-forms*

In the above discussion about derivation in Portuguese, it is obvious that suffixes have inherent syntactic categories; they also choose different categories, i.e.:

- they derive nouns and adjectives from verb stems and verb roots (like *-dor*, *-mento* or *-ão*),
- they derive nouns and adjectives from nouns and adjectives roots (as *-al* or *-idade*) and
- they derive verbs from nouns and adjectives roots (as *-iz-* or *-ific-*)

Evidence from suffixes added to *words* can only be taken from a lexical representation where the suffix is adjoined to an inflected base-form. This is what happens in derived words with *z*-evaluative suffixes (e.g. *-zinho* [zíɲu] in *cãozinho* 'little dog' or *-zito* [zítu] in *papelzito* 'small piece of paper') and the adverbial suffix *–mente*.[7] In fact, words like *cãezinhos* [kɐ̃jzíɲuʃ] 'small dogs' or *belamente* [bɛlɐmḗtɨ] 'beautifully' give evidence of the inflected form of the base: in the first example the noun has the plural form, *cães* [kɐ̃jʃ] (from *cão*, singular), with complete assimilation of the plural suffix /s/ to the following consonant of the suffix; in the second example, the adverbial suffix is added to the singular feminine form of the adjective, *bela*, and never to the masculine (**belomente*).[8] Thus, in these cases there is no doubt that the suffix chooses the word as the base-form.

The other kind of affixes, prefixes, is also attached to words. They never change

---

[7] There is a word *mente* 'mind'. However, in the formation of adverbs, *-mente* functions as a suffix like the z-evaluative suffixes such as *-zinho* or *-zito*.

[8] Obviously, we cannot deduce the inflected form if the adjective is 'uniform', like *feliz* 'happy', whose corresponding adverb is *felizmente* 'happily'.

the syntactic category of the base-form; they choose verbs (as in *refazer* 'redo' [re[fazer]$_V$]$_V$) and non-verbs (as in *desprazer* [des[prazer]$_N$]$_N$ 'displeasure' or *indesejável* [in [desejável]$_{Adj}$]$_{Adj}$ 'undesirable'). In 5.3.2. we shall discuss the problems concerned with the level of their adjunction.[9]

5.2. THE STRUCTURE OF LEXICAL REPRESENTATIONS

5.2.1. Lexical phonology

In this book, we have taken for granted the basic proposals arising in lexical phonology, namely the existence of two different levels, the lexical and post-lexical levels in the derivation of the word-form. Also, we accept a structured interaction of morphological and phonological rules (see Kiparsky, 1982a and b; Mohanan, 1986; for an overview see Anderson (1988), Goldsmith (1990), Durand (1990) and Spencer (1991)).

We recall that generative grammar during the 1960s applied its theoretical principles to explain how the phonological component worked; it succeeded remarkably well in Chomsky and Halle (1968). The model considers that the constitution of the word is mostly effected through the syntactic component's output. The presence of allomorphs is interpreted as the result of applying phonological rules upon the underlying representations, thus reducing the allomorphy to the operation of phonological rules (for Portuguese, see Mateus, 1975 and Andrade, 1977).

Later on, and particularly on the grounds of 'lexicalist hypothesis' (Chomsky 1970), morphology acquired an independent status and morphological rules have been viewed as obeying different conditions from those governing sound structure. Aronoff's proposal of word-formation processes based on the word is the most highly developed study from this theoretical viewpoint. The most significant outcome is that morphology is no longer integrated in phonology as it used to be in the SPE 'syntax first' theory. The development of lexical phonology came after these studies.[10]

Any explanation of the structure of lexical representations needs to be based on a study of how morphological and phonological rules interact. Let us look at some examples of derived nouns.

(i) We stated above that derivational suffixes precede inflectional ones in word-formation. However, words formed with *z*-evaluative suffixes (as *-zinho* or *-zito*) attached to nouns ending in stressed nasal diphthongs with an alternation between singular and plural forms (e.g. *cão / cães*, see 4.2.1.3) show the allomorph of the plural base-form (say, *-ãe*) preceding the derivational suffix (*cãezinhos* and *cãezitos*).

Furthermore, the unstressed vowel of the derived word corresponding to the

---

[9] In Portuguese there are no *infixes* either with a morphemic or a morphological function.

[10] Lexical phonology had also been called lexical morphology, and lexical phonology and morphology. We have adopted lexical phonology, which is the most common designation, owing to the fact that the main interest of our analysis focuses on the phonological phenomena.

stressed one in the base-form is not reduced (e.g. *papel* [pɐpέɫ] / *papelzito* [pɐpɛɫzítu] and not *[pɐpiɫzítu]). It is worth noting that the formation of derived words with another evaluative suffix, *-inho* (and *-ito*, *-ico* and similar ones) is subject to the EP unstressed vowel rules (see *papel* [pɐpέɫ] / *papelinho* [pɐpiɫíɲu]), while this does not happen with the *z*-evaluative suffixes.

(ii) In adverbs derived with the *-mente* suffix, as we have seen above, the adjective (that is, the base-form of the word) takes the feminine form. Once more, the base-form of these derived words is not subject to the EP unstressed vowel rules (cf. *bela* [bέlɐ] 'beautiful' (fem.) / *belamente* [bɛlɐmɐ́ti], not *[biɫɐmɐ́ti] 'beautifully', vs. *beleza* [biɫézɐ] 'beauty').[11]

We assume that the regular phonological processes apply on the complete structure of lexical representations. In the derived words with *z*-evaluative and *-mente* suffixes it is necessary to block these processes or to allow the allomorphy of nasal endings in the plural. One way of explaining this exceptional behaviour is by setting up a special kind of derived boundary, represented by [=], that interacts with a stress cyclic application to block the EP unstressed rules (as it is done in SPE model, see Mateus (1975)). As this is the only case where this boundary is necessary, the solution appears to be *ad hoc* and not demanded by the entire model.

If, instead, we integrate this derivation in the lexical phonology model,[12] we may now state that the word-formation process giving rise to those kinds of derived words is located at a different level from that accommodating other suffixes to be applied, the former affixes having the status of phonological words.[13] Thus, in Portuguese, word-formation with derivational and inflectional suffixes (except for *z*-evaluatives and adverbial *–mente*) belongs to the lexical level and they are subject to all regular phonological processes. Word-formation with the adjunction of the mentioned specific suffixes takes place in the end of the lexical component and they are subject to the post-lexical phonological rules after the word formation.

In demonstrating the suitability of the lexical phonology model, the reader may recall the well-known example of the English trisyllabic laxing rule (TSL) and its relationship with the flapping rule: the first rule needs morphological (and lexical) information while the second rule only needs phonological information. This

---

[11] In view of the unstressed vowel not being subject to the unstressed vowel system, in traditional Portuguese grammar these kinds of words are the only ones that are said to have a secondary stress. This 'secondary stress' was formerly indicated, in the orthography, with the diacritic (`) (e.g. *cafèzinho* 'little (cup of) coffee', or *sòmente* 'only').

[12] Work on lexical phonology has been proceeding ever since the beginning of the 1980s, even though previous studies—such as those of Siegel (1974), Allen (1978) and Lieber (1980)—had already put forward some proposals which have now been integrated into the model. But it is in Kiparsky (1982) and in Mohanan (1982) that the most significant aspects of lexical phonology were first developed.

[13] Rubach (1995: 1.2.) also says that 'some affixes may have the status of phonological words and consequently they may form separate domains for the application of cyclic rules.' Even if this statement is included in the discussion of cyclic-rule application, it is worth noting that it is basic to the claim about 'the non-isomorphic nature of concepts such as the morphological word versus the phonological word' (ibid.). According to Selkirk (1986) such cases are the marked ones.

means they have different grammatical status. In the SPE model they are treated in the same way, that is, in phonological terms and the suffixes which do not spark off the TSL rule are singled out as exceptions to it (for the discussion of this problem see Kiparsky, 1982b and Kenstowicz, 1994: 195–8). Furthermore, TSL relates segments that belong to the underlying English structure while the flapping rule gives rise to the appearance of an allophone, [ɾ], which is not phonologically distinctive.

In Portuguese there are some similar cases, already mentioned above and given below in (9).

(9) *elegant-e* [iliɡə́t-ɨ] 'elegant'
    -ia   *elegânc-ia* [iliɡə́s-iɐ] 'elegance'

    president-e [pɾizidə́t-ɨ] 'president'
    -ia   *presidênc- ia* [pɾizidə́s-iɐ] 'presidency'

    abundant-e [ɐbũdə́t-ɨ] 'abundant'
    -ia   *abundânc-ia* [ɐbũdə́s-iɐ] 'abundance'

    resident-e [ʀizidə́t-ɨ] 'resident'
    -ia   *residênc-ia* [ʀizidə́s-iɐ] 'residency'

These pairs show that, as in English, there are a number of pairs demonstrating the application of a spirantization rule (SP) on the last root consonant, /t/. This rule changes /t/ into [s] when the /ia/ suffix is added—a suffix beginning with an /i/ followed by another vowel.

If the phonological context were responsible for this change, there would be no exceptions, or the exceptions could be explained in phonological terms. In fact, when the /t/ root consonant is preceded by an /s/ (phonetically realized as an [ʃ]), there is no application of the rule (e.g. *modest-o* [mudéʃt-u] 'modest' / *modést-ia* [mudéʃt-iɐ] 'modesty'). The application of the /t/ → [s] rule in this derivation can be prevented by sole reference to the phonological context. Notice that so far the suffix attached to the stem is not stressed.

Nevertheless, there are cases where the final /t/ is not preceded by an /s/ and, yet, the rule does not apply: see (10).

(10) *idiot-a* [idiɔ́t-ɐ] 'idiot'
    -ia   *idiot-ia* [idiut-íɐ] 'idiocy'

    valent-e [vɐlə́t-ɨ] 'brave'
    -ia   *valent-ia* [vɐlə́t-íɐ] 'bravery'

    servent-e [siɾvə́t-ɨ] 'servant'
    -ia   *servent-ia* [siɾvə́t-íɐ] 'service'

All these words have stressed suffixes, unlike the examples in (8), and we may presume that this fact could well prevent the application of the rule.

However, this is not true since there are stressed suffixes in derived words that trigger the spirantization rule: see (11).

(11) *democrat-a* [dɨmukɾát-ɐ] 'democrat'
 -ia   *democrac-ia* [dɨmukɾɐs- íɐ] 'democracy'
 burocrat-a [buɾukɾát-ɐ] 'bureaucrat'
 -ia   *burocrac-ia* [buɾukɾɐs-íɐ] 'bureaucracy'

 diplomat-a [diplumát-ɐ] 'diplomat'
 -ia   *diplomac-ia* [diplumɐs-íɐ] 'diplomacy'

 necromant-e [nɨkɾumɐ̃́t-ɨ] 'necromancer'
 -ia   *necromanc-ia* [nɨkɾumɐ̃s-íɐ] 'necromancy'

 profet-a [pɾufét-ɐ] 'prophet'
 -ia   *profec-ia* [pɾufɨs-íɐ] 'prophecy'

Due to the fact that stressed and non-stressed suffixes both give rise to the rule, we conclude that derivations like *servente* [sɨɾvɐ̃́tɨ] / *serventia* [sɨɾvɐ̃tíɐ], without consonant alternation, are exceptions to the application of this rule.[14]

The spirantization of /t/ (a [–continuant] consonant) before a vowel consists of the spreading of the [+continuant] feature of the vowel over to the previous consonant. Besides this, other [–continuant] consonants are subject to the spreading of vowel features when preceding suffixes beginning with /i/ followed by another vowel (*-ia*) or followed by a consonant (*-ista*, *-ismo*, *-idade*). In these cases, two rules are applied: a spirantization rule that changes /k/ into [s] (see (12)) and a velar softening rule (VS) that changes /g/ into [ʒ] (see (13)).

(12) *católic-o* [kɐtɔ́lik-u] 'Catholic'
 -ismo   *catolic-ismo* [kɐtulis-íʒmu] 'Catholicism'

 eléctric-o [ilétrik-u] 'electric'
 -ista   *electric-ista* [ilɛtris-íʃtɐ] 'electrician'
 -idade *electric-idade* [ilɛtris-idádɨ] 'electricity'

(13) *psicólog-o* [psikɔ́lug-u] 'psychologist'
 -ia   *psicolog-ia* [psikuluʒ-íɐ] 'psychology'
 -ismo   *psicolog-ismo* [psikuluʒ-íʒmu] 'psychologism'
 -ista   *psicolog-ista* [psikuluʒ-íʃtɐ] 'psychologist'

Yet, the application of these rules has exceptions. See (14).

---

[14] In Villalva (1994a) another explanation is given for derived words like *presidência* and *abundância* (and also *segurança* 'security'). The author presents several arguments to prove that the suffixes are *-ncia* and *-nça* including two morphemes, *-nt* and *-ia*, that have been amalgamated through the application of a no longer productive Spirantization rule. Thus, for Villalva, these suffixes are attached to verb stems (e.g. [[abund a]*ncia*]). Although this is an interesting argument on which to base the statement that morphemes and suffixes may not be isomorphic (two morphemes, one suffix), we believe that this kind of derivation (e.g. *abundant-e* / *abundânc-ia*) is still very productive in Portuguese and that the application of the spirantization rule is grounded in intuition and tradition. Moreover, as the spirantization of the [t] before a stressed suffix is not analysed (for instance, *democrat-a* / *democrac-ia*), it seems that the same rule still works in the other cases.

(14) *monarc-a* [munáɾk-ɐ] 'monarch'
  -ia   *monarqu-ia* [munaɾk-íɐ] 'monarchy'

  fidalg-o [fidáɫg-u] 'noble'
  -ia   *fidalgu-ia* [fidaɫg-íɐ] 'nobility'

  tabac-o [tɐbák-u] 'tobacco'
  -ista   *tabaqu-ista* [tɐbɐk-íʃtɐ] 'smoker'

  intrig-a [ĩtɾíg-ɐ] 'intrigue'
  -ista   *intrigu-ista* [ĩtɾig-íʃtɐ] 'schemer'

All the suffixes we have discussed so far and which are responsible for this alternation, begin with an /i/. The suffix -*ia* may be unstressed (cf. (9)) or stressed (cf. (11) and (13)); -*ismo*, -*ista* and -*idade* are always stressed. Thus, the question does not lie in the metrical context but in the segmental and morphological context: some features of the vowel spreading over the final root consonant when there is a morphological boundary. As these root consonants are [–continuant], the [+continuant] feature of the vowel spreads over in every case.

The remaining problem which still has to be discussed from a phonological point of view concerns the place of articulation. In word formation processes, rules that attach derivational suffixes are lexical and so there may be exceptions. Even though the segments of the suffixes are unspecified in the lexicon, they acquire full specification after they are added to the root (see 2.4.2 for what has been said about underspecification).

Alternation [t] ~ [s], exemplified in (9) and (11), only occurs when the /i/ of the suffix is followed by another vowel, while the examples in (12) do not have this restriction. Thus, it is enough to represent this one vowel in the formalization of the process.[15]

The diagram below (15) depicts the /t/ spirantization in a formal representation. As it is a plosive, /t/ is identified only as [–continuant] but it has to be specified as [–voice]. The [+continuant] feature of the vowel spreads over the consonant. As /t/ is an unmarked coronal, the C-place is filled by default, with the coronal node and the [+anterior] feature: owing to the fact that it is a [+continuant], the consonant is realized as an [s]. With respect to the /i/ of the suffix, we assume that the vowel obtains full specification when it is added on to by the word-formation rule already studied in connection with inflection suffixes. The vowel is therefore specified for the feature [back] and in the height node in this assimilation process.

[15] The other high vowel, say, /u/, does not cause this assimilation (cf. *batatudo* /batat+udo/ [bɐtɐtúdu] 'muscle-bound').

(15)

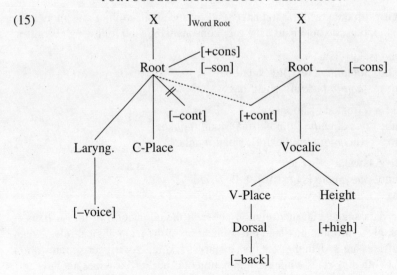

In the alternations exemplified in (12) and (13) (/k/ spirantization and /g/ softening), the vowel also spreads the [+continuant] feature over the consonant. However, these plosives are not coronal as it will be expected by default (both are dorsal), and therefore have to be identified as [+back]. See the representations in (16).

(16)   /k/   →   [s], /g/ → [ʒ]

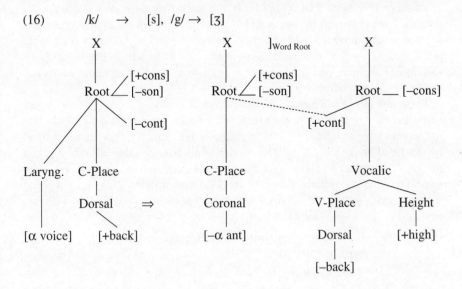

The configuration of this process shows an opposition in the values of [voice] and [anterior] features, represented by the variable α.

There are other suffixes, namely evaluatives like *-inho*, *-ito*, *-ico* etc., which also begin with the vowel [i] and never call for the application of any phonological rule and, thus, do not change the root consonant. See the following examples:

(17) *saco* [sáku] 'bag'
      -inho   *saquinho* [sɐkíɲu] 'small bag'
      -ito   *saquito* [sɐkítu] 'small bag'

      macaco [mɐkáku] 'monkey'
      -inho   *macaquinho* [mɐkɐkíɲu] 'small monkey'
      -ito   *macaquito* [mɐkɐkítu] 'small monkey'

      sueco [swέku] 'Swede'
      -inho   *suequinho* [swɛkíɲu] 'little Swede'
      -ito   *suequito* [swɛkítu] 'little Swede'

These data suggest an interrelation between the adjunction of the suffixes—morphological information—and the application of the phonological rules: when some suffixes are added, the root consonants /t/, /k/ and /g/ trigger spirantization and velar softening rules while the adjunction of other suffixes does not have this effect.

Lexical Phonology merely puts forward a model where morphology and phonology interact. Furthermore, the importance of the idiosyncratic properties of the lexical items in this phonological theory allows us to account for the different behaviour of the root consonant with respect to the application of phonological rules. Such properties are marked in the items although obviously not in all of them. The items that do not have this mark, therefore, do not call for the rule: they are presented in (10) and (14) above. It is worth noting, however, that the word-formation rules adding either *-ia*, *-ismo* or *-inho*, *-ito* suffixes all apply at the lexical level. The same happens with *-elho* as in *garot-elho* 'small boy', *-udo* as in *panç-udo* 'paunchy' or *-ota* as in *cas-ota* 'small or tumbledown house' which are all evaluative suffixes.

These last sets of suffixes still have other specific properties: they never choose verbs and they never change the syntactic category of the base. This means that they do not have an inherent syntactic category. Furthermore, they are not marked by gender although they accept the gender of the base and they absorb the class marker *-o* for masculine and *-a* for feminine. Moreover, they are peripheral with respect to other derivational suffixes (see (18a) with suffixes *-eiro*, *-eza*, *-ção* and the evaluative *-inho/a* and *-ito/a*), and they accept recursivity (cf. (18b) with two evaluatives *-ic-* + *-ito*, *-ic-* + *-inho* and *-ot-* + *-inha*).[16]

(18) a. *engenheirinho* [ẽʒiɲɐjɾíɲu] 'engineer' (depreciative)
          engenheirito [ẽʒiɲɐjɾítu]
          $[[[[[engenh]_{NR} eir]_{NR} inh/it]_{NR} o]_{St}]_W$

[16] There are two other suffixes that also accept recursivity: those occurring in *sensibilizável* [[[[sensi]bil]iz a]vel] 'able to lead to awareness' and *leccionação* [[[[lec]cion]a]ção] 'the act of teaching'. In fact, /bil/ and /vel/ are allomorphs of the same suffix, as well as /cion/ and /ção/. The difference between these suffixes and evaluatives is that they can occur twice but with different realizations according to their position in the word.

certezinha [sɨɾtɨzíɲɐ] 'certainty' (reinforcement)
[[[[[cert]$_{Adj\ R}$ ez]$_{N\ R}$ inh]$_{N\ R}$ a]$_{St}$]$_W$

b. *burriquinho* [buʀikíɲu] 'small donkey'
burriquito [buʀikítu]
[[[[[burr]$_{NR}$ iqu]$_{N\ R}$ inh/it]$_{N\ R}$ o]$_{St}$]$_W$

casotinha [kɐzɔtíɲɐ] 'tiny little house'
[[[[[cas]$_{N\ R}$ ot]$_{N\ R}$ inh]$_{N\ R}$ a]$_{St}$]$_W$

Moreover, words with these suffixes are not in the dictionary owing to the fact that they are the result of a productive word-formation processes. Due to all these peculiarities, we can say, as Villalva does (1994a: ch.5), that they are neither derivational nor inflectional, but *modifiers*.[17]

Finally, classes 1, 2 and 3 of nominals (see above 4.2) behave differently with respect to derivation with modifiers:

- class 1 nouns and adjectives normally attach suffixes like *-inho* to the root (e.g. *livrinho* [livɾíɲu] 'small book', *casinha* [kɐzíɲɐ] 'small house', *pentinho* [pẽtíɲu] 'small comb');
- class 2 nouns and adjectives give preference to *z*-evaluative suffixes, but they can also attach the other evaluative suffixes (e.g. *amorzinho* [ɐmoɾzíɲu] 'little darling', *animalzinho* [ɐnimáɫzíɲu] 'small animal', *papelzinho* [pɐpɛɫzíɲu] or *papelinho* [pɐpɨlíɲu] 'bit of paper');
- class 3 only accepts *z*-evaluative suffixes (e.g. *cafézinho* [kɐfɛzíɲu] 'small (cup of) coffee', *sonzinho* [sõzíɲu] 'faint sound', *chapéuzinho* [ʃɐpɛwzíɲu] 'small hat').

As it will be seen further on, we assume that derivational suffixes and prefixes are different from modifiers because of their inherent properties which have to be indicated in the lexicon (see below in 5.2.2, and particularly in (19)). We prefer to adopt this solution rather than make a distinction between strata in the lexical component, as put forward in other studies about Portuguese.[18] The properties we refer to in 5.2.2 for different suffixes—the fact that they have syntactic categories or the place they may occupy in the internal structure of the word or, even, the base-form they chose—are idiosyncratic properties of the suffixes themselves and do not necessarily mean that they belong to different strata.

5.2.2. An outline of some basic claims

Ever since the theory of lexical phonology was first introduced, it has been the subject of numerous discussions, in which many of its claims have been

---

[17] The concept of *modifier* entails the discussion of the head and other specific morphological questions. We have not dealt with these questions in this book, but we have kept the term *modifier* for the sake of argument.

[18] See Mohanan (1995) about the different lexical domains depending on the morpheme properties. See also Lee (1994) about the domains of word-formation processes in Portuguese.

challenged.[19] Its most important contribution undoubtedly lies in the fact that it represents a model for organizing the grammar, thus allowing independent morphological and phonological rules to interact. Furthermore, the separation between lexical and post-lexical levels has made it possible to solve several problems in the word-formation processes.

In the 'classical' presentation of lexical phonology the interaction between morphology and phonology is closely related to level ordering, due to the fact that, following Kiparsky (1982a), the output of certain phonological rules is available as input for morphological processes. This hypothesis must be tested in different languages and it has not yet been proved that it is essential to the theory as a whole (see Booij (1989) where it is discussed in connection with strong and weak verbs in Dutch). In Portuguese it is not clear that the application of phonological rules is essential for some morphological rules to work. However, there is evidence that morphology creates the objects on which the rules of phonology operate (cf., for instance, spirantization and softening rules in (15) and (16); see also 4.2.2.1.2. for the adjunction of inflectional suffixes leading to their full specification at the lexical level).

The cyclic application is an important claim within the theory. Ever since Mascaró (1976), it has been assumed that the theory accommodates two classes of rules: cyclic and non-cyclic. The condition for cyclic application—derived environments—can be reduced to a condition on rule application, the Strict Cycle Condition (SCC). Cyclic application means that the phonological rules apply after every step in the word-formation process creating a 'derived environment', even if there is no affix at all in the surface word (as in Portuguese non-verbs like $[[[amor]_R]_{St}]_W]$ that do not show any phonetic segment following the root consonant). Non-cyclic application occurs following all the morphological processes, at the post-lexical level. Kiparsky (1982, 1985) offers different arguments to justify why cyclicity is inherent to lexical rules while post-lexical rules have a non-cyclic application: if cyclicity interacts with word-formation processes, then post-lexical rules are non-cyclic because they have no access to the internal constituents of a word, due to the erasure of the brackets (Bracket Erasure Convention, BEC).

Another claim made by classical lexical phonology is that the application of post-lexical rules is automatic and free from exception as they are post-syntactic. This last property of the post-lexical rules—having no exceptions—is a natural consequence of the BEC, since these rules have no access to the internal constituents of the word or to the properties of the lexical items. Seen in this light, spirantization and softening rules in Portuguese can only be lexical rules.

The conditions deciding on cyclic application, the SCC, and the fact that only lexical rules may have exceptions, constitute two claims which have been challenged during the last few years. First of all—and for those authors who believe in the existence of more than one lexical 'stratum'—it seems that some lexical strata are non-cyclic, and each stratum can be specified as being cyclic or non-

---

[19] For a recent discussion about the basic claims of lexical phonology, see Roca (1994), Kenstowicz (1994) and Mohanan (1995).

cyclic.[20] Besides, it is not clear for all post-lexical rules that they are non-cyclic (this is the case of the syllable parsing rule[21] which is cyclic at any level).[22] Another possibility, which has come to light in different languages, has to do with the exceptions witnessed in post-lexical rules.

Finally, Kiparsky (1982, 1985) and Mohanan (1982) propose that lexical rules are structure-preserving; that is, they cannot change one segment into another segment that does not belong to the underlying system of the language. The Structure Preserving Principle (SPP) is thus obeyed. This claim has been likewise discussed, for instance, in Mohanan and Mohanan (1984) where it is shown that in Malayalam, lexical rules expand the points of articulation of nasal consonants from an underlying number of three to seven. In Portuguese, we do not have any arguments against the statement above: segments resulting from the application of lexical rules are structure-preserving as, for instance, theme vowel assimilation, vowel harmony, spirantization and velar softening rules—in sum, all the phonological processes that are morphologically conditioned.

The problem of considering that suffixes preceding other suffixes in the word belong to different strata also deserves attention. From our point of view, order in word-formation results from the selection restrictions of the affixes, namely the syntactic category of the base-form. Thus, if no other properties distinguish them, they can belong to the same stratum, which means that there is only one stratum at the lexical level, which is the domain of application to all these processes.

To summarize, we adopt a model compatible with the interaction between morphological and phonological rules with a cyclic and non-cyclic application: words are built up through the interaction of morphological rules (which determine the addition of the constituents) and phonological rules (which obey the conditions of word well-formedness in Portuguese). This perspective does not mean an input–output sequence for every operation or the necessary existence of different lexical strata with a sequential modularity, which orders application in classical Lexical Phonology. However, it allows the domains of rule application to be co-present in the word-formation process. Morphological and phonological rules apply when the idiosyncratic properties of the morphemes trigger the domain for their application.[23]

Understanding how the application of lexical rules works implies knowing about the nature of the lexicon. In the light of what has been presented above, all morphemes of a language—roots and affixes—are listed in the lexicon and identified by their inherent properties as well as by their idiosyncratic selection

[20] See Halle and Mohanan (1985) and Halle and Vergnaud (1987) for a slightly different position.

[21] In Portuguese, syllable parsing may integrate the high vowels in the onset as in *piar* [piár]→[pjár], corresponding to the phonetic realization in two different registers. This process is also cyclic.

[22] According to Halle and Vergnaud (1987), the distinction between cyclic and non-cyclic strata 'is the manner in which the rules in a stratum take account of the morphological composition of the string' (77–8).

[23] In general, we agree with the proposal for the organization of the grammar presented in Paradis and La Charité, (1993: 144).

restrictions.[24] It is worth noting that, among these idiosyncratic properties, there are some related to stress. In other words, some vowels belonging to the roots or to the suffixes are 'unstressable'. In the list below, semantic features and argument structure have been excluded, as we are not concerned with them.

(19) *Properties of the items listed in the lexicon*
      (categories, subcategories and selection restrictions)

Roots
Category and subcategory
Syntactic category (noun, adjective, verb, adverb, preposition)
Morpho-syntactic category (gender)
Morphological subcategory (class marker–nouns; TV-verbs)

Inherent properties
Non-inflected adjectives for gender
Verb irregular inflection
Unstressable vowels

Affixes
Inflectional suffixes
Plural (non-verbs)
TMA and PN (verbs)

Derivational affixes and modifiers
Morphological category (prefix, suffix)

Prefixes
Inherent properties
Relation to the base (close to the root, peripherality)
Recursivity

Selection restrictions
Syntactic category: category of the base (noun, adjective, verb, and adverb)
Morphological category: category of the base (root, etc.)

Suffixes
Inherent properties
Syntactic category (noun, adjective, verb, adverb)
Morpho-syntactic category (gender)
Morphological subcategory (class marker–nouns; TV-verbs)

---

[24] According to Lieber (1989: 99), the morpho-syntactic features for main categories constitute the *categorial signature*; derivational affixes are also given full categorial signature and inflectional affixes are only specified for the positive values of the features they bear. This notion is related to the fact that such features *percolate* from one level to the higher level in the whole word-formation process. We do not need to deal with this concept here and for our purpose it is enough to identify the properties of the items. See Villalva (1994a: ch.4) and (1994b) for the categorial signature in Portuguese and for a discussion about the properties of the suffixes.

Morphological function (head, modifiers)
Recursivity
Unstressable vowels

Selection restrictions
Syntactic category / categories of the base (noun, adjective, verb)
Morphological category of the base (root, stem, word)

The *lexical level* is the domain of base-form syllable parsing. This cyclic rule applies before any morphological or phonological rule and, during the generation of the word, it applies after every step that sets up a new environment (see Chapter 3). Apart from this, the lexical level is the domain of morphological rules which attach inflectional suffixes (theme vowel and tense–mood–aspect or person–number suffixes; class markers and gender and number suffixes) and derivational affixes to non-verb roots and to verb roots and stems.

As we pointed out above, the lexical level is equally the domain of the application of TV deletion and vowel harmony rules in Portuguese verbs (cf. 4.2.2.1 and 4.2.2.2 for the discussion of the rules). Unstressed vowel rules and nasalization (see Chapter 7) also belong to the lexical level as well as the other morphology sensitive phonological rules.

Derivational affixes and modifiers, which are added at the lexical level (except *z*-evaluative and *-mente* suffixes) may obey their inherent properties that establish their order with relation to the base. For example, in the word *religiosidade*, 'religiousness', whose structure is $[[[[religi]_{NR} os]_{Adj\ R} idad]_{NR} e]_{St}]_W$, the suffix *-os-*, which categorizes adjectives, has to precede *-idad-* that categorizes nouns. Some suffixes can be recursively added (e.g. *-bil-* and *-vel*, allomorphs of the same suffix, occur twice in *sensibilizável*, 'able to lead to awareness, $[[[[sens\ i]_{Vb\ St} bil]_{Adj\ R} iz\ a]_{Vb\ St} vel]_{Adj\ R}$). In the composition of the string, the adjunction of a suffix can create a new root for the possible application of a suffix (cf. *religiosidade*) or it creates a verb stem if TV is adjoined (cf. *sensibiliz-a-r*).

Phonological rules like spirantization and velar softening apply at the lexical level when specific suffixes are adjoined (see (15) and (16)), and their results are maintained in the adjunction of other suffixes (cf. *presidencial* 'presidential' $[[[[president]_{N\ R} i(a)]_{N\ R} al]_{Adj\ R}]_W$.

Irregular verbs are marked in the lexicon and they do not trigger the vowel harmony rule. Their respective items are marked for morphological irregularities with diacritics, and the various inflectional suffixes make subcategories for those particular roots and stems. This proposal is close to Lieber's (1989, 103) for Latin *strong* verbs. Irregularity in verbs concerns namely:

- the inflected forms of the strong verbs with alternation in the root vowel and/or consonant of the present vs. past verb stems—like *ter* 'to have' (*tenho/tive*), *vir* 'to come' (*venho/vim*), *pôr* 'to put' (*ponho/pus*), *ver* 'to see' (*vejo/vi*), *querer* 'to want' (*quero/quis*), *saber* 'to know' (*sei/soube*),
- the strong past participles that are chosen by certain suffixes—as *convert-er / convers-or* and

• the suppletion of some verbs—like *ir* 'to go' (*vou* / *fui*) and *ser* 'to be' (*sou* / *seja* / *fui*, present indicative / present subjunctive / past).

The *post-lexical level* is the domain wherein phonological processes related to syllable position apply (see Chapter 7 for the formal representation of these processes).

Derived words with *z*-evaluative and *-mente* suffixes belong to the syntactic level because of their particular properties, namely because they choose the word as their base-form, where the class marker and the regular inflectional suffixes have already been attached. Yet, they are also subject to the post-lexical rules. The specific morphological category of the base they are attached to is part of their respective inherent properties and their selection restrictions. It should be pointed out that *z*-evaluative suffixes are normally attached to non-verbs of classes 2 and 3, that is, to those with final root consonants, stressed vowels and diphthongs; they are also attached to many derived nouns and adjectives.

Post-lexical phonological rules (e.g. onset and coda rules as well as gliding rules) apply after the morpho-syntactic word is built up, that is, after all affixes are added. These rules apply non-cyclically except for syllable parsing.

Lexical phonology is intimately connected with autosegmental theory and the concept of underspecification. As the reader may have noted, filling-rules and changing-rules that apply to root consonants and suffixes provide clear evidence in favour of this theory; lexical and post-lexical levels are the domains at which such rules apply.

6

WORD STRESS IN PORTUGUESE

In this chapter we present the facts about word stress in Portuguese, first in the noun and then in the verb system.

6.1. NOUN SYSTEM

For the majority (over 70 per cent) of nouns, adjectives and adverbs ending in an oral vowel, stress falls on the syllable before the last, as in (1).

(1) mod*e*lo[1] [mudélu] 'model' N
     rapar*i*ga [ʀɐpɐɾíɡɐ] 'girl' N
     beld*a*de [bɛɫdádɨ] 'beauty' N
     colh*e*ita [kuʎéjtɐ] 'harvest' N
     inclem*e*nte [ĩklɨmẽtɨ] 'severe' Adj
     corr*e*cto [kuʀέtu] 'correct' Adj
     empr*e*go [ẽpɾéɡu] 'job' N
     sinc*e*ro [sĩsέɾu] 'sincere' Adj
     provoc*a*nte [pɾuvukẽtɨ] 'provocative' Adj
     bel*i*che [bɨlíʃɨ] 'bunk' N

   In contrast, nouns and adjectives ending in a consonant are generally stressed on the last syllable, as we see in (2).

(2) hospit*a*l [ɔʃpitáɫ] 'hospital' N
     gramatic*a*l [ɡɾɛmɐtikáɫ] 'grammatical' Adj
     pap*e*l [pɐpéɫ] 'paper' N
     subt*i*l [subtíɫ] 'subtle' Adj
     carac*o*l [kɐɾɛkɔ́ɫ] 'snail' N
     az*u*l [ɐzúɫ] 'blue' Adj
     marqu*ê*s [mɐɾkéʃ] 'marquis' N
     ingl*ê*s [ĩɡléʃ] 'English' N, Adj
     fel*i*z [fɨlíʃ] 'happy' Adj

---

[1] All stressed vowels are in italic, independently of the fact that some of them may be orthographically marked.

rapaz [ʀɐpáʃ] 'boy' N
capataz [kɐpɐtáʃ] 'foreman' N
paul [pɐúł] 'swamp' N
juiz [ʒwíʃ]² 'judge' N
colher [kuʎɛ́ɾ] 'spoon' N
prazer [pɾɐzéɾ] 'pleasure' N

Comparing (1) with (2), one could argue that Portuguese is a language in which stress is quantity-sensitive. Nevertheless, this is not our assumption since, as we shall see later, we think that there is evidence to the contrary. There are more than a thousand words stressed on the final syllable, even when this is an open one. Let us consider the examples in (3).

(3)   café [kɐfɛ́] 'coffee' N
      maré [mɛɾɛ́] 'tide' N
      chaminé [ʃɐminɛ́] 'chimney' N
      jacaré [ʒɐkɐɾɛ́] 'alligator' N
      dominó [dɔminɔ́] 'dominoes' N
      avó [ɐvɔ́] 'grandmother' N
      alvará [ałvɐɾá] 'charter' N
      guaraná [gwɐɾɐná] 'guarana' N
      guarani [gwɐɾɐní] 'Guarani' N
      jabuti [ʒɐbutí] 'giant tortoise' N
      javali [ʒɐvɐlí] 'wild bear' N
      avô [ɐvó] 'grandfather' N
      robô [ʀobó] 'robot' N
      peru [pɨɾú] 'turkey' N
      caju [kaʒú] 'cashew fruit' N
      baú [baú] 'trunk' N
      sabiá [sabjá] 'thrush' N

We consider that the words in (2) and (3) demonstrate identical behaviour with relation to stress and that final stress has nothing to do with syllable weight. We assume that the difference between (2), (3) and (1) is due to morphological reasons. Every word stressed like those of (1) ends in a vowel, /a/, /o/, /e/, that is, a class marker, while the words stressed in (2) and (3) lack this class marker (cf. 4.2.1). The morphological canonical form of nouns and adjectives is thus

(4)   Nouns: [stem]₁, [class]₂, ([number]₃)_{N Adj}

For nouns, the absence of a class marker restricts stress location to the final syllable. Moreover, final stress on nouns shows up only when the form lacks a class marker. Thus one may say that the alternation between final and penultimate

---

² Excepting the sequences [kwV] and [gwV], every word with a glide in prevocalic position may have an alternate pronunciation with a high vowel, [i] or [u].

stress for nouns and adjectives is in fact morphologically conditioned, namely by the presence or absence of a class marker.

The words in (5), ending in a diphthong, present normal stress on the penulti-mate, as the phonetic glide is the realization of the class marker. As we know, the class marker is a vowel but it may surface as a glide.

(5) carap*a*u [kɐɾɐpáw] 'horse-mackerel' N
     aten*e*u [ɐtɨnéw] 'athenaeum' N
     mausol*é*u [mawzuléw] 'mausoleum' N
     faris*e*u [fɐɾizéw] 'Pharisee' N
     pigm*e*u [pigméw] 'pygmy' N
     povar*é*u [puvɐɾéw] 'mob' N

Most of the words ending in a nasal vowel, like those of (6) behave exactly like those of (2) because the phonetic nasal vowel is a sequence of an oral vowel plus a nasal autosegment.

(6) jard*i*m [ʒɐɾdí] 'garden' N
     varand*i*m [vɐɾẽdí] 'balcony' N
     frenes*i*m [fɾɨnɨzí] 'frenzy' N
     at*u*m [ɐtú] 'tuna' N
     com*u*m [kumú] 'common' Adj
     bomb*o*m [bõbó] 'chocolate' N
     maç*ã* [mɐsé] 'apple' N
     irm*ã* [iɾmé] 'sister' N
     rom*ã* [ʀumé] 'grenade' N

For words having a nasal diphthong in final position, normally they are stressed like those of (5), on the second phonological vowel, or like those of (2), in cases where the glide has been inserted (see Nasalization, 7.2).

(7) nataç*ã*o [nɐtɐséw̃] 'swimming' N
     naç*ã*o [nɐséw̃] 'nation' N
     tuf*ã*o [tuféw̃] 'typhoon' N
     desd*é*m [diʒdéj̃)] 'disdain' N
     ref*é*m [ʀɨféj̃)] 'hostage' N

These regularities—stress on the final syllable if there is no class marker but stress the penultimate if there is a class marker—are valid for about 80 per cent of the native vocabulary. This means that we are still left with a significant number of words whose stress does not obey the normal parameters. So, we have words with a class marker that are not stressed on the penultimate syllable as we also have words with no class marker that are not stressed on the final syllable. That is, words that are exceptions to (1) and (2), stressed on the third from the end if they have a class marker and on the second if they have a defective class marker, respectively.

In any case stress can never be further than the third syllable from the right edge of the word, as the words in (8) show.

(8) último [uɫtimu] 'ultimate' N
     júbilo [ʒúbilu] 'exultation' N
     divórcio [divɔ́ɾsju] 'divorce' N
     árabe [áɾɐbɨ] 'Arab(ic)' N, Adj
     angélico [ẽʒéliku] 'angelic' Adj
     plástico [pláɾʃtiku] 'plastic' N, Adj
     óptico [ɔ́tiku] 'optical' Adj
     linguístico [lĩgwíʃtiku] 'linguistic' Adj
     catástrofe [kɐtáʃtɾufɨ] 'catastrophe' N
     catastrófico [kɐtɐʃtɾɔ́fiku] 'catastrophic' Adj
     calorífero [kɐluɾífiɾu] 'heater' Adj
     lanígero [lɐníʒiɾu] 'lanigerous' Adj
     meritório [miɾitɔ́ɾju] 'meritorious' Adj
     árido [áɾidu] 'arid' Adj
     urticária [uɾtikáɾjɐ] 'nettle rash' N
     sábia [sábjɐ] 'wise (fem)' N, Adj

Exceptions to (7), that is words having an unstressed nasal diphthong are, for example, those in (9):

(9) órfão [ɔ́ɾfẽw̃] 'orphan (m)' N, Adj
     sótão [sɔ́tẽw̃] 'loft' N
     orégão [ɔɾégẽw̃] 'oregano' N
     ordem [ɔ́ɾdẽj̃] 'order' N
     viagem [vjáʒẽj̃] 'travel' N
     garagem [gɐɾaʒẽj̃] 'garage' N
     selagem [sɨláʒẽj̃] 'stamping' N
     vertigem [viɾtíʒẽj̃] 'vertigo' N

The words in (10), though ending in a consonant, are stressed on the penultimate, not the final.

(10) frágil [fɾáʒiɫ] 'fragile' Adj
     útil [útiɫ] 'useful' Adj
     fútil [fútiɫ] 'futile' Adj
     cônsul [kṍsuɫ] 'consul' N
     fácil [fásiɫ] 'easy' Adj
     móvel [mɔ́vɛɫ] 'mobile' N, Adj
     amável [ɐmávɛɫ] 'kind' Adj
     açúcar [ɐsúkɐɾ] 'sugar' N
     lápis [lápiʃ] 'pencil' N
     íman [ímɐn] 'magnet' N

glúten [glúten] 'gluten' N
abdómen[3] [ɐbdɔ́mɛn] 'abdomen' N

As we saw, only the words in (8), ending with an oral vowel, can be stressed on the antepenultimate. All the other groups are stressed on the last or the penultimate.

So, in the noun system, phonetically stress may fall on the last syllable, as in (2), (3), (5), (6), and (7), on the penultimate one, as in (1), (9), and (10), or on the antepenultimate as in (8). In any case, we are always left with three possible locations for stress. Stress may not retract further than the third syllable to the left of the end of the word.

6.2. VERB SYSTEM

As we will see, verb forms are, mostly (in 75 per cent of cases) stressed on the syllable preceding the final one, that is the second from the right edge of the word.

Let us recall the main single verb tenses in Portuguese (cf. 4.2.2.1), illustrating with a verb from each conjugation: *falar*, 'to speak', *bater*, 'to beat, to strike', and *partir*, 'to break, to leave'.

(11) Present Indicative[4]

falo [fálu]	bato [bátu]	parto [pártu]
falas [fáleʃ]	bates [bátiʃ]	partes [pártiʃ]
fala [fále]	bate [báti]	parte [párti]
falamos [felémuʃ]	batemos [betémuʃ]	partimos [pertímuʃ]
falam [fálew̃]	batem [bátej̃]	partem [pártej̃]

Phonetically, every form is stressed on the penultimate.

In the present subjunctive, whose forms are given in (13), every form is also stressed on the penultimate syllable.

(12) Present Subjunctive

fale [fáli]	bata [báte]	parta [párte]
fales [fáliʃ]	batas [báteʃ]	partas [párteʃ]
fale [fáli]	bata [báte]	parta [párte]
falemos [felémuʃ]	batamos [betémuʃ]	partamos [pertémuʃ]
falem [fálej̃]	batam [báte w̃]	partam [párte w̃]

[3] In certain EP dialects, *íman* may be [ímẽ̞] and *abdómen*, [ɐbdɔ́m(i)]. In BP, the three last words of (10) may be pronounced with a nasal vowel instead of an oral vowel followed by [n]. Otherwise, in EP, for words ending in an unstressed nasal vowel, we only find the word *órfã*, [ɔ́rfẽ̞], 'orphan (fem)'.

[4] In this tense, as well as in all the others, the different forms correspond to: 1st, 2nd and 3rd singular, 1st and 3rd plural. As already noted, 2nd person plural is of a very restricted usage (cf. 4.2.2). Nevertheless, concerning stress and other general phonological processes its behaviour is perfectly regular.

For the imperfect indicative, imperfect subjunctive, and pluperfect whose forms are given in (13), (14) and (15), respectively, we have a form, which is stressed on the antepenultimate.

(13) Imperfect Indicative

falava [fɐlávɐ]	batia [bɐtíɐ]	partia [pɐɾtíɐ]
falavas [fɐlávɐʃ]	batias [bɐtíɐʃ]	partias [pɐɾtíɐʃ]
falava [fɐlávɐ]	batia [bɐtíɐ]	partia [pɐɾtíɐ]
falávamos [fɐlávɐmuʃ]	batíamos [bɐtíɐmuʃ]	partíamos [pɐɾtíɐmuʃ]
falavam [fɐlávẽw̃]	batiam [bɐtíẽw̃]	partiam [pɐɾtíẽw̃]

(14) Imperfect Subjunctive

falasse [fɐlásɨ]	batesse [bɐtésɨ]	partisse [pɐɾtísɨ]
falasses [fɐlásɨʃ]	batesses [bɐtésɨʃ]	partisses [pɐɾtísɨʃ]
falasse [fɐlásɨ]	batesse [bɐtésɨ]	partisse [pɐɾtísɨ]
falássemos [fɐlásɨmuʃ]	batêssemos [bɐtésɨmuʃ]	partíssemos [pɐɾtísɨmuʃ]
falassem [fɐlásẽj̃]	batessem [bɐtésẽj̃]	partissem [pɐɾtísẽj̃]

(15) Pluperfect Indicative

falara [fɐláɾɐ]	batera [bɐtéɾɐ]	partira [pɐɾtíɾɐ]
falaras [fɐláɾɐʃ]	bateras [bɐtéɾɐʃ]	partiras [pɐɾtíɾɐʃ]
falara [fɐláɾɐ]	batera [bɐtéɾɐ]	partira [pɐɾtíɾɐ]
faláramos [fɐláɾɐmuʃ]	batêramos [bɐtéɾɐmuʃ]	partíramos [pɐɾtíɾɐmuʃ]
falaram [fɐláɾẽw̃]	bateram [bɐtéɾẽw̃]	partiram [pɐɾtíɾẽw̃]

In these last three tenses, 1st person plural is stressed on the antepenultimate rather than on the penultimate, as is the case elsewhere. In the 1st conjugation, these tenses have a marker of the C(onsonant)V(owel) form, /va/, /se/ and /ɾa/, respectively. In the 2nd and 3rd conjugations tense markers are /ia/, /se/ and /ɾa/.

In the perfect, we have the following forms:

(16) Past Perfect Indicative

falei [fɐléj]	bati [bɐtí]	parti [pɐɾtí]
falaste [fɐláʃtɨ]	bateste [bɐtéʃtɨ]	partiste [pɐɾtíʃtɨ]
falou [fɐló]	bateu [bɐtéw]	partiu [pɐɾtíw]
falámos [fɐlámuʃ][5]	batemos [bɐtémuʃ]	partimos [pɐɾtímuʃ]
falaram [fɐláɾẽw̃]	bateram [bɐtéɾẽw̃]	partiram [pɐɾtíɾẽw̃]

Here, 1st and 3rd singular are phonetically final stressed. Several remarks must be made. As a matter of fact, at the phonological level, the stressed vowel is the second from the end.

---

[5] In Brazilian Portuguese, this past form is homophonous with the 1st person plural of the present indicative as occurs in the second and third conjugations. The same occurs in some northern dialects of European Portuguese.

In the 1st person singular of the 2nd and 3rd conjugations, (*bati* and *parti*) as well as the 3rd singular of the 1st conjugation (*falou*), final stress is due to the phenomenon of coalescence (cf. 4.2.2.1.2).

In the case of the 1st person singular of the 1st conjugation (*falei*) as well as the 3rd singular of the 2nd and 3rd conjugations (*bateu* and *partiu*) stress seems to be final but the phonetic glide of these forms is a phonological vowel.

In the future we find the following:

(17) Future Indicative

falar*ei* [felɐɾéj]	bater*ei* [betɨɾéj]	partir*ei* [pertɨɾéj]
falar*ás* [felɐɾáʃ]	bater*ás* [betɨɾáʃ]	partir*ás* [pertɨɾáʃ]
falar*á* [felɐɾá]	bater*á* [betɨɾá]	partir*á* [pertɨɾá]
falar*emos* [felɐɾémuʃ]	bater*emos* [betɨɾémuʃ]	partir*emos* [pertɨɾémuʃ]
falar*ão* [felɐɾë̃w̃]	bater*ão* [betɨɾë̃w̃]	partir*ão* [pertɨɾë̃w̃]

With relation to all the other forms already seen, 3rd person singular and plural in the future behave in a peculiar way as they are final stressed. But the future tense is peculiar not only with relation to stress.

In the first place we may note that all the forms show an /ɾ/ after the theme vowel. In second place, in case of cliticization, clitics may appear inside the verb form. So we have, *falar-te-ei*, 'I will talk to you' but not **falarei -te*. As clitics appear after the /ɾ/ we may conclude that it does not belong to the future marker; otherwise we could find **fala-te-rei*, 'I will talk to you'. This leads us to consider that the future is composed of the infinitive form, and that it is to this form that the tense and person markers are added. Yet another reason resides in the fact that when the form is pronounced without enclisis, the theme vowel, /a/, as unstressed, is raised, *falarei*, [felɐɾéj]; if there is enclisis, the theme vowel behaves as if it were stressed, that is, without raising, *falar-te-ei* [felaɾtiéj], or [felaɾtjéj].

The future tense and person markers are in fact the present indicative of the verb *haver*, 'to be there' (cf. 4.2.2.1.3). Historically, the future derives from a periphrastic construction of the kind *hei (de)*[6] *falar*, '(I) shall speak', *hás (de) falar*, 'You will speak', etc. The forms with enclisis were *hei (de) te falar* or *hei (de) falar-te*, etc. So, even if this periphrastic form is historically grounded, it is on purely synchronic facts that we assume it (cf. 4.2.2.1.3).

The conditional, whose forms are given in (18), is formed of the infinitive but now followed by forms of the imperfect of the verb *haver*, 'to be there'.

(18) Conditional

falar*ia* [felɐɾíɐ]	bater*ia* [betɨɾíɐ]	partir*ia* [pertɨɾíɐ]
falar*ias* [felɐɾíɐʃ]	bater*ias* [betɨɾíɐʃ]	partir*ias* [pertɨɾíɐʃ]
falar*ia* [felɐɾíɐ]	bater*ia* [betɨɾíɐ]	partir*ia* [pertɨɾíɐ]
falar*íamos* [felɐɾíɐmuʃ]	bater*íamos* [betɨɾíɐmuʃ]	partir*íamos* [pertɨɾíɐmuʃ]
falar*iam* [felɐɾíɐ̃w̃]	bater*iam* [betɨɾíɐ̃w̃]	partir*iam* [pertɨɾíɐ̃w̃]

---

[6] Until the fifteenth century these forms were used without *de*.

Future and conditional paradigms may be seen as exceptions, since clitics may appear internally, that is, in between a verb formative identical to the Infinitive and the specific endings of the future and the conditional.

(19) falar-te-*í*amos '(we) would speak to you'
     comê-lo-*i*as '(you) would eat it'
     sabê-lo-*e*mos '(we) will know it'
     contar-te-*e*i '(I) will tell you'

Clitics differ in a crucial way from 'normal' suffixes, as they never induce a stress shift. Clitics are immune to stress and may be said to be invisible to stress processes.

(20) d*i*zem '(they) say'   pap*e*l 'paper'
     d*i*zem-no '(they) say it'   papel*a*da 'pile of papers'
     d*i*zem-no-lo '(they) say it to us'   papelar*i*a 'stationer's (shop)'

Stress positions that are deeper than the antepenultimate one require a comment. A cliticized antepenultimate accentuation, given that cliticization is postaccentual and that clitics are inert to stress, will surface as ante-antepenultimate (*dáva]mo] -lo]*), '(we) were giving it'. It is possible to have even apparently deeper stresses by adjoining supplementary clitics, (*dáva]mo] -no]-lo]*), '(We) were giving it to ourselves'.

Assuming that clitics are attached after stress assignment, though having no effect on stress position, we can state that stress in verbs is reduced to the 'last, penultimate and antepenultimate syllable' schemata.

As already noticed, (cf. 4.2.2.1.1), Portuguese has, in contrast to the other Romance languages, the peculiarity of having a personal infinitive, i.e. an infinitive followed by person markers.

(21) Personal Infinitive

fal*a*r [fɐlár]	bat*e*r [bɐtér]	part*i*r [pɐrtír]
fal*a*res [fɐlárɨʃ]	bat*e*res [bɐtérɨʃ]	part*i*res [pɐrtírɨʃ]
fal*a*r [fɐlár]	bat*e*r [bɐtér]	part*i*r [pɐrtír]
fal*a*rmos [fɐlárrmuʃ]	bat*e*rmos [bɐtérmuʃ]	part*i*rmos [pɐrtírmuʃ]
fal*a*rem [fɐlárrẽj̃]	bat*e*rem [bɐtérẽj̃]	part*i*rem [pɐrtírẽj̃]

In this tense, 1st and 3rd singular behave like most noun forms ending in a consonant, those that have a defective class marker, in the sense that they are stressed on the final.

Besides the forms considered, verbs also have a gerund, a present participle and a past participle, all stressed on the penultimate, and a future subjunctive that in regular verbs presents the same forms as the personal infinitive (cf. 4.2.2.1).

(22) a. Gerund
    amando [ɐmɐ̃́du]   batendo   partindo

    b. Present Participle
    amante [ɐmɐ̃́tɨ]

    c. Past Participle
    amado [ɐmádu]   batido   partido

6.3. WHY PORTUGUESE IS NOT QUANTITY-SENSITIVE

Like nouns, verbs may be phonetically stressed on one of the three last syllables. They are normally stressed on the last but one. They are stressed on the last, excepting some forms of the future, as we have seen, in case of coalescence or if there is a diphthong, and they may be stressed on the antepenultimate if the tense marker is of the imperfect or pluperfect form. In other words, a verb form is always stressed on the last vowel of the stem or on the vowel following it. In this last case the vowel is either a tense marker, as in the 1st and 2nd plural of the present subjunctive, or the theme vowel, as in the imperfect, imperfect subjunctive and the pluperfect.

Given this stress pattern, and in coherence with Latin diachrony, we may ask if we are not dealing with a quantity-sensitive stress system. Although the quantity-sensitive hypothesis has been assumed by some researchers we think that there are arguments against it. Among these one may recall the existence of minimal pairs such as:

(23) a. júbilo [ʒúbilu] 'exultation' N
    jubilo [ʒubílu] '(I) exult' V

    b. divórcio [divɔ́rsju] 'divorce' N
    divorcio [divursíu] '(I) get divorced' V

    c. último [úɬtimu] 'ultimate' Adj
    ultimo [uɬtímu] '(I) ultimate' V[7]

    d. sábia [sábjɐ] 'wise' (fem) Adj
    sabiá [sabjá] 'thrush' N
    sabia [sɐbíɐ] 'I, s/he knew, tasted' V

Since the quantity-sensitive hypothesis implies a phonological conditioning of stress location, it is hard to account for such alternations without positing idiosyncratic lexical marks or some post-stress abstract process leading to similar surface forms from different post-stress representations. More generally, the pure quantity-sensitive hypothesis seems, in principle, to be incompatible with the coexistence of two stress subsystems, one for nouns one for verbs.

A vast majority of noun and verb forms with more than two syllables are

---

[7] These alternations are like those in English where stress location distinguishes between a verb and noun: *export*, *import*, *torment*, etc.

stressed on the penultimate, independently of whether this or the last syllable is open or closed. Under these circumstances, it is hard to accept quantity as a conditioning factor.

Outside the stress system, quantity has never been shown to play any role in Portuguese phonology. If some phonologists wish to consider an alternation between long and short vowels, they must recognize that when a vowel is long then it is systematically stressed. Therefore, there is general agreement that duration is a by-product of stressing. If so, length cannot be assigned the role of an explanatory principle of stress location.

To sum up, we conclude that the stress system in Portuguese is not quantity sensitive.

Given this first result, a morpholexical conditioning is likely to be called into play to account for the complex structure of stress facts. We will discuss this hypothesis at length below.

From a general point of view, as has been shown in 4.2., morphological composition is relatively homogenous among nouns, adjectives and verbs. As is well known, one of the main problems of Portuguese morphology (and one that is particularly relevant to stress analysis) is the defective character of class and tense markers. Consider the following examples in (24), where the first four words lack the general class marker and the last four the present tense marker:

(24) a. café [kɐfé] 'coffee'
        hospital [ɔʃpitáɫ] 'hospital'
        avô [ɐvó] 'grand-father'
        javali [ʒɐvɐlí] 'wild boar'

    b. falo [fálu] '(I) speak'
        ataca [ɐtákɐ] '(s/he, it) attacks'
        sabe [sábɨ] '(s/he, it) knows, tastes'
        moras [mɔɾɐʃ] '(you) live, reside'

In nouns, the absence of a class marker restricts stress location to the final syllable. Moreover, final stress on nouns shows up only when the form lacks a class marker. Thus one may say that the alternation between final and penultimate stress for nouns and adjectives is in fact morphologically conditioned, namely by the presence or absence of a class marker. This is not the case for verbs. Absence of a tense marker does not seem to have any effect on stress position, (see (24b)). To illustrate this striking difference, let us consider the following pairs. In (25a) the absence of a class marker in the first noun induces a final rather than penultimate stress. On the other hand, in (25.b) both verbs exhibit penultimate stress, although the first form lacks a tense marker.

(25) a. café [kɐfé]   vs.   modelo [mudélu]
        papá [pɐpá]   vs.   papa [pápɐ]

    b. falo [fálu]   vs.   falaras [fɐláɾɐʃ]
        leva [lévɐ]   vs.   levavas [lɨvávɐʃ]

Finally, let us notice that tense markers, except in the future, conditional and present subjunctive, are always unstressed, independently of their position in the word.

Let us recall the canonical form for nouns, adjectives and verbs:

(26) a. Nouns: $[\text{stem}]_1, ([\text{class}]_2, [\text{number}]_3)_{\text{N A}}$
     b. Verbs: $[\text{stem}]_1, (\text{class})_2, ([\text{tense}]_3, [\text{person-number}]_4)_{\text{V}}$

(27) javalí $[\text{javali}]_{1\text{ N}}$ [ʒɐvɐlí] 'wild boar'
     gatos $[\text{gat}]_1\,\text{o}]_2\,\text{s}]_{3\text{ N}}$ [gátuʃ] 'cats'
     francês $[\text{francês}]_1\,]_{\text{A}}$ [fɾɐ̃séʃ] 'French' (masc. sg.)
     francesas $[\text{frances}]_1\,\text{a}]_2\,\text{s}]_{3\text{ A}}$ [fɾɐ̃sézɐʃ] 'French' (fem. pl.)
     falamos $[\text{fal}]_1\,\text{a}]_2\,\text{mos}]_{4\text{ V}}$ [fɐlɐ́muʃ] '(we) speak, spoke'
     fales $[\text{fal}]_1\,\text{e}]_3\,\text{s}]_{4\text{ V}}$ [fáliʃ] '(that you) speak'
     comamos $[\text{com}]_1\,\text{a}]_3\,\text{mos}]_{4\text{ V}}$ [kumɐ́muʃ] '(let us) eat'

6.4. WORD STRESS IN PORTUGUESE AND GENERATIVE PHONOLOGY

Within SPE type phonologies, word stress became a central concern of research. Mateus (1975) and Andrade (1977) propose accounts of the stress system. Although Mateus describes the nominal system in a more detailed way than Andrade, their conclusions are by and large convergent. Both agree that there are two different stress systems, one for verbs and another for nouns and adjectives.

The rule that accounts for stress location in verb forms can be said to be:

(28) $V \rightarrow [+ \text{stress}] / \underline{\hspace{1cm}}((+CV)C_oV)C_o\#]_V$

and the most common one for noun and adjective forms:

(29) $V \rightarrow [+ \text{stress}] / \underline{\hspace{1cm}}C_oVC_o\#]_{N, A}$

with two other rules that apply to forms marked in the lexicon as exceptions to (29): one for words stressed on the last syllable and another one for words bearing stress on the antepenultimate syllable.

To sum up, almost every analysis of Portuguese word stress faces two problems. The first one resides in the apparent discrepancies between the nominal and the verbal system. Any attempt to unify the stress system, by positing fairly abstract rules, morphological marks or whatever, will encounter a second problem: although their composition is very similar, derivational morphemes do not act the same way in both subsystems. Namely, some morphemes appear to be immune to stress in the noun system but not in the verb system, as, for example -ic in *fábrica / fabrica*.

6.5. SECONDARY STRESS AND ECHO STRESS

Apart from the fact that all authors recognize the existence of a secondary stress in derived words with the suffix *-mente* or with suffixes that have a *-z-*, it can be said that in the majority of previous studies Portuguese has been analysed as a mono-accentual language, that is to say, one without secondary rhythmic stress nor accentual echoes. There are some exceptions to this trend, namely Mateus (1975), who considers four degrees of non-main stress, Delgado-Martins (1983), and Andrade and Viana (1988a, 1988b). The latter show the phonetic existence of echoes of the main stress on each even syllable, leftwards. The stress echoes present themselves as a rhythmic wave (or a rhythmic principle of alternation between strong and weak beats). In most cases, they are phonetically marked by the relative duration of the syllables that occupy that position. (To explain this rhythmic wave going from right to left, Andrade and Viana (1988b) offered an analysis in terms of grid and constituents.). Besides this, there may also be a non-rhythmic initial secondary stress.

As we know, the existence of stress echoes has often been analysed in terms of constituents. These constitute a central element in Halle and Vergnaud's model (1987). This is not an obligatory conclusion since models such as those of Hayes (1980), Prince (1983, 1990) or Laks (1990), which do not make appeal to constituency, but to a rhythmic primitive, treat stress echoes without reference to the internal organization of the phonetic chain in terms of constituents.

Leaving the debate aside, let us underline the importance of this rhythmic notion for stress in Portuguese and the fact that it implies the notion of anchoring (or, if we prefer, that of trigger of echo stresses). Thus it is only once we have a clear understanding of main stress assignment that echo stresses can be analysed. On the other hand, the fact that main stress provokes rhythmic echoes enlightens us on its nature as well as on its function in the phonological system of a given language. Being an almost fixed stress, it assigns a demarcating role and allows the perception of the morphological composition. This morphological-lexical information is central from the point of view of comprehension.

In Portuguese, a native speaker is capable of distinguishing between a noun and a verb, between a vowel that is a class marker and a vowel that is not a class marker, etc., simply on the basis of the main stress position (e.g. júbilo [ʒúbilu] (N) vs. jubilo [ʒubílu] (V)). The existence of an echo of the main stress reinforces its informative power, organizing the phonetic chain as a rhythmic domain in which it occupies the last stressed place. This analysis is also supported by the impossibility of having a secondary stress (not related to the main one) or an echo of stress (related to main stress) at the right of the main stress. The fact that stress cannot go to the left further than the last, or the next to last syllable of the stem constitutes a further argument in favour of its analysis in demarcating terms.

These observations lead us to analyse more closely the relations between morphological composition and stress. Andrade (1983) presents an analysis that takes into consideration morphological composition. In this study, the stress system of

Portuguese is analysed in terms of trees and constituents, taking into account the morphological structure of the words and assigning a fundamental role to the notion of 'derivational stem'[8] which is somewhat different from the what is commonly referred to as stem. Look for example, at the derivational stems of the words below:

	Word	Derivational stem
(30)	jacaré 'alligator'	jacaré]
(31)	principal 'principal'	principal]
(32)	disciplina 'discipline'	disciplin]a
(33)	categórico 'categorial'	categóric]o
(34)	fonologia 'phonology'	fonologi]a
(35)	composicionalidade 'compositionality'	composicionalidad] e

Thus, the derivational stem corresponds to what remains of the word once we strip the class, number and person markers off. It is, we assume, the basic domain of stress. The apparent complexity of the facts, as one can see, can be reduced to an essential principle: main stress falls on the last vowel of the stem, or on the one before the last if there is an extrametrical vowel.

In this analysis, the right-to-left rhythmic wave cannot be considered a primitive of the stress system but only as a derived effect. Therefore, it is not possible to formalize the regularity according to which main stress falls systematically on the first vowel to the left of the syllable that contains an extrametrical vowel.

In fact, the analysis presupposes two phenomena: in the first place, the assignment of extrametricality, and in second place, the determination of stress placement. This regularity is strong enough for us to postulate that, in fact, it constitutes a single phenomenon: the appearance of a lexically marked morpheme as unstressed imposes the assignment of main stress on its left.

It seems desirable to unify these two phenomena into a single one: the assignment of stress prominence as a consequence of the assignment of lexical atonicity. Finally, the appeal to the notion of extrametricality and its particular use leads us to distinguish two metrical domains. In *falávamos*, for example, the first domain is formed by the stem followed by all the other morphemes except the person and number morphemes. Given the morpheme -*va* is in final position in its domain, its extrametricality may be taken into consideration. But, as -*mos* is, in this analysis, an element dominated by -*la*, it is necessary to consider the whole word as a second metrical domain.

The problem now is that the morpheme -*va* is no longer in final position and, therefore, it should lose its extrametricality. One of the consequences of this analysis is that, independent of their number, morphemes placed at the right of the main stress are in fact being formally treated as extrametrical, given that they are always unstressed. It is their position relative to main stress that explains their atonicity. On the other hand, the atonicity of alternate syllables to the left of the

---

[8] See Harris (1983) for Spanish.

main stress results from the propagation of the rhythmic wave. Keeping the essential intuitions presented in this study, our analysis intends to solve these difficulties, assigning chief importance to the notion of rhythmic wave.

6.6. WORD STRESS AND THE RHYTHMIC WAVE

6.6.1. Nouns and adjectives

We start with the following Rhythmic Principle:

(36) Stress in Portuguese results from the right–left expansion of a rhythmic wave whose initial beat is a trough.

In a 'grid only' framework we parameterize the model in the following way:

(37) In L_0 project the syllables; on L_0, right-to-left perfect grid, trough; on L_1, End Rule, right.

L_0, or line 0, is the line on which every syllable in a word projects a position. L_1 is the line on which rhythmic peaks are marked, L_2 the line on which the strengthened element of L_1 appears.

These parameters would produce, for example, the results in (38).

(38)   a.   b.

L_2 *   *

L_1 . * .   . * . * .

L_0 x x x   x x x x

                 model]o   organizad]o

Within this analysis, main stress assignment and its rhythmic echoes are the result of a double process (Perfect Grid and End Rule). As shown in Laks (1990), this result is not satisfactory as long as main stress assignment and rhythmic echoes are due to two formally distinct processes, and as long as main stress is seen as one of the rhythmic stresses especially promoted. In order to unify these two processes as well as to derive echo stresses as echoes of main stress and take into account the fact that the rhythmic wave presents a decrease of intensity at the edges as it proceeds, we will say that the rhythmic wave peak-trough directly assigns an absolute prominence to the first peak, fusing in this way the effects of PG and ER. We modify (36) into (39).

(39) The rhythmic wave is triggered by trough-first anchored at right, first peak strong.

The parameterization of the model will then be:

(40) In L_0 PG right–left, trough, first peak strong.

(41)   a.   b.

                  *   *

                . * .   . * . * .

              x x x   x x x x x

              model]o   organizad]o

Note that in these examples the rhythmic wave is anchored on the right. We state that when there is no explicitly specified anchorage point as such, it is the right limit that starts the wave.

This first principle of the rhythmic wave (right-to-left, first peak strong, anchored to the right), describes the cases where stress falls on the penultimate syllable of nouns and adjectives. But stress is word final in a certain number of cases. These words have the peculiarity of possessing what we call a defective class marker. To account for the words stressed on the last syllable with the help of the Stress Principle (see (37)) it is enough that we assume that the class marker, though phonetically null, has a rhythmic position. Let us reconsider the proposed parameterization:

(42)   a.   b.   c.   d.

               *   *   *   *

             . * .   * . * .   . * .   * . * .

           x xx   x xx x   x x x   x x x x

           café]⁹   hospital]   model]o   african]o

But we must consider a number of nouns and adjectives that are exceptions to the stress schema that we have just seen. These exceptions are regular in the sense that only the nouns and adjectives that have an explicit class marker are subject to being stressed on the antepenultimate syllable, while those that have a defective class marker may, at the most, be stressed on the penultimate syllable. The treatment of these exceptions clearly depends of the lexicon. We assume that a lexical entry may constrain the rhythmic wave. This constraint is evidenced by the fact that a vowel of a given lexical entry may have a pre-assigned rhythmic trough. Consider útil, (util].]), or aristocrático (aristocratic]o]). In order to correctly derive the stress pattern of these examples it is necessary and sufficient that we specify the anchoring mode of the rhythmic wave produced by principle (39).

(43) Anchoring Principle: (39) is anchored to the first position corresponding to its initial tempo; in the absence of such a position, it anchors to the right limit.

In this way, when a word has no pre-assigned lexical troughs, the rhythmic wave

⁹ In the lexical entries, the phonetically null class markers are depicted by a dot. In a certain sense this represents what Harris (1995) calls a V slot.

anchors on the right limit of the word, as we have already seen. Nevertheless, when the word has one or more lexically pre-assigned troughs, the rhythmic wave anchors on the first trough it encounters when it starts propagating. Recall that this trough position corresponds to its initial beat:

(44)   a.   b.   c.

                            .   . .

Entry:[10]   útil].   catástrof]e   catastrófic]o

The result of (38) and (42) will then be:

(45)   a.   b.   c.
              *   *   *
              * . .   . * . .   * . * . .

              x x x   x x x x   x x x x x
Stress   útil.   catástrofe   catastrófico

Let us observe that one of the effects of the anchoring principle is that when a word has a lexically pre-assigned trough, the positions placed at its right are not affected by the rhythmic wave. This is inherent in the fact that the wave anchors to the first trough position and proceeds from right to left. The positions placed at the right are not affected and are considered to be troughs by default. Let us also note that when a word has several lexically pre-assigned troughs, the rhythmic wave may cause a lexically pre-assigned trough to become stressed if it is in an odd position relatively to the anchoring point of the wave (cf. *catastrófico*), since the rhythmic wave anchors on the first trough it may encounter. In (45c) we have 2 troughs: /i/ anchors the wave and, consequently, the second trough, carried by the /o/, is turned into a peak by the wave. The final /o/ is not affected by the entire process and becomes a trough by default.

The assignment of lexical troughs deserves a commentary. As a number of authors have noted, a certain number of morphemes are stress-repellent. This is, for example, the case in Portuguese of *-ico*, *-voro*, *-gero*, etc, like in *atómico*, *carnívoro* and *lanígero*, respectively. In the cases where several troughs occur, it is sufficient that these morphemes be lexically assigned troughs, for the rhythmic wave, anchoring on the first trough, to reorganize them correctly. This phenomenon is not an arbitrary one. As has already been remarked, in fact, accentuation specifies the form of the terminal part of the intonational curve, 'rhythmic coda' of the curve. So, Latin, for example, imposes a trough rhythmic coda. That is, in other words, the accentual curve in Latin may not be flat; it always needs a resting position. This is the case of Portuguese, too, with the difference that this rhythmic coda (peak–trough) may be assigned to a non-final word position. Thus

---

[10] From now on, a lexical entry consists of a line of segmental bracketed material and optionally of a rhythmic line on which pre-assigned lexical troughs are noted by dots.

we may have penultimate stress in words with a defective class marker, _útil_ [útiɫ], (util].]), or antepenultimate stress, _aristocrático_ (aristocratic]o]) as it may be assigned to a previously trough position, which satisfies the form of the rhythmic coda.

As a final comment on the accentuation of nouns and adjectives, let us remember that it is possible to have a secondary stress on the first syllable of the word, whatever its initial parity with the anchoring point of the rhythmic wave. This initial secondary stress is, thus, non-rhythmic. In case the initial syllable is in an odd position in relation to the anchoring point, its accentual prominence is directly assigned by the rhythmic wave. On the other hand, when its position is even (relative to the anchoring point of the rhythmic wave) it will be assigned a trough. In this case, it is necessary to assign it a peak corresponding to the secondary prominence. In a 'grid only' frame, this is done by invoking End Rule Initial. The accentual peak assigned by ER will be directly adjacent to the peak assigned by the rhythmic wave. We should note that, in Portuguese, these secondary peaks may co-exist, and initial stress may reduce to a trough the peak normally assigned by the rhythmic wave.

So, in the examples below, _africano_ [ɐfɾikénu] 'African', has an initial peak directly assigned by the rhythmic wave. On the contrary, _armoricano_ [ɐɾmurikénu] 'Armorican', has an initial peak assigned by End Rule Initial.

(46) L_2 *   *

     L_1 * . * .   * . . * .

     L_0 x x x x   x x x x x

    Stress: africano   armoricano

To summarize, final, penultimate and antepenultimate stressing in Portuguese nouns and adjectives is adequately analysed by the application of two simple principles: a rhythmic wave principle and an anchoring principle. It is necessary, however, to state that defective class markers are associated with a rhythmic position and that a certain number of morphemes may bear a lexically pre-assigned trough.

6.6.2. Verbs

We have seen that verbs may present stress on the last, penultimate, or antepenultimate syllables.

(47) part_i_ [pɐɾtí] '(I) broke, left'
     fal_a_mos [fɐlámuʃ] 'We spoke'
     atacávamos [ɐtɐkávɐmuʃ] 'We were attacking'

Besides some forms in the future tense, stress on the final syllable is found only in forms in which tense, person and number markers are amalgamated in a single morpheme, which surfaces phonetically without a vowel (but as a glide or nothing) *parti*, [pɐɾtí] *bateu*, [bɐtéw] *falei*, [fɐléj] *falou*, [fɐló].[11] We assume that these markers consist of a single vowel (/i/ or /u/) that will become a glide or will be deleted. With the single application of the rhythmic wave principle and the anchoring principle, we deduce the stress pattern on the last syllable.

(48)   a.   b.   c.   d.

         . * .   . * .   . * .   . * .

         x x x   x x x   x x x   x x x

         parti]i   fala]i   bate]u   falo]u

Penultimate stress corresponds to the regular pattern, according to which the rhythmic wave anchors, by default, on the right limit (*falamos*, *partimos*).

Antepenultimate patterns raise a problem, since, by default, the rhythmic wave may produce only penultimate stress. One can not simply say that antepenultimate stress in verbs can be explained by the presence of an actualized tense marker (*falávamos*, *acabássemos*). We assume that the tense marker has a lexical trough on which the rhythmic wave may anchor.

(49)   a.   b.

  Entry: falávamos   acabássemos

              *   *

            . * . .   * . * . .

            x x x x   x x x x x

  Stress: falávamos   acabássemos

This generalization requires some explanation and some restriction. If the present indicative is distinguished from the present subjunctive by the fact that the latter has a tense marker, it is necessary to assume that this is the only marker which is not a trough, as is shown by *falamos*, *falemos*.

We have, in this way, a tripartition of tense markers. The present indicative is opposed to the present subjunctive because this latter tense has a tense marker which is absent in the first one. Except for the future,[12] all other tenses are opposed to those in the present by the fact that they have a tense marker, which is a lexical trough (cf. 4.2.2).

---

[11] This is the case of the perfect, in the 1st and 3rd persons singular. In *bateu* and *falei*, ⟨u⟩ and ⟨i⟩ represent a phonetic glide. In the dialect we are describing, there is no glide in *falou*, as the diphthong [ow] does not exist, as neither [ij], nor [uw] (see Chapter 2).
    One could also suppose that these amalgamated tense, person and number markers assign a rhythmic position which is phonetically empty to the form in question.
[12] Remember that future tense person markers are the present indicative forms of the verb *haver*, 'to be there'.

(50)

	a.	b.	c.	d.
Entry:	fala]m	fale]mos	falásse]mos	falava]
	*	*	*	*
	*	*	*	*
	x x	x x x	x x x x	x x x
Stress:	falam	falemos	falássemos	falava[13]

Noun–verb minimal pairs that present a stress alternation (cf. (23)) are obviously a morphological problem. This is a problem related to the derivation noun–verb and verb–noun. In fact, both cases can be found. There are nouns, which derive from verbs, and verbs that are derived from nouns (cf. 5.1.2). Generally, nouns derived from verbs present no stress alternation—*ataque* [ɐtákɨ], 'attack', / *atacar* [ɐtɐkáɾ], '(to) attack'—but when a verb is derived from a noun there may be a stress alternation, *jubilar* [ʒubiláɾ], '(to) jubilate' / *júbilo* [ʒúbilu], 'jubilation'. This is consistent with our analysis. In the case of verbs there is no lexically pre-assigned trough. In these circumstances we can understand that whenever a noun is built on a verb there is no lexically pre-assigned trough. On the contrary, when a verb is derived from a noun we may have two different cases:

• The noun has no lexically pre-assigned trough. It may, as such, serve as a verb base. For example, *marca* [máɾkɐ], 'mark' /*marcar* [mɐɾkáɾ], '(to) mark'.
• The noun has a lexically pre-assigned trough. We make the assertion that it is submitted to a generalization grounded on the fact that verb roots have no lexically pre-assigned trough, *fábrica*, [fábɾikɐ], 'factory'/ *fabricar*, [fɐbɾikáɾ], 'to produce'.

This fact may be proven with a neologism test. If a native speaker of Portuguese is asked to create a verb from a (non-existent) noun with stress on the antepenultimate syllable, he will necessarily regularize the root, *piranético/piraneticar*. If the same speaker is asked to create a noun from a (non-existent) verb he may eventually stress the antepenult, if the root ends, for example, in -ic, which is one of the suffixes that have a lexically pre-assigned trough, *mageticar / magético*.

We arrive at a result that is notable for its simplicity and coherence. Portuguese stipulates that the rhythmic coda of the word is necessarily descending (of the type peak–trough), this decrease may operate over several syllables (peak–trough–trough). The apparent complexity of the stress system and its apparent heterogeneity, which oppose nominal stress to verb stress, are actually surface facts.

Thus, with regard to stress in Portuguese, two and only two principles are at work:

1. The rhythmic wave right-to-left, trough, first peak prominent (39).

---

[13] Note that this analysis, which assigns a lexical trough to the tense markers, solves the problems raised with extrametricality. It also correctly leads us to consider a number of apparently regular penultimate stresses as being, in fact, the result of the application of processes that produce an antepenultimate stress, as is the case of *falava* where /va/ is assigned a lexical trough.

2. The wave anchoring principle (43), which places the initial trough on the first pre-assigned trough to be found or, in case of its absence, on the right margin of the word.

These two principles interfere with some morphological peculiarities: the fact that defective class markers present a phonetically empty rhythmic position and some tense markers have a lexically pre-assigned trough. Suffixes and lexical entries may also have pre-assigned troughs. This entails the modification of surface stress patterns.

Finally, the Portuguese stress system appears to be a simple rhythmic system partially masked by morphology.

PHONOLOGICAL PROCESSES

7.1. INTRODUCTION

In the previous chapters a difference has been established among phonological processes that are (a) morphologically conditioned, (b) conditioned by morphology and lexical marks in relation to prosody and (c) merely conditioned by prosodic factors. The former was described in Chapters 4 and 5. The two latter are discussed in the present chapter.

Processes conditioned by inflectional and derivational morphology pertain to the lexical domain. Generally, these processes result from the application of word-formation rules; some of them, however, depend on idiosyncratic properties of the lexical items. As was mentioned in Chapters 4 and 5, such processes are common to both varieties of Portuguese, EP and BP.

Other phonological processes depend on main stress placement and they have to take account of morphological information and/or lexical properties. These processes also belong to the lexical level. They may have exceptions and they must look at the internal structure of the word. Nasalization (cf. 7.2) and Unstressed Vowel System (cf. 7.3) discussed in this chapter, are such processes.

Finally, there are processes conditioned only by the syllabic position of the segments, namely nuclei and codas (cf. 7.4). This set of processes pertains to the post-lexical level and they are free from exception.

The reader will be aware that phonological processes applying on unstressed vowels and those associated with syllable position are responsible for significant differences between European and Brazilian Portuguese. In fact, EP idiosyncrasies mainly concern unstressed vowels, many of which are extremely reduced and often deleted, while BP differs from EP with respect to the phonetic characteristics of consonants in syllable onset as well as in syllable coda. Due to these two broad aspects of Portuguese phonology foreign listeners first encountering the two varieties of Portuguese get the strange impression that they are facing two different languages. Even though we recognize the striking differences at the phonetic level, we assume that there is one single underlying system for the distinct varieties of Portuguese.

7.2. NASALIZATION

One of the most challenging aspects of Portuguese is nasalization. Within standard generative theory this process has been described as the assimilation of nasality by vowels when they are followed by a nasal consonant: as a sequence of the assimilation, the nasal consonant gets deleted. Arguments against the evidence of lexical nasal vowels have been presented in 2.2.2.4, where some of the studies showing this classical view are presented.

Within the multilinear framework, nasalization is analysed as the spreading of the feature [nasal] of a floating autosegment that anchors to a syllable constituent. The latter may be either the nucleus or the onset. We recall, here, some data on nasal vowels (cf. above 2.2.2).

(1) a. Stressed   b. Final stress
    [ḗ] *an*tes 'before'   [ḗ] rom*ã* 'pomegranate'
    [ẽ́] *cen*tro 'centre'
    [ĩ́] *cin*co 'five'   [ĩ́] f*im* 'end'
    [ṍ] ap*on*ta 's/he points'   [ṍ] t*om* 'tone'
    [ṹ] af*un*da 's/he sinks'   [ṹ] com*um* 'common'

(2) Pre-stressed
    [ẽ] *an*dar 'to walk'
    [ẽ] rem*en*dar 'to patch'
    [ĩ] f*in*dar 'to finish'
    [õ] p*on*tinho 'small point'
    [ũ] af*un*dar 'to sink'

Akin to what happens with tone stability, the nasal feature of the segment is preserved in spite of its non-association to a skeletal position. The domain of the floating nasal autosegment is the nucleus to its left: it spreads its nasal feature over it.

The nasal floating segment differs from the underspecified segments /l/, /ɾ/ and /s/ discussed below in 7.4.1.1 and 7.4.1.2 in that the former has no position in the skeleton, while the latter do. With respect to the liquids and the fricative, when their position in the skeleton is associated with the coda, they have a consonantal realization (see (20)–(24) and (26)). In the only case where there is no realization—zero realization of the /ɾ/, see (23)—the root is delinked from its skeletal position, but no feature is spread.

The nasalization process differs from the processes just mentioned: in fact, the feature nasal is always maintained, whether it is spread over the preceding vowel (such as in (3)), or it is realized as a nasal consonant (as it is represented in (6)). See in (3), below, the representation of these two kinds of floating segments, nasal and liquids/fricative, prior to their associations.

(3) a. Nasalization

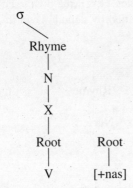

b. Liquids and fricative

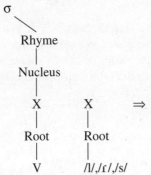 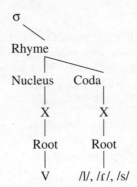

See now the examples in (4) and (5).

(4) a. [ẽ] irmã 'sister'　　　　b. [ɐn] irmanar 'fraternize'
　　　[ẽ] sã 'healthy' (fem.)　　　[ɐn] sanidade 'sanity'
　　　[ĩ] fim 'end'　　　　　　　[in] finalizar 'finalize'
　　　[õ] som 'sound'　　　　　　[un] sonoro 'sonorous'

(5) a. [ẽw̃] pão 'bread'　　　　b. [ɐn] panificação 'bakery'
　　　[ẽw̃] limão 'lemon'　　　　[un] limonada 'lemonade'
　　　[ẽw̃] irmão 'brother'　　　[ɐn] irmanar 'to fraternize'

The occurrence of final nasalized diphthongs in (5a) has already been explained in 4.2.1.2.2: the nasal auto-segment anchors in the nucleus and the phonetic glide also becomes nasalized. The problem we face now is the presence of the nasal consonant in the examples included in (4b) and (5b). Apparently, it is the same floating segment that is realized as a consonant. This is true in these words because the nuclei in (4b) and (5b) are followed by an empty onset, unlike the examples in (1) and (2), where the nuclei were in word-final position or followed by a lexically filled onset. Due to the fact it is attached to an onset, the nasal auto-segment has to be realized as a consonant. Given the unmarked consonants are anterior coronals, the consonant is specified by default as an [n]. See the representation in (6).

(6)

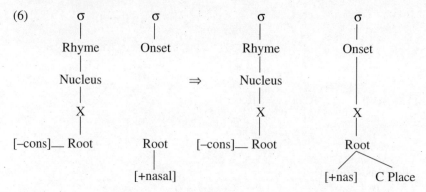

In the alternations of the prefix /in/ or /en/ (see (7) below) there is a good evidence of both realizations of the nasal autosegment. We see in (7a) that the nasal segment anchors in the nucleus because the onset of the following syllable is filled. In (7b) the segment of the same prefix fills the empty onset and it is realized as a coronal consonant.

(7) a. [ĩ] *in*tenção 'intention'
         [ĩ] *in*capaz 'unable'
         [ĩ] *im*pério 'empire'

         [ẽ] *en*riquecer 'to enrich'
         [ẽ] *en*fiada 'file'
         [ẽ] *em*barcação 'ship'

     b. [in] *in*acabado 'unfinished'
         [in] *in*oportuno 'inopportune'
         [in] *in*existente 'inexistent'

         [in] *en*amorar 'to fascinate'
         [in] *en*altecer 'to exalt'

There are, however, some words that do not evidence any nasalization even though they are related to others that present a phonetic realization of the nasal autosegment (e.g. *lua* [lúɐ] 'moon' / *lunar* [lunáɾ] 'lunar', *boa* [bóɐ] 'kind' / *bondade* [bõdádɨ] 'kindness'). We propose that the empty onset is only filled in derived words like *irmanar* [[[irman]$_{Root}$ a]$_{St}$ r]$_W$ or *inacabado* [[in [acab]$_{Root}$ a]$_{St}$ do]$_W$ or *lunar* [[lun] $_{Root}$ a]$_{St}$ r]$_W$ and not in inflectional ones such as *lua* [[lu]$_{Root}$ a]$_W$.[1] In this specific case, the process of onset filling is morphologically conditioned.

---

[1] On this question see Andrade and Kihm (1987).

Let us now look at the diphthongs in (8) (also previously included in (5a)).

(8) [ẽw̃] p*ão* 'bread'
    [ẽw̃] lim*ão* 'lemon'
    [ẽw̃] irm*ão* 'brother'

In these examples, lexically, only the diphthong of *irmão* has two skeletal positions, due to the fact that the glide results from the attachment of the class marker: [irma[+nasal]$_{Root}$ o]$_W$. The other [ẽw̃] diphthongs correspond to a single skeletal position.

There is another type of nasal diphthong that also corresponds to a single skeletal position. We recall some examples previously presented, in 3.2.2.1.

(9) [ẽj̃][2] hom*em* 'man'
    [ẽj̃]   prend*em* 'they fast'
    [ẽw̃] falar*am* 'they have talked'
    [ẽw̃] pair*am* 'they soar'

These diphthongs occur at the end of words carrying stress on the penultimate syllable. The glide of these final unstressed diphthongs, either in words like *homem* or in verbal endings like in *pairam*, is epenthetic. This means that it does not exist in the lexical representation but that it is introduced after the spreading of nasality by the diphthongization rule represented in (10). The inserted glide in verb forms has the same V-place as the preceding vowel (e.g. *prendem* / prend e+[+nasal]/ [prẽdẽj̃], *falaram* /fal a+ra [+nasal]/ [fɐláɾẽw̃]). See (10).

(10)   V [+nasal] #   ⇒   V G [+nasal] #

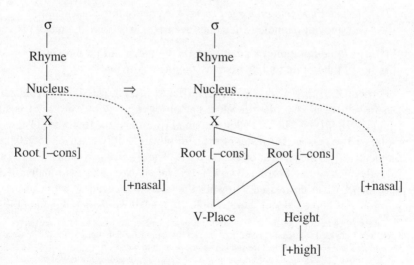

---

[2] As has been said earlier on, the nasal diphthong [ẽj̃] in European Portuguese corresponds to the Brazilian [ẽj̃].

There is strong evidence for the proposed floating segment in the cases mentioned above, where it is realized as a projection of the nasal feature and does not correspond to any skeletal position. Autosegmental theory is clearly a more adequate framework to account for nasalization than other previous generative theories.

In (11) we have included some examples where nasal consonants are not floating autosegments, but are lexically specified.[3]

(11)
Labial	Coronal	Dorsal
ca*m*a [m] 'bed'	ca*n*a [n] 'cane'	ca*nh*a [ɲ] 'white rum'
u*m*a [m] 'one'	u*n*a [n] 'unified'	u*nh*a [ɲ] 'nail'

7.3. UNSTRESSED VOWELS

7.3.1. General processes

European Portuguese is a language whose unstressed vowels are reduced and frequently deleted.[4] This is most remarkable in post-stressed and final position. We shall see further on that some exceptions to this reduction occur namely in prestressed syllable (see 7.3.3).

In (12) we include a short sentence with two phonetic transcriptions corresponding to the EP pronunciation: one of them tentatively represents a monitored pronunciation, (13a), the other corresponds to what is usually called fast-speech, (13b). It should be noted that the phonological processes under discussion in this sentence may be observed in words produced in isolation.[5]

(12) *O estudo da fonologia exige precisão, rigor e muita paciência.*
'The study of phonology demands accuracy, strictness and much patience.'

(13) a. [u ʃtúdu dɐ funuluʒíɐ izíʒɨ pɾɨsizɐ̃w̃ ʀigóɾ i mũ ĩtɐ pɐsiésiɐ]
(13) b. [u ʃtú dɐ fnulʒíɐ izíʒ pɾsizɐ̃w̃ ʀigóɾ i mũĩtɐ pɐsjésjɐ]

Portuguese [ɨ] can always be deleted ([izíʒɨ] / [izíʒ]; [pɾɨsizɐ̃w̃] / [pɾsizɐ̃w̃]). Unstressed [u] is also often deleted, namely when it is in word final position ([ʃtúdu] / [ʃtúd]) or when it follows a labial ([funuluʒíɐ] / [fnulʒíɐ]). These two unstressed vowels are the result of the neutralization of two sets of vowels: most frequently, [ɨ] is the realization of non-high [–back] vowels (/ɛ/ and /e/, see (14a)); [u] is the realization of [+round] vowels (/ɔ/, /o/, /u/, see (14b)). Normally, /i/ does not change when unstressed.[6] Vowel /a/ is always realized as [ɐ] in unstressed position. See some pairs of morphologically related words in (14a) and (14b).

---

[3] In Brazilian Portuguese, the lexical nasal consonant spreads the nasal feature over the preceding vowel when stressed (e.g. *cama* [kɐ̃mɐ]). Moreover, in many Brazilian dialects, the dorsal nasal consonant loses its [+consonant] feature and is realized as a glide: *unha* [új̃ɐ].

[4] See above (2.2.2.3) on the difference between EP and BP, regarding unstressed vowels.

[5] Processes that apply in connected speech–external sandhi– are treated in the next section.

[6] In some contexts, especially in final position, unstressed /i/ can also be realized as [ɨ]: fer*i*r [í] 'to hurt' / fer*e* [ɨ] 's/he, it hurts'.

(14) a. d*e*do [é]   d*e*dada [ɨ] 'finger' / 'fingerprint'
      bat*e*r [é]   bat*e* [ɨ] 'to beat' / 'you beat'
      f*e*sta [ɛ]   f*e*stejo [ɨ] 'feasting' / 'festivity'
      m*e*l [ɛ]   m*e*lado [ɨ] 'honey' / 'sweetened with honey'
      f*i*ta [í]   f*i*tinha [i] 'band' / 'small band'

    b. f*o*go [ó]   f*o*gueira [u] 'fire' / 'bonfire'
      p*o*rta [ɔ]   p*o*rteira [u] 'door' / 'doorkeeper'
      f*u*ro [ú]   f*u*rado [u] 'hole' / 'pierced'
      g*a*to [á]   g*a*tinho [ɐ] 'cat' / 'small cat'
      vir*a*r [á]   vir*a* [ɐ] 'to turn' / 'you turn'

Generally, when unstressed, EP [–back] and [+round] vowels are high.[7] In other words, the general rule of unstressed vowels is a *raising rule*. Non-back vowels are also retracted, in most cases.

As said above, nasal vowels are always non-low.[8] When unstressed, they do not trigger the raising rule:

(15) v*e*nto [ẽ́]   v*e*ntoso [ẽ] 'wind' / 'windy'
     c*a*nto [ẽ́]   c*a*ntar [ẽ] 'song' / 'to sing'
     p*o*nto [ṍ]   ap*o*ntar [õ] 'point' / 'to point'

7.3.2. Regular exceptions

Unstressed vowels in (16) are not reduced. See the examples.

(16) s*a*lto [á]   s*a*ltar [a] 'leap' / 'to jump'
     m*a*l [á]   m*a*ldade [a] 'evil' / 'badness'
     r*e*lva [ɛ]   r*e*lvado [ɛ] 'grass' / 'grassplot'
     b*e*lo [ɛ]   b*e*ldade [ɛ] 'beautiful' / 'beauty'
                      incr*í*vel [ɛ] 'incredible'
                      am*á*vel [ɛ] 'kind'

     g*o*lpe [ɔ]   g*o*lpear [ɔ] 'stroke' / 'to strike'
     v*o*lta [ɔ]   v*o*ltar [ɔ] 'return' / 'to return'
     s*o*lta [ó]   s*o*ltar [o] 'free' / 'to untie'
     v*o*lvo [ó]   v*o*lver [o] 'I revolve' / 'to revolve'
                      álc*o*ol [ɔ] 'alcohol'

All of these vowels are nuclei of closed syllables with an /l/-filled coda.

Vowels that belong to syllables whose nucleus contains a glide are also exceptions to the general process of unstressed vowels[9]. See (17).

---

[7] In BP (dialects under study) the same vowels are mid.

[8] A low nasal vowel, [ã], occurs at the phonetic level in connected speech, as we will see below in 7.5.

[9] Portuguese dialects that have the diphthong [ow], do not reduce the diphthong [ow] in unstressed position: m*o*uro [ów] 'Moor' / m*o*uraria [ow] 'quarter where the Moors lived'. The EP dialects under study do not have this diphthong, but the resulting vowel [o] is not raised when unstressed.

(17) b*ai*rro [áj]   b*ai*rrista [aj] 'district' / 'regionalist'
     g*ai*ta [áj]   g*ai*tinha [aj] 'flute' / 'small flute'
     c*oi*ta [ój]   c*oi*tado [oj] 'pain' / 'poor fellow'
     c*oi*sa [ój]   c*oi*sinha [oj] 'thing' / 'little thing'
     b*oi* [ój]   b*oi*ada [oj] 'ox' / 'herd of oxen'

     c*au*sa [áw]   c*au*sar [aw] 'cause' / 'to cause'
     p*au*sa [áw]   p*au*sado [aw] 'pause' / 'paused'
     d*eu*s [éw]   end*eu*sar [ew] 'god' / 'to deify'
     pn*eu* [éw]   pn*eu*mático [ew] 'tyre'

Unstressed vowels in words like *invasor* [ĩvazóɾ] 'invader', *objecção*
[ɔbʒɛsẽ̃w] 'objection', or *adopção* [ɐdɔsẽ̃w] 'adoption' (see Chapter 2, note 7)
are exceptional cases as non-high vowels are maintained unreduced in the pre-
stressed position. They result from historical factors in EP and must be marked in
the lexicon.

7.3.3. Vocalic processes and lexical phonology

Unstressed vowels that are followed by a glide or belong to a syllable closed by
an /l/ are immune to the application of the general raising rule. The same happens
to the true exceptions (e.g. *invasor* [ĩvazóɾ] or *objecção* [ɔbʒɛsẽ̃w], see above)
that are marked in the lexicon in order not to undergo the raising rule. The remaining unstressed vowels trigger this specific rule.

As has been said above (see 2.4.1), the raising rule deals only with features
depending on the class node height: in EP all [–high] vowels, that is /e, ɛ, o, ɔ, a/
become [–low], and /e, ɛ, o, ɔ/ also become [+high] (see 7.3.1); in BP /e, ɛ, o, ɔ/
become [–low] and /a/ is not raised.

Given the exceptions mentioned above, we may conclude that the raising rule
applies in the lexical component (see Vigário (1997a) in support of this and for
further arguments). Unlike the rules analysed previously, this is a changing rule:
it changes the values of height features. Again, its application argues in favour of
the independency of the class node height. The rule in question provides further
support to the proposal that (a) height and V-place are two independent class
nodes and (b) the height node is specific to vocalic segments.

Due to the fact that the central vowel [ɨ] does not occur in BP, and has restricted
occurrence in EP (it only may occur between consonants and in word final position, after a consonant), we may conclude that its retraction is post-lexical.
Moreover, in fast speech this vowel is always deleted. We can hypothesize that
the deleted vowel is a [–back] vowel, [i], which centralizes (becomes [+back])
only in monitored pronunciation. In any event, this centralization belongs to the
post-lexical component.

7.4. PROCESSES CONDITIONED BY SYLLABLE STRUCTURE

7.4.1. Consonants in coda

In Portuguese, as in many languages, only coronals can fill a syllable coda at the lexical level. As most phonologists point out, coronal consonants are the least marked ones: they undergo place assimilation and neutralization more often than non-coronals; they are also the most frequently occurring consonants in natural languages. Unmarked coronals are [+anterior], universally. Thus, we take the view that coronal consonants are underspecified at the lexical level for C-place in EP.[10] Given the fact that codas are associated with coronals, we obviously agree with the following Coda Condition

'Codas may not have place features' (Yip, 1991: 62)

Consonants in coda are floating segments up to the post-lexical level, where they are associated to their position in the syllable (see *coda association convention* in 3.4). As a consequence of their syllabification, these consonants trigger specific coda rules: the latter fill the blank values of place.

7.4.1.1. Liquids

In Chapter 3 we listed the most frequent realizations in European Portuguese and Brazilian Portuguese of the underspecified liquids occurring in syllable coda. The examples given then are repeated below in (18a and b).

(18) EP BP[11]

a. *par* [páɾ] [páɾ] 'pair'
       [páʀ]
       [páx]

   ser [séɾ] [séɾ] 'being'
       [séʀ]
       [séx]

   cor [kóɾ] [kóɾ] 'colour'
       [kóʀ]
       [kóx]

   vir [víɾ] [víɾ] 'to come'
       [víʀ]
       [víx]

   parte [páɾ]te [páɾ]te 'part'
       [páʀ]te
       [páx]te

---

[10] Cf. 2.4. with respect to underspecification; and on coronals see Paradis and Prunet, 1991: 1–25.

[11] The alternations in the realization of the tap and the trill in BP are described in Callou and Leite, 1990: 72–6. The authors also refer that this consonant may be realized as an *aspiration* and may have *no phonetic realization*; when the following word begins with a vowel it is realized as a tap. See also above, 2.2.1.1.

	corte [kɔ́ɾ]te	[kɔ́ɾ]te 'cut'
		[kɔ́R]te
		[kɔ́x]te
	perda [péɾ]da	[péɾ]da 'loss'
		[péR]da
		[péx]da
	curta [kúɾ]ta	[kúɾ]to 'short'
		[kúR]to
		[kúx]to

	EP	BP
b.	*mal* [máɫ]	[máw] 'evil'
	mel[méɫ]	[méw] 'honey'
	sol [sɔ́ɫ]	[sɔ́w] 'sun'
	funil [funíɫ]	[funíw] 'funnel'
	malta [máɫ]ta	[máw]ta 'people' (pop.)
	feltro [féɫ]tro	[féw]tro 'felt'
	polpa [póɫ]pa	[pów]pa 'pulp'

To explain the phonetic realizations of liquids in coda it is worth saying that /ɾ/ and /l/ are sufficiently specified by two features: [+consonant] and [+sonorant]. Nasals are also [+sonorant] but they are marked with respect to the other sonorants: segments are [−nasal] by default unless they are specified as [+nasal]. As we said in 2.4.2, specification as [+lateral] distinguishes /l/ from /ɾ/.

Let us now examine the examples included in (18a) above. In EP the specification of an underlying /ɾ/ in coda position is the result of the application of a default rule. As we see in (19), this rule fills in the value of the feature that depends on the coronal node.

(19) *Default rule:* [ɾ]: rhotic in coda in EP

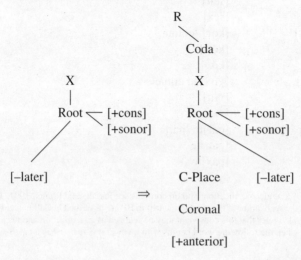

In BP there are other realizations of /ɾ/ as we see in (18a): [ʀ] and [x]. These realizations are [+back] and result from the application of specific coda rules (see the representation of these rules in (20) and (21) below). With respect to the other liquid, /l/, it also has a [+back] realization both in BP and in EP, namely either as a velarized lateral, [ɫ], or as a back glide, [w] (see again the examples in (18b)). Thus, phonetically, coda liquids in general are backed, relatively to their default specifications.

It is worth pointing out that the different realizations of the liquids in this position do not result from a changing-rule but from a *filling-rule* that fills the feature [back] with a [+] (see below, rules (20) and (21)). The realization of /ɾ/ as [x] also involves the *delinking* of the feature [sonorant].

Fricatives can be [+voice] or [–voice]. Rule (21) fills the voice feature with a [–].

(20) *Coda rule:* /ɾ/ → [ʀ] (BP – uvular rhotic)

(21) *Coda rule:*/ɾ/ → [x] (BP – velar voiceless fricative)

The other two realizations of /ɾ/, aspiration and zero (see note 11), also result from the delinking of a set of class nodes: [h] involves the delinking of [+consonant], and consequently, the dissociation of C-Place, whereas in the case of the zero realization, it is the root that is dissociated. These processes are represented in (22) and (23).

(22) *Coda rule:* /ɾ/→ [h] (BP – aspiration)

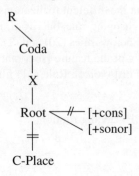

(23) *Coda rule:* /ɾ/→ ø (BP – zero realization)

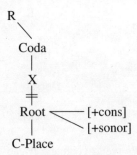

It must be pointed out that the delinking of [+sonorant] in (21) and of [+consonant] in (22) (an aspiration is a sonorant but it is not a consonant) provides an argument in favour of our proposal that [consonant] and [sonorant] are two separate features directly depending on the root.

At the phonetic level, EP laterals are velarized in syllable coda: in fact they are assigned the secondary place features [+back] and [+high] that depend from the vocalic node.

Phonetically, European Portuguese coda laterals correspond to back glides in Brazilian Portuguese. Similarly to what happens with inflection of nominals ending in /l/ (see above 4.2.1.2.1), the [+consonant] feature of the lateral is delinked. As was said earlier on, only consonants may occur in coda. Thus, the resulting glide is automatically associated with the nucleus. Due to the fact that the realization of this lateral in coda is [+back], the resulting segment is the phonetic [+back] glide, an [w].

See in (24a) and (24b) the representation of EP velarization and BP gliding of the lateral in syllable coda.

(24) a. EP lateral velarization

b. BP lateral gliding

The disassociation of the [+consonant] feature in (24b) entails that the segment loses its lateral feature: it is no longer a consonant and it becomes dominated by the vocalic node.

7.4.1.2. *Fricative /s/*

The fricative occurring in syllable coda is also a coronal; similarly to coda /ɾ/ and /l/, it has no place features at the lexical level. Place features are introduced by default when a specific rule does not apply. In fact, in the Portuguese dialects under study, the fricative in syllable final position triggers a specific rule: it is realized as [–anterior], namely as an alveopalatal (see 2.3). It is, thus, produced with a more retracted articulation than the unmarked one ([+anterior]). Furthermore, when followed by another consonant, the fricative agrees in voicing with the following consonant. See examples in (25).

(25) Fricative /s/ in coda

    a. [ʃ] [–voice]

        tasca [táʃkɐ] 'tavern'
        aspecto [ɐʃpétu] 'aspect'
        susto [súʃtu] 'fright'
        peste [péʃtɨ] 'plague'
        asfixia [ɐʃfiksíɐ] 'asphyxia'
        nascer [nɐʃséɾ] 'to born'

    b. [ʒ] [+voice]

        sismo [síʒmu] 'seism'
        Israel [iʒʀɐél] 'Israel'
        desdita [dɨʒdítɐ] 'misfortune'
        esbater [iʒbɐtéɾ] 'to fade'
        deslize [dɨʒlízɨ] 'slip'
        rusga [ʀúʒgɐ] 'clamour'
        Lisboa [liʒbóɐ] 'Lisbon'
        desnudar [dɨʒnudáɾ] 'to undress'

This assimilation process is represented in (26):

(26) Fricative /s/ assimilation

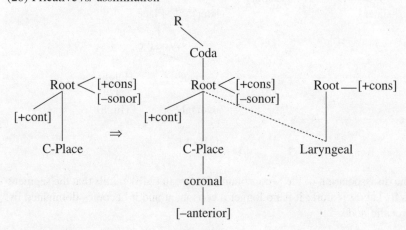

7.4.2. Brazilian plosives in onset

In most dialects of BP, coronal plosives in syllable onset occur as affricates when followed by an [i]. This takes place independently of stress placement, as examples in (27a) and (27b) indicate.

(27) a. Stressed [i]   Unstressed [i]

     tia [t͡ʃ]ia 'aunt'   *bate* ba[t͡ʃ]e 's/he beats'
     atira a[t͡ʃ]ira 's/he shoots'   *atirar* a[t͡ʃ]irar 'to shoot'
     sentia sen[t͡ʃ]ia 's/he felt'   *sentimento* sen[t͡ʃ]imento 'feeling'
     tira [t͡ʃ]ira 'band'   *tirar* [t͡ʃ]irar 'to take away'

    b.

     dia [d͡ʒ]ia 'day'   *pede* pe[d͡ʒ]e '(s/he) asks'
     dita [d͡ʒ]ita 'fortune'   *sede* se[d͡ʒ]e 'thirst'
     bendita ben[d͡ʒ]ita 'blessed'   *bendizer* ben[d͡ʒ]izer 'to bless'
     acredita acre[d͡ʒ]ita 's/he believes' *acreditar* acre[d͡ʒ]itar 'to believe'

As has been said in 2.2.1.2, given the fact that [t] and [d] occur in different contexts, while [t͡ʃ] and [d͡ʒ] only appear in this specific context in question, we may conclude that the phonological segments are /t/ and /d/ and the affricates emerge as a result of the environment. Linguists do not agree with respect to the representation of these contour segments:[12] some analyses propose two roots linked to one skeletal position, others characterize them by a sequence of features linked to a single root node (for discussion of these two proposals see Clements and Hume, 1995: 254–6).

In order to choose between the two types of analyses, it is worth comparing these affricates with light diphthongs. These latter occur in unstressed final position of 3rd person plural of verb forms or result from morphological alternation with a single vowel (see 3.3.1 on this question). In these cases both the vowel and glide are linked to a single skeletal position; but they are associated with separate root nodes because they have different places of articulation (e.g. *falam* fal[ẽw̃]). Affricates are different: phonetically, they have a stop phase followed by a fricative release, but both elements correspond to a single C-place node. Thus we agree with different authors who consider these consonants as consisting of 'a single root node dominating a single specification for place but two specifications for continuancy' (Broselow, 1995: 187). In Portuguese, place specification results from the spread of the vowel features—[+high] and [–back]. The representation of the BP affricates is as in (28).

---

[12] As far as affricates are concerned, we do not make a distinction between contour segments and complex segments; cf. Kenstowicz (1994: 498–506).

(28) Brazilian affricates

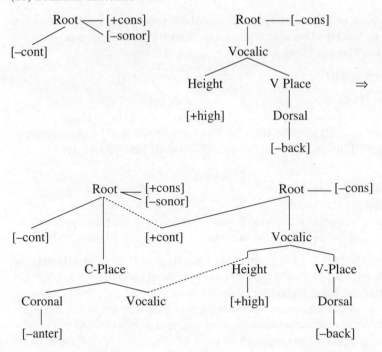

7.5. CONNECTED SPEECH (EUROPEAN PORTUGUESE)

In connected speech, the fact that the end of a word is in contact with the beginning of the following one may induce some phonetic modifications with relation to the pronunciation of words in quotation form–external sandhi. Naturally, this will only take place if there is a prosodic relationship between successive words.

Let us consider the cases where some modification may occur:
• the first word ends in a consonant and the second one begins with a consonant;
• the first word ends in a vowel or a glide and the second one begins with a vowel.
Phonologically, the only word final consonants are, as we have seen, /l/, /ɾ/ and /s/ (see 3.2.3). Their behaviour is perfectly regular. See in (29) final /l/ and /s/:[13]

(29) a. mi*l f*olhas [míɫfóʎɐʃ] 'thousand leaves'
         mi*l v*acas [míɫvákɐʃ] 'thousand cows'

    b. doi*s p*atos [dójʃpátuʃ] 'two ducks'
        doi*s l*ivros [dójʒlívɾuʃ] 'two books'
        dua*s a*lmas [dúɐzáɫmɐʃ] 'two souls'

---

[13] As we see in (29b), it does not matter if the fricative is spelled with a ⟨s⟩ or a ⟨z⟩.

dez patos [déʃpátuʃ] 'ten ducks'
dez livros [déʒlívɾuʃ] 'ten books'
dez almas [dézáɫmɐʃ] 'ten souls'

Final /ɾ/ behaves according to the kind of word initial rhotic the speaker uses (see above, 2.2.1.1). If the speaker has a multiple alveolar one, [r], final /ɾ/ disappears; otherwise it is kept.

(30) por regra [puɾ régɾɐ] [purégɾɐ] 'by rule'
por regra [puɾ ʀégɾɐ] [puɾʀégɾɐ] 'by rule'

In other cases, when consonants come in contact in final and initial position due to vowel deletion, if both have in common the major and place features, one of the following phenomena takes place: they either become a single consonant, (31a), or a geminate, (31b).

(31) a. dois chás [dójʃáʃ] 'two teas'
dois gémeos [dójʒémjuʃ] 'two twins'

b. sabe bem [sáb:ẽj] 'knows well, tastes good'
disse sim [dís:ĩ] 'said yes'
amor de Deus [d:éwʃ] 'God's love'

Sequences like /sʃ/, [ʃʃ] and /sʒ/, [ʒʒ] are always simplified, even in careful speech.[14] Other sequences result in a geminate as it is shown in (31b).

As a matter of fact, stress plays a more important role than our description suggests. If phrase stress is not on the second word, that is, if the second word is not in phrase final position, both consonants just become a single one, as we see in (32).

(32) Faculdade de Letras[15] [fɐkuɫdádlétɾɐʃ] 'Faculty of Letters'
cidade luz[16] [sidádlúʃ] 'light city'
cidade de luz [sidádlúʃ] 'city of light'
cidade do Cabo [sidádukábu] 'Capetown'

sabe bem demais [sábẽjdmájʃ] 'tastes too good'
sabe bestialmente bem [sábʃtjáɫmétbẽj] 'tastes terribly good'

disse sinceramente não [dísĩsɛɾɐmétnẽw̃] 'said sincerely no'
disse semelhante coisa [dísmʎẽtkójzɐ] 'said such a thing'
dissemelhante coisa [dismʎẽtkójzɐ] 'inequal thing'

---

[14] In casual speech, /ss/, [ʃs], and /sz/, [ʒz], are also simplified, in [ʃ] and [ʒ], respectively: dois sapatos [dójʃɐpátuʃ], 'two shoes', dois zeros [dójʒɛɾuʃ], 'two zeros'. In word internal position a similar thing happens: nascer [nɐʃséɾ], 'to be born', piscina [piʃsínɐ], 'swimming pool', are normally pronounced [nɐʃéɾ] and [piʃínɐ]. In northern and eastern dialects they are realized as [nɐséɾ] and [pisínɐ].

[15] Another case of haplology is Campo Pequeno [kẽpu] [pikénu], 'Small field, a Lisbon's Quarter', which is practically always pronounced [kɐpkénu]. See also Viana (1892), Andrade and Viana (1992) and Frota (1994).

[16] This example just serves to show that it is homophonous with the next one.

With respect to non-consonantal segments, the most common changes are shown in (33)–(39).

(33) a anona [anónɐ] 'one anon'
    disse a Anita [dísanítɐ] 'Anita said'

(34) diga Aldina [dígałdínɐ] 'say Aldina'
    diga aldeia [dígałdéjɐ] 'say village'

(35) disse à Anita [dísanítɐ] 'said to Anita'
    disse à Nita [dísanítɐ] 'said to Nita'
    à animal [animáł] 'as an animal'

(36) a. da Antónia [dãtɔ́njɐ] 'Antónia's'
       casa antiga [kázãtígɐ] 'old house'

    b. água é líquido [ágwélíkidu] 'water is liquid'
       rapariga honesta [ʀɐpɐrígɔnéʃtɐ] 'honest girl'

(37) a. salto alto [sáłtwáłtu] 'high jump'
       quarto acto [kwártwátu] 'fourth act'
       mato esta [mátwéʃtɐ] 'I kill this one'
       casaco amplo [kɐzákwɐ̃plu] 'large coat'

    b. como uvas pretas [kómúvɐʒprétɐʃ] 'I eat black raisins'
       salto altíssimo [sáłtałtísimu] 'a very high jump'
       salto alto demais[sáłtáłtdmájʃ] 'an excessively high jump'
       casaco amplíssimo [kɐzákɐ̃plísimu] 'very large coat'
       casaco amplo demais[kɐzákɐ̃pludmájʃ] 'an excessively large coat'
       mato esta mosca [mátéʃtɐmɔ́ʃkɐ] 'I kill this fly'

(38) táxi amarelo [táksjɐmɐrélu] 'yellow taxi'
    júri actual [ʒúɾjɐtwáł] 'present jury'

As can been seen in (33)–(38), [ɐ], [u] and [i] are the only unstressed vowels occurring in final position. In the previous sets, second word initial vowels are unstressed except for some of the examples in (36b) and (37b), and the items of (37a).

With respect to (33)–(37), it may be observed that whenever the initial vowel is unstressed, the final one is not present. If the initial vowel of the second word is stressed (some examples in (36b), (37a) and (37b)), the final vowel of the first word may disappear ((36b), (37b)) or become a glide ((37a)).

How can we predict when a final unstressed vowel disappears altogether?

The answer has once more to do with stress, but not only with word stress. If the initial vowel of the second word is unstressed or bears a stress which is not the phrasal stress, then the word final vowel disappears; otherwise it is kept: *salto altíssimo* [sáłtałtísimu], *casaco amplo demais* [kɐzákɐ̃pludmájʃ], but *salto alto* [sáłtwáłtu].

Grammatical monosyllables like *que* [kɨ] 'that', *se* [sɨ] 'if' and *de* [dɨ] 'of' have a glide before a word initial vowel (see (39)).[17]

(39) qu*e* eu vá [kjewvá] 'that I go'
o facto d*e* eu falar [ufáktudjewfɐláɾ] 'the fact that I speak'
s*e* eu falar [sjewfɐláɾ] 'if I speak'
porqu*e* é que foi [puɾkjɛ́kfój]] 'why did you go'
o qu*e* é que foi [ukjɛ́kfój] 'what was it'

Numerals have a specific behaviour. *Doze* 'twelve', *treze* 'thirteen', *catorze* 'fourteen', *quinze* 'fifteen' and *vinte* 'twenty' have a [j] whenever the following word begins with a vowel (see (40a)), while *sete*, 'seven', *nove*, 'nine', *dezassete* 'seventeen' and *dezanove* 'nineteen' do not alternate (see (40b)).

(40) a. doze horas [dózjɔ́ɾɐʃ] '12 hours'
treze horas [tɾézjɔ́ɾɐʃ] '13 hours'[18]
catorze horas [kɐtóɾzjɔ́ɾɐʃ] '14 hours'
quinze horas [kĩzjɔ́ɾɐʃ] '15 hours'
vinte horas [vĩtjɔ́ɾɐʃ] '20 hours'

b. sete horas [sétɔ́ɾɐʃ] '7 hours'
nove horas [nɔvɔ́ɾɐʃ] '9 hours'
dezassete horas [dzɐsétɔ́ɾɐʃ] '17 hours'
dezanove horas [dzɐnɔ́vɔ́ɾɐʃ] '19 hours'

Another interesting fact concerns certain verb forms before a phonetic [u] or [ɐ].

(41) a. disse o Júlio [dísuʒúlju] 'Júlio said'
disse asneiras [dísɐʒnéjɾɐʃ] 's/he said foolishness'
disse-o [dísju] 's/he, you said it'

b. feche o livro [féʃulívɾu] 'close the book'
feche uniforme [féʃunifɔ́ɾm] 'close uniformly'
feche-o [féʃju] 'close it'

c. passe a camisa [pásɐkɐmízɐ] 'iron the shirt'
passe acima [pásɐsímɐ] 'pass above'
passe-a [pásjɐ] 'pass it'

The glide appears obligatorily every time the following [u] or [ɐ] are pronouns, not when they are determiners or anything else, (see above the third example of (41a), (41b) and (41c)). In other words, the glide appears every time both vowels belong to the same phonological word, but not between boundaries (*passe-a*

[17] Probably because [ɨ] in lexical words normally has no phonetic realization in final position, a number of dialects and styles has no [j] even in grammatical words. That is why the examples in (39) may have no [j].

[18] For example, *treze e quinze* [tɾézikĩz] is ambiguous as it may mean '3 hours and 15 minutes' or '13 hours and 15 minutes'.

[passe-a], *passe a camisa* [passe] [a camisa], *disse-o* [disse-o], *disse asneiras* [disse] [asneiras]).[19]

We summarize the changes of (33)–(39), according to the final and initial word sounds, in Table 7.1.

TABLE 7.1

	Word-final position	Word-initial position	Result
(33)	ɐ	ɐ	a
(34)	ɐ	a	a
(35)	a	ɐ	a
(36a)	ɐ	ẽ	ã
(36b)	ɐ	V	V
(37a)	u	V	wV
(37b)	u	V	V
(38)	i	V	jV
(39)	ɨ	V	jV

7.6. CONCLUSION

We have presented an overview of the phonology of Portuguese which has included interrelated aspects of morphology. We hope that the data offered in the course of our discussion are sufficiently enlightening to allow a fair assessment of the richness of Portuguese phonology. We also hope to have demonstrated that current theoretical models for analysing human languages can satisfactorily explain the peculiarities of this Romance language.

[19] See the analysis of this problem also in Vigário (1997a).

REFERENCES

Abaurre, M. B. M. (1991), 'Análise fonológica do comportamento de elementos átonos nas unidades rítmicas (pés) do Português Brasileiro falado: ênclises e próclises fonológicas'. MS, Campinas: UNICAMP–IEL.

Albano, L. (1992), 'A sílaba portuguesa como questão empírica na fonologia'. D. E. L. T. A., 8: 105–24 (São Paulo, special issue).

Ali, M. de Said (1921–3), Gramática histórica da língua portuguesa. São Paulo: Melhoramentos.

Allen, M. (1978), 'Morphological Investigations'. Ph.D., Connecticut University.

Anderson, S. R. (1985), Phonology in the Twentieth Century. Chicago: University of Chicago Press.

Anderson, S. R. (1988), 'Morphological Theory', in F. Newmeyer (ed.): 146–91.

Anderson, S. R. (1992), A-Morphous Phonology. Cambridge: Cambridge University Press.

Andrade, A. (1987), 'Um estudo experimental das vogais anteriores e recuadas em português. Implicações para a teoria dos traços distintivos'. MS, INIC, Centro de Linguística da Universidade de Lisboa.

Andrade, A. (1992), 'Ainda as vogais de Sagres', Actas do 8º Encontro da Associação Portuguesa de Linguística (Lisbon, 1993): 37–58.

Andrade, A. (1994), 'Reflexões sobre o 'e mudo' em Português Europeu', in I. Duarte and I. Leiria (eds) (1996), Vol. 2: 303–44.

Andrade, E. d' (1977), Aspects de la phonologie (générative) du Portugais. Lisbon: INIC, Centro de Linguística da Universidade de Lisboa.

Andrade, E. d' (1981), 'As alternâncias vocálicas no sistema verbal do Português', Boletim de Filologia (Lisbon), XXVI: 69–81 (Republished in Temas de Fonologia, 95–106.)

Andrade, E. d' (1983), 'L'accent de mot en Portugais'. MS, Univeristy of Lisbon.

Andrade, E. d' (1988), 'O acento de palavra em Português', in J. Staczek (ed.), On Spanish, Portuguese and Catalan Linguistics. Washington: Georgetown University Press: 17–38

Andrade, E. d' (1992), Temas de Fonologia. Lisbon: Colibri.

Andrade, E. d' (1994), 'Na onda do acento', in I. Duarte and I. Leiria (eds), Vol. 2: 157–74.

Andrade, E. d' (1997a), 'Sobre a alternância vogal/glide em Português', Actas do 13º Encontro da Associação Portuguesa de Linguística (Lisbon): 91–102.

Andrade, E. d' (1997b), 'Some remarks about stress in Portuguese', in F. Martínez-Gil and A. Morales-Front (eds): 343–58.

Andrade, E. d' and Kihm, A. (1987), 'Fonologia autosegmental e nasais em português', Actas do 3º Encontro da Associação Portuguesa de Linguística (Lisbon): 51–60.

Andrade, E. d' and Laks, B. (1987), 'Fonologia métrica e análise aritmética da quantidade', Actas do 3º Encontro da Associação Portuguesa de Linguística (Lisbon): 39–50.

Andrade, E. d' and Laks, B. (1991), 'Na crista da onda: o acento de palavra em português', *Actas do 7º Encontro da Associação Portuguesa de Linguística* (Lisbon): 15–26.

Andrade, E. d' and Laks, B. (1996), 'Stress and constituency: the case of Portuguese', in J. Durand and B. Laks (eds), *Current Trends in Phonology: Models and Methods*, ESRI, Vol. 1: 15–41. Manchester: University of Salford.

Andrade, E. d' and Viana, M. C. (1988a), 'O ritmo e o acento em Português', in *Actas do 2º Encontro Regional da Associação Portuguesa de Linguistica* (Lisbon). In press.

Andrade, E. d' and Viana, M. C. (1988b), 'Ainda sobre o acento e o ritmo em português', *Actas do 4º Encontro da Associação Portuguesa de Linguística* (Lisbon): 3–16.

Andrade, E. d' and Viana, M. C. (1992), 'Que horas são às (1)3 e 15?', *Actas do 8º Encontro da Associação Portuguesa de Linguística* (Lisbon): 59–66.

Andrade, E. d' and Viana, M. C. (1993a), 'Sinérese, diérese e estrutura silábica', *Actas do 9º Encontro da Associação Portuguesa de Linguística* (Coimbra): 31–42.

Andrade, E. d' and Viana, M. C. (1993b), 'Subrodas da translineação', in *Actas de EPLP '93* (Lisbon): 209–14.

Archangeli, D. B. (1988), 'Aspects of Underspecification Theory', *Phonology Yearbook,* 5: 183–207.

Arnauld, A. and Lancelot, C. (1660), *Grammaire générale et raisonnée*. Paris.

Aronoff M. (1976), *Word Formation in Generative Grammar*. Cambridge, Mass.: The MIT Press.

Aronoff, M. and Oehrle, R. (eds) (1984), *Language Sound Structure*. Cambridge, Mass.: MIT Press.

Aurélio, Buarque de Holanda F. (1986), *Novo Dicionário da Língua Portuguesa*. Rio de Janeiro: Nova Fronteira.

Baldinger, K. (1963), *La formación de los dominios lingüisticos en la Peninsula Iberica.* Madrid: Gredos. (First published in Germany, 1958).

Barbeiro, L. F. (1986), 'O papel da sílaba na análise dos procesos fonológicos e fonéticos'. M.A. thesis, University of Lisbon.

Barbosa, J. Soares (1822), *Grammatica philosophica da lingua portugueza ou principios de grammatica geral aplicados à nossa lingoagem*. Lisbon.

Barbosa, J. Morais (1962), 'Les voyelles nasales portugaises: interprétation phonologique', *Proceedings of the 4th International Congress of Phonetic Sciences* (Helsinki, 1961): 691–708. The Hague: Mouton.

Barbosa, J. Morais (1965), *Études de phonologie portugaise*. Lisbon: Junta de Investigações Científicas do Ultramar. (2nd edn, Universidade de Évora, 1983.)

Barbosa, J. Morais (1988), 'Notas sobre a pronúncia portuguesa nos últimos cem anos', *Biblos*, 64: 329–82.

Barros, J. de (1540), *Grammatica da lingua portuguesa com os mandamentos da santa madre igreja*. Lisbon: Luis Rodrigues.

Basbøll, H. (1988), 'Phonological Theory', in F. Newmeyer (ed.): 192–215.

Bell, A. and Hooper, J. (eds) (1978), *Syllables and Segments*. Amsterdam: North-Holland.

Bisol, L. (1989), 'O ditongo na perspectiva da fonologia atual', *Delta* 5/2: 185–224.

Bisol, L. (1994a), 'Ditongos derivados', *Delta* 10/2: 123–140.

Bisol, L. (1994b), 'O acento e o pé binário', *Letras de Hoje*, 29: 25–36. Porto Alegre: EDIPUCRS.

Bisol, L. (ed.) (1996), *Introdução a estudos de fonologia do Português Brasileiro*. Porto Alegre: EDIPUCRS.

Bisol, L. and Hora, D. (1993), 'Palatalização da oclusiva dental e fonologia lexical', *Actas do 9⁰ Encontro da Associação Portuguesa de Linguistica* (Lisbon): 61–80.

Blevins, J. (1995), 'The Syllable in Phonological Theory', in J. Goldsmith (ed.), 206–44

Bloch, B. and Trager, G. (1942), *Outlines of Linguistic Analysis*. Baltimore: LSA.

Bloomfield, L. (1933), *Language*. New York: Holt, Reinhart and Winston.

Bonet, E. and Mascaró, J. (1997), 'On the representation of contrasting rhotics', in F. Martínez-Gil and A. Morales-Front (eds): 103–26.

Booij, G. (1992), 'Lexical Phonology and Prosodic Phonology', in W. U. Dressler *et al.* (eds), *Phonologica 1988*, 49–62. Cambridge: Cambridge University Press.

Booij, G. (1989), 'Complex verbs and the theory of level ordering', *Yearbook of Morphology*, 2: 21–30.

Booij, G. (1994), 'Lexical Phonology: A Review', *Lingue e Stile*, 29/4: 525–55.

Booij, G. and Rubach, J. (1987), 'Postcyclic versus Postlexical Rules in Lexical Phonology', *Linguistic Inquiry*, 18: 1–44.

Booij, G. and Marle, J. van (eds) (1989), *Yearbook of Morphology*, 2. Dordrecht: Foris.

Bosch, A., Need, B., and Schiller, E. (eds) (1987), *Papers from the Parasession on Autosegmental and Metrical Phonology*. Chicago: Chicago Linguistics Society.

Broselow, E. (1995), 'Skeletal Positions and Moras', in J. Goldsmith (ed.): 175–205.

Cagliari, L. (1977), 'An Experimental Study of Nasality with Particular Reference to Brazilian Portuguese'. Ph.D. thesis, University of Edinburgh.

Cagliari, L. C. (1997), *Fonologia do Português. Análise pela geometria de traços*. Campinas.

Callou, D. and Leite, Y. (1990), *Iniciação à fonética e à fonologia*. Rio de Janeiro: Jorge Zahar.

Câmara, J. Mattoso (1953), *Para o Estudo da Fonêmica Portuguesa*. Rio: Simões.

Câmara, J. Mattoso (1970), *Estrutura da Língua Portuguesa*. Petrópolis, RJ: Vozes.

Carvalho, J. Brandão de (1989), 'Phonological Conditions on the Portuguese Clitic Placement: On Syntactic Evidence for Stress and Rhythmical Patterns', *Linguistics*, 27: 405–36.

Chomsky, N. (1970), 'Remarks on Nominalisation', in R. Jacobs and P. Rosenbaum (eds): 194–221.

Chomsky, N. and Halle, M. (1968), *The Sound Pattern of English*. New York: Harper and Row.

Cintra, L. F. Lindley (1971a), 'Nova proposta de classificação dos dialectos galego-portugueses'. *Boletim de Filologia*, 22: 81–116.

Cintra, L. F. Lindley (1971b), 'Observations sur le plus ancien texte portugais non-litéraire: la *Notícia de Torto*', *Actele celui de-al XII-lea Congres International de Lingvistica si Filologie Romanica* (Bucharest): 161–74.

Clements, G. N. (1985), 'The Geometry of Phonological Features', *Phonology Yearbook*, 2: 225–52.

Clements, G. N. (1988), 'Towards a Substantive Theory of Features Specification', *Proceedings of the 18th Annual Meeting of the North East Linguistics Society*. Amherst, Mass.: Graduate Linguistic Student Association.

Clements, G. N. (1991), 'Place of Articulation in Consonants and Vowels: A Unified Theory', *Working Paper 5, Cornell Phonetics Laboratory*: 77–123.

Clements, G. N. and E. Hume (1995), 'Internal organization of speech sounds', in J. Goldsmith (ed.): 245–306.

Clements, G. N. and Keyser, S. J. (1983), *CV Phonology: A Generative Theory of the Syllable*. Cambridge, Mass.: MIT Press.

Colman, F. (1983), 'Vocalisation as nucleation', *Studia Linguistica*, 37: 30–48.

Costa, A. J. (1977), 'Os mais antigos documentos escritos em Português—revisão de um problema histórico-linguístico', *Revista Portuguesa de História*, 17 (1979): 263–340. Reprinted in *Estudos de cronologia, diplomática, paleografia e histórico-linguísticos*. (1993: 169–256). Porto, Sociedade de Estudos Medievais.

Cunha, C. and Cintra, L. F. Lindley (1984), *Nova gramática do português contemporâneo*. Lisbon: Sá da Costa.

Delgado-Martins, M. R. (1973), 'Análise acústica das vogais tónicas em português', *Boletim de Filologia*, 22: 303–14.

Delgado-Martins, M. R. (1976), 'Vogais e consoantes do português: estatística de ocorrência, duração e intensidade', *Boletim de Filologia*, 24: 1–11.

Delgado-Martins, M. R. (1982), *Aspects de l'accent en portugais: Voyelles toniques et atones*. Hamburg: Buske.

Delgado-Martins, M. R. (1983), *Sept études sur la perception*. Lisbon: Laboratório de Fonética da Faculdade de Letras.

Delgado-Martins, M. R. (1994), Relação fonética/fonologia: a propósito do sistema vocálico do Português. In I. Duarte and I. Leiria (eds) (1996): Vol I, 311–25.

Duarte, I and Leiria, I. (eds) (1996), *Actas do Congresso Internacional sobre o Português* (1994). Lisbon: Colibri.

Durand, J. (1990), *Generative and Non-Linear Phonology*. New York: Longman.

Ellison, M. and Viana, M. C. (1996), 'Antagonismo e elisão das vogais átonas em PE', *Actas do 11º Encontro Nacional da Associação Portuguesa de Linguística* (Lisbon) Vol. 3: 261–82. Lisbon: APL/Colibri.

Ewen, C. and Anderson, J. (eds) (1985), *Phonology Yearbook*, 2. Cambridge: Cambridge University Press.

Figueiredo, Cândido de (1899), *Dicionário da Língua Portuguesa*. Lisbon: Livraria Tavares Cardoso e Irmão (last revised edn, 1922).

Fromkin, V. (ed.) (1985), *Phonetic linguistics: Essays in Honour of Peter Ladefoged*. Orlando: Academic Press.

Frota, S. (1994), 'Os domínios prosódicos e o Português Europeu', *Actas do 10º Encontro da Associação Portuguesa de Linguística* (Évora): 221–38.

Fudge, E. C. (1987), 'Branching structure within the syllable', *Journal of Linguistics*, 23: 359–77.

Girelli, C. A. (1988), 'Brazilian Portuguese Syllable Structure'. Ph.D. dissertation, University of Connecticut.

Goldsmith, J. (1990), *Autosegmental and Metrical Phonology*. Oxford: Basil Blackwell.

Goldsmith, J. (ed.) (1995), *The Handbook of Phonological Theory*. Oxford: Basil Blackwell.

Goldsmith, J. (1995), 'Phonological Theory', in J. Goldsmith (ed.): 1–23.

Halle, M. (1991), 'Phonological Features', in W. Bright (ed.), *Oxford International Encyclopedia of Linguistics*: 207–12. Oxford: Oxford University Press.

Halle, M. and Mohanan, K. P. (1985), 'Segmental phonology of modern English', in *Linguistic Inquiry*, 16: 57–116.

Halle, M. and Vergnaud, J.-R. (1987), *An Essay on Stress*. Cambridge, Mass: MIT Press.

Harris, J. W. (1974), 'Evidence from Portuguese for the "Elswhere Condition"', *Linguistic Inquiry*, 5: 61–80.

Harris, J. W. (1983), *Syllable Structure and Stress in Spanish*. Cambridge, Mass.: MIT Press.

Harris, J. W. (1984), 'Autosegmental Phonology, Lexical Phonology and Spanish Nasals', in M. Aronoff and R. T. Oehrle (eds): 67–82.

Harris, J. W. (1985), 'Spanish Diphthongisation and Stress: A Paradox Resolved', *Phonology Yearbook*, 2: 31–45.

Harris, J. W. (1995), 'Projection and head marking in the computation of stress in Spanish', in J. Goldsmith (ed.): 867–87.

Harris, Z. (1951), *Methods in Structural Linguistics*. Chicago: University of Chicago Press.

Hayes, B. (1980), *A Metrical Theory of Stress Rules*. New York: Garland.

Head, B. (1984), 'Propriedades fonéticas e generalidades de processos fonológicos: o caso do "r-caipira"', *Cadernos de Estudos Linguísticos*, 13. Campinas: UNICAMP–IEL.

Head, B. (1965), 'A Comparison of the Segmental Phonology of Lisbon and Rio de Janeiro'. Ph.D. dissertation, University of Texas at Austin.

Hernandorena, C. L. (1994), 'A geometria dos traços na representação das palatais na aquisição do português', *Letras de Hoje*, 29: 159–67. Porto Alegre: EDIPUCRS.

Hockett, C. F. (1947), 'Problems of morphemic analysis', *Language*, 23: 321–43.

Hockett, C. F. (1954), 'Two models of grammatical description', *Word*, 10: 210–34.

Hora, D. (1993), 'A palatalização das oclusivas dentais: uma abordagem não-linear', *Delta*, 9/2: 175–94.

Hulst, H. G. van der (1984), 'Vowel Harmony in Hungarian: A Comparison of Segmental and Autosegmental Analyses', in H. G. van der Hulst and N. Smith (eds): 267–303.

Hulst, H. G. van der and Smith, N. (eds) (1982), *The Structure of Phonological Representations*, Part I. Dordrecht: Foris.

Hulst, H. G. van der and Smith, N. (1982), 'An Overview of Autosegmental and Metrical Phonology', in H. G. van der Hulst and N. Smith (eds): 1–45.

Hulst, H. G. van der and Smith, N. (eds) (1984), *Advances in Non-Linear Phonology*. Dordrecht: Foris.

Hulst, H. G. van der and Smith, N. (eds) (1988), *Features, Segmental Structure and Harmony Processes*, Part I. Dordrecht: Foris.

Hyman, L. (1988), 'Underspecification and Vowel Height Transfer in Esimbi', *Phonology Yearbook*, 5/2: 255–73.

Inkelas, Sh. (1995), 'The Consequences of Optimalization for Underspecification', *Proceedings of the 24 North-East Linguistic Society*. Amherst, Mass.: Graduate Linguistics Students Association.

Jacobs R. and Rosenbaum, P. (eds) (1970), *Readings in English Transformational Grammar*. Waltham, Mass.: Ginn.

Jakobson, R and Halle, M. (1956), *Fundamentals of Language*, Vol. 1: *Janua Linguarum*. The Hague: Mouton.

Jakobson, R., Fant, G. and Halle, M. (1952), *Preliminaries to Speech Analysis*. Cambridge, Mass.: MIT Press.

Jespersen, O. (1912), *Lehrbuch der Phonetik*. Berlin.

Jong, K. de (1995), 'On the Status of Redundant Features: The Case of Backing and Rounding in American English', in B. Connell and A. Arvaniti (eds), *Papers in Laboratory Phonology IV: Phonology and Phonetic Evidence*: 68–86. Cambridge: Cambridge University Press.

Kahn, D. (1976), 'Syllable-based Generalizations in English Phonology'. Ph.D. dissertation, Massachusetts Institute of Technology.

Kaisse, E. and Shaw, P. (1985), 'On the Theory of Lexical Phonology', *Phonology Yearbook*, 2: 1–30.

Keating, P. (1988), 'The phonology-phonetics interface', in F. Newmeyer (ed.): 281–302.

Kenstowicz, M. (1994), *Phonology in Generative Grammar*. Oxford: Basil Blackwell.

Kibbee, D. and Wanner, D. (eds) (1991), *New Analyses in Romance Linguistics*. Amsterdam: Benjamins.

Kiparsky, P (1982), 'Lexical Phonology and Morphology', in I.-S. Yang (ed.): 3–91.

Kiparsky, P. (1985), 'Some Consequences of Lexical Phonology', *Phonology Yearbook*, 2: 85–138.

La Charité, D. (1993), 'On the Need for Negative Constraints and Repair: Consonant Mutation in Setswana', *Canadian Journal of Linguistics*, 38/2: 257–78.

La Charité, D. and Paradis, C. (1993), 'Introduction—The Emergence of Constraints in Generative Phonology and a Comparison of Three Current Constraint-Based Models', in C. Paradis and D. La Charité (eds): 127–53.

Lacerda, A. (1970 and 1975), 'Objectos verbais e significado elocucional. Toemas e entoemas, entoação', offprints from *Revista do Laboratório de Fonética Experimental de Coimbra*, 7 and 8.

Ladefoged, P. (1975), *A Course in Phonetics*. New York: Harcourt, Brace and Jovanovich.

Lahiri, A. and Evers, V. (1991), 'Palatalization and Coronality', in C. Paradis and J.-F. Prunet (eds), 79–100.

Laks, B. (1990), 'Constituance et métrique', in B. Laks and A. Rialland (eds): 25–58.

Laks, B. and Rialland. A. (eds) (1990), *Architecture des représentations phonologiques*. Paris: CNRS.

Lee, S.-H. (1992), 'Fonologia Lexical do Português', *Cadernos de Estudos Linguísticos*, 23. Campinas: UNICAMP–IEL.

Lee, S.-H. (1994), 'A Regra do Acento do Português: outra alternativa', *Letras de Hoje*, 29: 37–42. Porto Alegre: EDIPUCRS.

Lee, S.-H. (1995), 'Morfologia e Fonologia Lexical do Português do Brasil'. Ph.D. dissertation, Campinas: UNICAMP.

Lieber, R. (1980), 'On the organization of the lexicon'. Ph.D. dissertation, Massachusetts Institute of Technology.

Lieber, R. (1989), 'On percolation', *Yearbook of Morphology*, 2: 95–138.

Lieberman, P. (1967), *Intonation, Perception and Language*. Cambridge, Mass.: MIT Press.

Lipski, J. M. (1973), 'The Surface Structure of Portuguese: Plurals and Other Things', *Linguistics: An International Review*, 111: 67–82.

Lopez, B. B. (1979), 'The Sound Pattern of Brazilian Portuguese'. Ph.D. dissertation, University of California at Los Angeles.

Lüdtke, H. (1952 and 1953), 'Fonemática portuguesa', *Boletim de Filologia*, 13: 273–88; 14: 197–217.

Major, R. C. (1985), 'Stress and Rhythm in Brazilian Portuguese', *Language*, 61: 259–82.

Martinet, A. (1960), *Éléments de linguistique générale*. Paris: Armand Colin. (Portuguese translation by J. Morais-Barbosa, *Elementos de linguística geral*. Lisbon: Sá da Costa, 1964.)

Martinet, André (1939), 'Un ou deux phonèmes?' *Acta Linguistica*, 1: 94–103.

Martínez-Gil, F. and Morales-Front, A. (eds) (1997), *Issues in the Phonology and Morphology of the Major Iberian Languages*. Washington: Georgetown University Press.

Martins, A. M. (1999), 'Ainda "Os mais antigos textos escritos em português": documentos de 1175 a 1252', in Lindley-Cintra: *Homenagem ao homem, ao mestre e ao cidadão*. Lisbon: Cosmos, FLUL (in press).

Mascaró, J. (1976), 'Catalan Phonology and the Phonological Cycle'. Ph.D. dissertation, Massachusetts Institute of Technology. Distributed by IULC.

Massini-Cagliari, G. (1995), 'Cantigas de Amigo: do Ritmo Poético ao Linguístico'. Ph.D. dissertation, Campinas: UNICAMP.

Mateus, M. H. M. (1975), *Aspectos da fonologia portuguesa*. Lisbon: Centro de Estudos Filológicos (2nd edn reviewed, *Textos de Linguística*, 6, 1982.)

Mateus, M. H. M. (1993), 'Onset of Portuguese Syllables and Rising Diphthongs', *Proceedings of the Workshop on Phonology* (Coimbra): 93–104.

Mateus, M. H. M. (1994), 'A silabificação de base em Português', *Actas do 10° Encontro da Associação Portuguesa de Linguística* (Évora): 289–300.

Mateus, M. H. M. (1995), 'Factos prosódicos nas gramáticas portuguesas', *Actas do 11° Encontro da Associação Portuguesa de Linguistica* (Lisbon): 123–42.

Mateus, M. H. M. (1996), 'Redundâncias lexicais e subespecificação: o sistema do Português', *Actas do 12° Encontro da Associação Portuguesa de Linguistica* (Braga): 203–14.

Mateus, M. H. M. (1996), 'Ainda a subespecificação na fonologia do Português', *Actas do 13° Encontro da Associação Portuguesa de Linguistica* (Lisbon): 63–74.

Mateus, M. H. M., Brito, A. M., Duarte, I., and Faria, I. (1983), *Gramática da língua portuguesa*. Coimbra: Almedina. (2nd revised edn, Lisbon: Caminho, 1989.)

McCarthy, J. (1986), 'OCP Effects: Gemination and Antigemination', *Linguistic Inquiry*, 7: 187–263.

McCarthy, J. (1988), 'Feature Geometry and Dependency: A Review', *Phonetica*, 43: 84–108.

Miguel, M. A. Cavaco (1993), 'Os Padrões das Alternâncias Vocálicas e da Vogal Zero na Fonologia Portuguesa'. Ph.D. dissertation, University of Azores, Ponta Delgada.

Miguel, M. A. Cavaco (1994), 'Interpretação fonológica de alguns plurais em Português', *Actas do 10° Encontro da Associação Portuguesa de Linguística* (Évora): 331–40.

Mohanan, K. P. (1982), 'Lexical Phonology'. Ph.D. dissertation, Massachusetts Institute of Technology. Distributed by IULC.

Mohanan, K. P. (1986), *The Theory of Lexical Phonology*. Dordrecht: Reidel.

Mohanan, K. P. (1991), 'On the Basis of Underspecification', *Natural Language and Linguistic Theory*, 9: 285–325.

Mohanan, K. P. (1995), 'The Organization of the Grammar', in J. Goldsmith (ed.): 24–69.

Mohanan, K. P. and Mohanan. T. (1984), 'Lexical Phonology of the Consonant System in Malayalam', *Linguistic Inquiry*, 15: 575–602.

Moors, C. ter (1984), 'Empty V-Nodes and their Role in the Klamath Vowel Alternations', in H. G. van der Hulst and N. Smith (eds): 313–31.

Morales-Front, A. and Holt, D. E. (1997), 'On the Interplay of Morphology, Prosody and Faithfulness in Portuguese Pluralization', in F. Martínez-Gil and A. Morales-Front (eds): 393–437.

Nascentes, A. (1953), *O linguajar carioca*. Rio de Janeiro: Simões.

Newmeyer, F. (ed.) (1988), *Linguistics: The Cambridge Survey*. Vol. I. Cambridge: Cambridge University Press.

Nogueira, R. de Sá (1938), *Elementos para um tratado de fonética portuguesa*. Lisbon: Imprensa Nacional.

Nogueira, R. de Sá (1942), *O problema da sílaba*. Lisbon: Livraria Clássica Editora.

Nunes, J. J. (1919), *Compêndio de Gramática Histórica Portuguesa*. Lisbon: Livraria Clássica Editora (4th edn, 1951).

Ohala, J. J. (1996), 'Doing without the Syllable', paper presented to the colloquium 'The Phonology of the World's Languages: The Syllable' (Pézenas, 1996).

Oliveira, Fernão de (1536), *Grammatica da lingoagem portuguesa*. Lisbon (3rd edn, Lisbon: José Fernandes Júnior, 1933.)

Paradis, C. (1993), 'Ill-formedness in the Dictionary: A Source of Constraint Violation', in C. Paradis and D. La Charité (eds): 215–34.

Paradis, C. and La Charité, D. (eds) (1993), 'Constraint-based Theories in Multilinear Phonology', *Canadian Journal of Linguistics*, 38: 2 (Special Issue).

Paradis, C. and Prunet, J.-F. (eds) (1991), 'The Special Status of Coronals: Internal and External Evidence', *Phonetics and Phonology*, 2. New York: Academic Press.

Parkinson, S. (1983), 'Portuguese Nasal Vowels as Phonological Diphthongs', *Lingua*, 61: 157–77.

Petrucci, P. R. (1992), 'Fatos de Estabilidade no Português Brasileiro', *Cadernos de Estudos Linguísticos*, 23. Campinas: UNICAMP–IEL.

Pike, K. (1947), *Phonemics: A Technique for Reducing Languages to Writing*. Ann Arbor: University of Michigan Press.

Pike, K. and Pike, E. V. (1947), 'Immediate Constituents of Mazateco Syllables', *International Journal of American Linguistics*, 13: 78–91.

Prieto, D. (1984), 'Prosodic Representation and Transformation in Galician Portuguese', in H. G. van der Hulst and N. Smith (eds): 143–60.

Prince, A. (1983), 'Relating to the grid', *Linguistic Inquiry*, 14: 19–100.

Prince, A. (1990), 'Quantitative consequences of rhythmic organization', in M. Ziolkowski, M. Noske and K. Deaton (eds), *Parasession on the Syllable in Phonetics and Phonology*: 355–98. Chicago: CLS.

Quícoli, A. C. (1990), 'Harmony, Lowering and Nasalization in Brazilian Portuguese', *Lingua*, 80: 295–331.

Redenbarger, W. (1981), *Articulator Features and Portuguese Vowel Height*. Cambridge, Mass.: Harvard University.

Roca, I. (1994), *Generative Phonology*. London: Routledge.

Rubach, J. (1985), 'Lexical Phonology: Lexical and Postlexical Derivations', *Phonology Yearbook*, 2: 157–72.

Rubach, J. (1993), *The Lexical Phonology of Slovak*. Oxford: Oxford University Press.

Rubach, J. (1995), 'Representations and the Organization of Rules in Slavic Phonology', in J. Goldsmith (ed.): 848–66.

Sagey, E. (1986), *The Representation of Features and Relations in Non-linear Phonology*. New York: Garland Press, 1991 (originally Ph.D. dissertation, MIT).

Selkirk, E. (1984a), *Phonology and Syntax: The Relation between Sound and Structure*. Cambridge, Mass.: MIT Press.

Selkirk, E. (1984b), 'On the major class features and syllable theory', in M. Aronoff and R. Oehrle (eds): 107–36.

Selkirk, E. (1986), 'On derived domains in sentence phonology', *Phonology*, 3: 371–405.

Siegel, D. (1974), 'Topics in English morphology'. Ph.D. dissertation, Massachusetts Institute of Technology.

Silva, A. de Morais (1948–59), *Grande dicionário da língua portuguesa*, 10th edition revised by J. P. Machado. Lisbon: Confluência (1st edition, 1789).

Spencer, A. (1991), *Morphological Theory*. Oxford: Basil Blackwell.

Steriade, D. (1987), 'Redundant Values', in A. Bosch, B. Need and E. Schiller (eds): 339–62.

Trubetzkoy, N. (1949), *Principes de phonologie*. Paris: Klincksieck. (First published in Germany as *Grundzüge der Phonologie*, 1939.)

Vago, R. M. (1988), 'The Treatment of Long Vowels in Word Games', in F. Newmeyer (ed.): 329–42.

Vasconcellos, J. Leite de (1901), *Esquisse d'une dialectologie portugaise*. Paris: Jules Aillaud. (3rd edn Lisbon: INIC, Centro de Linguística da Universidade de Lisboa, 1987.)

Viana, A. R. Gonçalves (1883), 'Essai de phonétique et de phonologie de la langue portugaise d'après le dialecte actuel de Lisbonne', *Romania*, XII (Paris). (Republished in *Estudos de Fonética Portuguesa*, Lisbon: Imprensa Nacional, 1973: 83–152.)

Viana, M. C. (1987), 'Para a Síntese da Entoação do Português'. Unpublished paper. Lisbon: Centro de Linguística da Universidade de Lisboa, INIC.

Vigário, M. (1997a), 'On the Prosodic Status of Stressless Function Words in European Portuguese', paper presented at the Conference on the Phonological Word (Berlin); to appear in T. A. Hall and U. Kleinhenz (eds), *Studies on the Phonological Word: Current Studies in Linguistic Theory*. Amsterdam: Benjamins.

Vigário, M. (1997b), 'Elisão da vogal não-recuada final e a palavra prosódica no Português Europeu', *Actas do 13º Encontro da Associação Portuguesa de Linguística* (Colibri): 359–76.

Vigário, M. and I. Falé (1993), 'A sílaba do Português Fundamental: uma descrição e algumas considerações de ordem teórica', *Actas do 9º Encontro da Associação Portuguesa de Linguística* (Coimbra): 465–77.

Vilela, M. (1990), *Dicionário do Português Básico*. Porto: ASA.

Villalva, A. (1990), 'Compounding in Portuguese', *Working Paper* 2. Lisbon: Instituto de Linguistica Teórica e Computacional.

Villalva, A. (1994a), 'Estruturas Morfológicas: Unidades e hierarquias nas palavras do Português'. Ph.D. dissertation, University of Lisbon.

Villalva, A. (1994b), 'Configurações não binárias em morfologia', *Actas do 10º Encontro da Associação Portuguesa de Linguística* (Évora): 583–94.

Wetzels, L. (1988), 'Contrastive and Allophonic Properties in Brazilian Portuguese Vowels', in D. Wanner and D. Kibee (eds), *New Analyses in Romance Linguistics*, LSRL, 18 (1991): 77–99. Philadelphia: Benjamins.

Wetzels, L. (1991), 'Harmonização vocálica, truncamento, abaixamento e neutralização no sistema verbal do português: uma análise auto-segmental', *Cadernos de Estudos Linguísticos*, 21. Campinas: UNICAMP–IEL.

Wetzels, L. (1992), 'Mid-Vowel Neutralization in Brazilian Portuguese', *Cadernos de Estudos Linguísticos*, 23. Campinas: UNICAMP–IEL.

Wetzels, L. (1997), 'The Lexical Representation of Nasality in Brazilian Portuguese', *Probus*, 9: 203–32.

Wiese, R. (1994), *The Phonology of German*. Oxford: Oxford University Press.

Williams, E. B. (1938), *From Latin to Portuguese. Historical Phonology and Morphology of the Portuguese Language*. Philadelphia: University of Pennsylvania Press.

Yang, I.-S. (ed.) (1982), *Linguistics in the Morning Calm*. Seoul: Hanshin.

Yip, M. (1991), 'Coronals, Consonant Clusters, and the Coda Condition', in C. Paradis and J.-F. Prunet (eds): 61–78.

NAME INDEX

SUBJECT INDEX